"Don't believe that there was a time not long ago when a socialist daily newspaper in New York City—published in Yiddish!—commanded the attention not only of millions of Jewish immigrants but also of presidents and foreign leaders? Read this magical book. It will transport you back to some of the most tumultuous decades the world has ever known, as seen through the life of a fearless newspaperman whose paper didn't simply cover events; it changed the course of them."

—JONATHAN MAHLER,
author *Ladies and Gentlemen, the Bronx Is Burning*

"A riveting account of Abraham Cahan's life and times. Cahan was as complex as he was courageous—Jewish immigrant, social democrat, labor organizer, anti-communist, our earliest neoconservative. Seth Lipsky is another fearless and brilliant newsman, and no one could have told Cahan's story better. This is a book to savor and remember."

—PETER KANN, Pulitzer Prize–winning reporter
and former publisher of *The Wall Street Journal*

"Abraham Cahan was at the forefront of the postwar battle against communist subversion of the labor movement and powerfully helped to save Europe from the tyrannies of Stalinism, though he had arrived in America as a revolutionary socialist on the run from the Tsarist secret police. Lipsky has given his story pulsating life."

—SIR HAROLD EVANS, editor at large, Reuters,
and author of *The American Century*

JEWISH ENCOUNTERS

Jonathan Rosen, General Editor

Jewish Encounters is a collaboration between Schocken and Nextbook, a project devoted to the promotion of Jewish literature, culture, and ideas.

>nextbook

PUBLISHED

THE LIFE OF DAVID · Robert Pinsky
MAIMONIDES · Sherwin B. Nuland
BARNEY ROSS · Douglas Century
BETRAYING SPINOZA · Rebecca Goldstein
EMMA LAZARUS · Esther Schor
THE WICKED SON · David Mamet
MARC CHAGALL · Jonathan Wilson
JEWS AND POWER · Ruth R. Wisse
BENJAMIN DISRAELI · Adam Kirsch
RESURRECTING HEBREW · Ilan Stavans
THE JEWISH BODY · Melvin Konner
RASHI · Elie Wiesel
A FINE ROMANCE · David Lehman
YEHUDA HALEVI · Hillel Halkin
HILLEL · Joseph Telushkin
BURNT BOOKS · Rodger Kamenetz
THE EICHMANN TRIAL · Deborah E. Lipstadt
SACRED TRASH · Adina Hoffman and Peter Cole
BEN-GURION · Shimon Peres with David Landau
WHEN GENERAL GRANT EXPELLED THE JEWS · Jonathan D. Sarna
THE BOOK OF JOB · Harold S. Kushner
THE WORLDS OF SHOLOM ALEICHEM · Jeremy Dauber
THE RISE OF ABRAHAM CAHAN · Seth Lipsky

FORTHCOMING

ABRAHAM · Alan M. Dershowitz

MOSES · Stephen J. Dubner

BIROBIJAN · Masha Gessen

JUDAH MACCABEE · Jeffrey Goldberg

MENACHEM BEGIN · Daniel Gordis

THE DAIRY RESTAURANT · Ben Katchor

FROM PASHAS TO PARIAHS · Lucette Lagnado

YOUR SHOW OF SHOWS · David Margolick

MRS. FREUD · Daphne Merkin

MESSIANISM · Leon Wieseltier

The Rise of Abraham Cahan

SETH LIPSKY

THE RISE OF ABRAHAM CAHAN

NEXTBOOK · SCHOCKEN · NEW YORK

A portion of this work appeared in the *Forward.*

Library of Congress Cataloging-in-Publication Data
Lipsky, Seth.
The rise of Abraham Cahan / Seth Lipsky.
pages cm
Includes bibliographical references and index.
ISBN 978-0-8052-4210-2
1. Cahan, Abraham, 1860–1951. 2. Jewish journalists—United States—Biography. 3. Authors, Yiddish—United States—Biography. 4. Forverts (New York, N.Y.). 5. Yiddish newspapers—United States. I. Title.
PJ5129.C27Z75 2013 839'.133—dc23 [B] 2013006773

www.schocken.com

Jacket photograph of Abraham Cahan courtesy of the Forward Association
Jacket design by Brian Barth

Printed in the United States of America
First Edition
2 4 6 8 9 7 5 3 1

For Amity

CONTENTS

The Rise of Abraham Cahan

PREFACE

A portrait of Abraham Cahan is the first thing that greets a visitor to the *Forward* in New York City. It attracted me from the moment that I, then a young newspaperman in my midthirties, first stopped by the paper's editorial rooms. It was early in 1983. Published in Yiddish and known as the *Forverts*, or *Jewish Daily Forward*, it had recently retreated to weekly publication with an English-language supplement. I was there on a quest to bring out a new, full-scale national Jewish newspaper in English, one that would start as a weekly, eventually become a daily publication, and most important, bear the legendary *Forward* name.

This was seen by many at the time as an improbable venture, but I had become an admirer of Cahan years before, though even today I'm not exactly sure how this came about. I admired him as a newspaperman: in particular, as editor of the Yiddish-language daily that he had helped found one hundred years earlier and had built into one of the first national newspapers, with a circulation of more than a quarter of a million and editions in Los Angeles, Chicago, Boston, and Philadelphia as well as New York. Cahan had edited the *Forward* for fifty years, right up to his death in 1951, and earned a place in the pantheon of America's greatest newspaper editors.

Beyond that, I was also attracted by Cahan's political story. He had stood with labor throughout its great awakening and the years during which it was being organized, but he had broken early with the hard-left factions and played a leading role in the long struggle against Communism. Although I myself was never a socialist or a member of a labor union, I had great sympathy for labor and its long march. The author to whom I thrilled as a young student was John Dos Passos. Like him,

I had moved to the right over the years, and as the Jewish story began to assert itself in the last quarter of the twentieth century, I perceived Cahan and what he built at the *Forward* as taking on, after a long decline, a new relevance.

This was partly because of the way the denouement of the Cold War had vindicated the anti-Communist crusaders with whom Cahan had made common cause and partly because of the way Cahan had confounded a left that was emerging in league with enemies of Israel. I quickly discovered other matters on which the *Forward* had much to offer, from the debate over immigration to the use of quotas in the struggle for racial integration to the way New York City was governed to the problem of public education to the question of culture and its importance in the pages of a major newspaper.

This was put into sharp relief for me one day in the summer of 1984, when I was still at *The Wall Street Journal* and nursing the idea of an English-language *Forward*. My future wife and I went for Sunday brunch to the home of the editor of the *Forward*, Simon Weber, and his wife, Sylvia. Among the other guests were the Nobel laureate and *Forward* writer Isaac Bashevis Singer and his wife, Alma. As we were seated at a table piled with smoked fish and bagels, I mentioned that the *Journal* had just come out, at least in principle, for open immigration into the United States.

"Oy," Singer said. "All those Mexicans."

I protested vehemently, slapping the table and declaring that I was shocked to find myself hearing such sentiments at the home of the editor of the *Forward* and from its greatest writer—indeed, from America's greatest immigrant writer.

Si Weber motioned me onto his balcony, which overlooked Brighton Beach, Brooklyn, where immigrant languages were spoken for miles in all directions. Then he shook his finger in my face and said, "I know you guys from *The Wall Street Journal*. All you want is cheap labor." As I tried to explain to him that, in fact, the *Journal* was one of the few newspapers to agree with the labor unions that rising wages were not the source of inflation, I realized that editing the *Forward* could be more fun than anything I'd yet imagined.

When I arrived at the paper, Cahan had been dead for nearly forty years, but his presence was still very much felt. His name was bandied about in editorial meetings. His books were on our shelves, and editors reminded young writers of his penchant for plain language. The story was still told of how, when a subeditor would come to Cahan with a question about clarity, he would send the fellow out to consult the elevator operator. On political matters, Cahan was cited both by readers who sent in letters to the editor and by older colleagues, men who worked in adjacent rooms on the Yiddish edition and wondered, as my colleagues and I did at the English-language paper, what the man whose portrait hung in the entryway would think about what was going on in the world today. Even members of the board of directors of the Forward Association cited Cahan as they wrestled with whether to continue to support the paper.

One morning, early in my tenure at the paper, I witnessed a curious thing. It occurred with the arrival at our offices of the newspaper's storied general counsel, Judith Vladeck, one of the country's leading labor lawyers. A grand figure of the old school, she swept out of the elevator. As she entered the premises, I was startled to see her lift her hand to avoid looking at the portrait of Cahan. Later she explained that, like others connected with the paper's traditions, she was not altogether an admirer of Cahan. Her own hero was B. Charney Vladeck, who happened to be her father-in-law and who, in the years between the First and Second World Wars, had served as the *Forward*'s business manager and whose politics were quite a bit to the left of Cahan's.

As the years passed, I discovered that the Cahan whose views my critics so often accused me of traducing was a Cahan they didn't agree with in the first place. After being accused of moving the paper too far to the right, I would seek guidance in the files from Cahan's era, only to discover editorials on the evils of Communism that sounded as though they had been written by members of the John Birch Society. Questioned on our devotion to coverage of books and the arts, I discovered in the files a Cahan who was obsessed with literature and theater and what we call today the culture wars. When some wondered whether I had taken the *Forward* too far from the Jewish beat, I discovered in Cahan an editor who moved broadly in society, dining with the likes of H. L. Mencken and gallivanting about town with his friends from the *Commercial Advertiser*.

Yet the further Cahan ranged, the more obsessed he seemed to become with remaining loyal to a core sensibility from his youth: to the memory of his parents, to certain elements of the shtetl, and even, it turned out, to the idea of Jewishness itself and to at least some of the laws handed down at Sinai. He had begun his journey by marching away from religion in the name of socialism, only to mount his last big fight against those who would abandon the Jewish religion in the name of harmony and integration—even while insisting, to the end, that he was not a religious man at all.

Cahan had begun to doubt religion as a youth, though his parents were fervently pious and gave him a religious education. Caught up in the political awakening that took hold in Russia and eastern Europe in the second half of the nineteenth century, he abandoned religious orthodoxy and plunged into the revolutionary, anticzarist movement, while also being tempted by the freedom and materialism of secular liberalism. As pogroms ignited a historic exodus of Jews from eastern Europe, Cahan escaped to America one step ahead of the czarist police.

In America, Cahan taught school and fell in with socialist activists—one of whom, Anna Bronstein, he married. They had no children but remained married for more than sixty years, until her death in 1947. Cahan began writing not only for socialist journals but also for the general press and in 1897 became the founding editor of the *Forward*. Working primarily, although not exclusively, in Yiddish—a language that, it has been said, he "had come to despise"—he went on to become one of the greatest newspapermen of all time.

Cahan covered the stirrings of revolution in Russia, the ideological maneuvering over World War I, the accession of political Zionism, the emergence of the ideas of social democracy in Europe and America, the rise of the free trade union movement, World War II, and the Holocaust. In some of these events and movements, he played a leading role. Animated by his socialist, pro-labor politics, the newspaper he built laid the foundations for the institutions that brought down the Soviet Union and defeated its international Communist movement by driving through its heart the stake of free labor. Along the way, Cahan built a separate reputation as a towering writer of fiction; a behind-the-scenes player in local, national, and world politics; and a leader of the anti-Communist labor movement. He wrote a two-volume history of the United States—in Yiddish.

But the most remarkable fact of Abraham Cahan's life was that, for all his worldly and political success, for all his freethinking and socialist idealism, he was never able to escape thinking of himself as a young yeshiva student from Vilna who prized, above all else, the wonder of Jewish life. In 1940, at age eighty, he excommunicated his star writer, Sholem Asch, for a flirtation with Jesus, going so far as to write a book denouncing him. He was capable of his own political surprises. On the eve of the Holocaust, Cahan mocked the only Jewish journalist of his own rank, Vladimir Jabotinsky, for his Zionist fervor—only to turn around weeks later, on Jabotinsky's death, and write a prophetic elegy to his greatest political opponent.

Finally, Cahan's life has much to teach us at a time when newspapers themselves are in a historic crisis, preoccupied with process and tactics and financial viability. For all his innovations as a newspaper builder, Cahan was one of those who understood the idea of the newspaper editor as a historical actor. He ranked with figures like William Lloyd Garrison and the greatest of the abolitionists, and Charles Dana, who worried less about his circulation than about the Union, and Theodor Herzl, who saw himself as not just covering a story but creating a state. Here, in Cahan, was a newspaperman who helped to reform his adopted country and open it to vast numbers of new citizens, while defeating its enemies at home and abroad.

1

Sometimes, when I think of my past in a superficial, casual way, the metamorphosis I have gone through strikes me as nothing short of a miracle. I was born and reared in the lower depths of poverty and I arrived in America—in 1885—with four cents in my pocket. I am now worth more than two million dollars and recognized as one of the two or three leading men in the cloak-and-suit trade in the United States. And yet when I take a look at my inner identity it impresses me as being precisely the same as it was thirty or forty years ago. My present station, power, the amount of worldly happiness at my command, and the rest of it, seem to be devoid of significance.

So Abraham Cahan began his literary masterpiece, *The Rise of David Levinsky*, a novel about a Jewish boy from Russia who comes to America, abandons his religious orthodoxy, and plunges into the world of business, only to find wealth but lose his soul. The novel, published in 1917 by Harper & Brothers when Cahan was fifty-seven, wasn't precisely autobiographical. Cahan had arrived in America in 1882 and had made his mark not in the cloak-and-suit trade but in the world of newspapers, politics, and literature. It is unlikely that he was worth anything near two million dollars, but he resided in a handsome house in Greenwich Village and moved comfortably at the highest levels of political life in New York and Washington.

Over the course of his life, however, Cahan went through a metamorphosis not unlike that of his fictional hero. He was born on July 7, 1860, in the Lithuanian village of Podberez'ye and spent his boyhood in Vilna. His father, Scharkne Cahan, was a religious teacher and tavernkeeper; his mother, Sarah Goldbreiter, was an educated woman who taught reading and writing to girls and kept house.

Cahan was blessed—or burdened—with an extraordinary memory. It stood him in good stead when, in his sixties, he sat down to write a memoir he called *Bleter Fun Mein Leben* (Pages from My Life). It ultimately ran to five volumes in Yiddish. The first two were eventually published in English in 1969 by the Jewish Publication Society under the title *The Education of Abraham Cahan*. Much of what we know of Cahan's early years comes from his astonishingly clear images that go back to when he was a young child. In the opening pages of the memoir, Cahan remarks that, after leaving Podberez'ye for Vilna at the age of five and a half, he did not see the hamlet again for fifty-eight years. Yet in the decades after he left, he retained a nigh photographic picture of the place.

"Had I been a painter," he wrote, "I could have pictured, anytime during those years, every detail of the town."

Cahan's earliest memory was of "an old sofa, torn and with its stuffing coming out." He remembered that it had "a large hole through which I had fallen" and remembered "standing inside the sofa." Years later, he asked his mother about the memory and a feeling of sadness that he associated with it. His mother "recalled the torn sofa but not any specific circumstances involving me," Cahan wrote. "She reckoned I was one-and-a-half years old at the time."

There were darker memories too, inevitable enough for a Jewish child growing up in nineteenth-century Russia. One day his mother took him to visit her father in Vilna, and en route they passed the bodies of Polish landowners hanging from several gallows that had been set up in a field of cabbage. The bodies were wrapped in white gowns that fluttered in the wind. "I remember," Cahan wrote, "a boot falling from one of the dead ones. I remember soldiers with their white trousers neatly tucked into their shiny black boots, marching past the gallows to the sound of blaring trumpets." He remembered his mother calling out for her sister ("Fayge! Fayge!"), from whom they had become separated in the milling crowd.

He was, at the time, all of three years old. He remembered the package of grits and a small pan for cooking it that his aunt Fayge gave his mother on the visit. He remembered standing at a window and looking out at a snow-covered market. "Somewhere, in one of the other houses, my father and several other Jews are in hiding," he wrote. "A town elder has been ordered to select Jews for service in the czar's army." That a three-year-old could know, let alone remember, about service in the czar's army, is hard to imagine. But Cahan claimed to remember being carried on his mother's hip: she held on to him with one hand and with the other offered food to a Jewish recruit who was in chains, on his way to serve in the army.

The danger of conscription was a constant presence in Cahan's youth. In 1827 Czar Nicholas I included Jews in Russia's conscription laws, requiring Jewish communities to produce candidates, from ages twelve to twenty-five, for Russia's military cantons, or training schools. The purpose of compulsory military service was less to defend Russia than to break the conscripts' ties to the Jewish community and to convert them to Christianity. Conditions were harsh, particularly for those who refused conversion, and suicide was not uncommon. The policy enforced strict quotas on Jewish communities, and leaders had to grapple with the task of implementing them. Some hired kidnappers (*khappers*, in Yiddish) to capture potential conscripts, many of whom ran away or disfigured themselves to avoid service. When quotas went unmet, boys as young as eight would be snatched in their stead.

Alexander II took the throne in 1855, upon his father's death, five years before Cahan's birth, and began to scale back some of Nicholas I's worst policies. He abolished the cantonist policy and decreased the period of military service to five years. He eased some restrictions on Jews, allowing Jewish businessmen to travel to parts of the empire from which they had been previously prohibited, and he opened the doors of some universities to a small percentage of Jews. Alexander II's reign was by no means a golden period of freedom for Jews, but the czar whom Benjamin Disraeli called the "kindliest prince who has ever ruled Russia" allowed Jews to hope, however modestly, that they might be witnessing the beginning of a new era in which they would be granted equal rights as Russian citizens.

Cahan's paternal grandfather, Reb Yankele, was a rabbi and was much revered by his family and the inhabitants of Podberez'ye. Cahan was admonished to persevere in his studies and to conduct himself in a manner befitting the grandson of a rabbi.

"The most intense of my first memories is of Friday, the eve of the Sabbath, when, as the twilight deepened, my father took me on his lap, telling me old legends and crooning ancient Hebrew songs," Cahan told Ernest Poole, who interviewed him for the magazine *Outlook* in 1911. When Cahan was four years old, his father wrapped him in his prayer shawl, as was the custom, and brought him to the *cheder* (a religious elementary school for boys). There his father broke down and sobbed. As far as he was concerned, his son had now "entered the service of God."

When Cahan was not quite six, his family moved from Podberez'ye to his mother's birthplace, Vilna. Only fourteen miles from Podberez'ye, it was, however, worlds away. "The Jerusalem of Lithuania," as Napoleon was said to have dubbed it, Vilna was a storied center of Jewish learning, best known as the home of the Vilna Gaon, the influential eighteenth-century rabbi. A great Talmudic scholar who was also well versed in secular subjects like mathematics and astronomy, the Vilna Gaon was considered a rationalist compared to the mystically inclined Hasidim, whom he battled.

Cahan's earliest impression of the city, which had a population of about 80,000, was not of its intellectual character but of something decidedly more earthbound. "The stench in the courtyards seemed to issue from the bricks of the buildings," he wrote in his memoir. Unlike Podberez'ye, which boasted gardens and fresh air, Vilna had only "streets and more streets." And no plumbing. Cahan's family had moved to Vilna because his mother's two uncles ran a thriving liquor business there. They owned distilleries several miles outside town and, in town, a wholesale liquor store and a tavern, behind which Cahan lived with his family between the ages of six and fourteen.

For all the stench, there was a good bit of warmth in the Cahan household. His mother kept her Sabbath candles on the chest of drawers in her bedroom, and on Fridays she moved them into the tavern, which became an extension of their home, and ushered in the Sabbath by saying the blessing over them. If a customer came in for a drink afterward, he could get it either on credit or against collateral. His parents would unpack the Passover dishes, and Cahan wrote of the fondness with which his mother handed him his own blue Passover goblet. He sensed tension between his parents, who worried about money. He was "pointed out" as a country cousin, he said, "a lower order of human being." But foreshadowing his greater assimilation in years to come, Cahan wrote that he picked up the new Vilna accent and idioms quickly. Soon he was "pointing out others as country cousins."

During the first half of the nineteenth century, Vilna had undergone sweeping changes. While the city still deeply felt the influence of rabbinical scholarship, it had also become a thriving center of the Haskala, as the Jewish enlightenment movement was called, which encouraged Jews to widen their scope of learning to include secular studies of all kinds. Even the Russian government recognized the importance of Vilna; during this time it opened several schools geared toward the Russification of the Jews. The result was that, at precisely the period during which Cahan arrived, a culture war was brewing, although its pattern was not always well defined. Cahan would become caught up in it and move into the secular camp—up to a point.

In his memoir, Cahan gave the impression that he sensed all this from the moment of his arrival in Vilna, even though he was not quite six years old. He wrote that it was common to see "two Jews stop in the street, begin to chatter like two turkeys about a passage in the Talmud, gather about them in short order a small crowd, and engage in heated debate, to the delight of the listeners." He reckoned that "a Vilna youth

[is] as skillful in the techniques of intellectual hairsplitting as an American boy is with a baseball."

Vilna boasted, in the Rabiner Institute, one of the two schools in Russia for training teachers to work with Jewish children in public schools. "Vilna, the city of the Gaon," Cahan wrote, "was now the city of Berka Michailishker (Adam Hacohen Lebensohn),* the great atheist." His father Scharkne would "often curse him with an intensity that reflected his respect for the atheist's excellence as a sage, grammarian, and Hebraist." Cahan's father told how "once a Jew visiting Berka Michailishker found on one of the tables a commentary on the Bible bound in red morocco leather. 'Why is it bound in red?' the pious Jew asked. To which the atheist replied, 'Originally it was white. But it was caught with so many lies that it turned red for shame.' "

Cahan's family home was situated in a lively part of town, on a square where several streets intersected. The air was filled with the noise and chatter of a busy marketplace, with peddlers, peasants, and salesmen hawking their wares—herring and salt and tobacco and soda and oats and hay. The Cahans' dark apartment was connected to the back of the tavern, which was a large room where brandy was on tap and platters of honey cake and roast goose and jellied calves' feet were displayed at the bar. Their customers were mostly workers from the marketplace, peddlers with long thick ropes around their waists who pushed two-wheeled carts. The tavern's patrons were proud that their barkeep was a son of a rabbi, but Cahan's father wished his customers were more educated and "respectable."

Scharkne Cahan was devoted to Jewish sacred music. He "treasured the singing and the rehearsals at which he spent many evenings with me on his lap," while his son was mesmerized, "transported," as he put it, "by music and brandy fumes to a fantasy world." Cahan's recollec-

* Abraham Lebensohn, also known as Adam Hacohen Lebensohn, described by the Jewish Encyclopedia as a "Russian Hebraist, poet, and grammarian." He was "popularly known by the surname Michailishker."

tions of this period are filled with references to the intensity of his religious feelings, but during this time he was also hearing the siren call of secularism.

Scharkne was no stranger to the conflict between the secular and religious. Cahan described him as a great learner, a yeshiva student who was never educated in secular topics but nonetheless thirsted for knowledge of the modern world. He read more philosophy than Talmud and was "irresistibly drawn to secular books printed in Hebrew, and he dreamed of helping me become an 'educated man.'" When his son Abraham was ten, the boy enrolled in a public school without his parents' permission. It was one of several government-operated schools in Vilna established for Jews, funded by taxes levied against the Jewish community.

There his clean-shaven Jewish teacher wore a blue frock coat with brass buttons and spoke in Russian; none of the students wore head coverings. Despite his yearning to learn Russian and other secular subjects, Cahan soon found himself homesick and fearful of his teacher's brass buttons, his Russian, and his seemingly foreign ways. After about a year, Cahan left the school, and his father hired two tutors—one to teach him Russian, and the other Hebrew grammar.

Cahan's education, and to some degree his life, remained divided between these two poles. His father toyed with the idea of sending him to the Rabiner school—where the teachers were also clean-shaven Jews who ignored the Sabbath—but lost his nerve. For someone of Cahan's generation, the world of his father was not simple: that older generation was also torn between religion and modernity. Cahan yearned to study at a secular institution but felt a great pull toward his religious upbringing. He called the period leading up to his bar mitzvah "the time of my greatest religious fervor." He was not the only one who felt this way. During the days between Rosh Hashanah and Yom Kippur, Jewish Vilna became "a preachers' market," and Cahan didn't miss a talk by any of them.

Cahan's brother, Isaac, was born in 1873. That winter a new law was introduced, imposing a general draft and abolishing the old practice of leaving to the community the selection of young men to fill the quota of military recruits. Also ended was the practice of allowing the wealthy to buy substitutes for military service. Eligible young Jewish men were now expected to serve the czar's army for five years and could not become officers. But a special dispensation could be granted to those with a secondary Russian education. So the new law fueled Jewish student enrollment in the Rabiner schools.

Meanwhile, Cahan's uncle's business spiraled downward, and he closed his wholesale brandy store. His parents took over the tavern, but they too struggled, and finally they gave up the business. Scharkne took a job as a bookkeeper at a small company that imported fruit from Crimea and southern Europe. Cahan liked to visit his father's office and breathe in the scent of oranges and apples and grapes from foreign lands. But the new employer was difficult, and Cahan witnessed him insulting and belittling his father, who soon lost the job. With money tight, his parents tried to apprentice Cahan to a cabinetmaker, but he rebelled in a demonstrative showdown with his mother. At fourteen, he entered the largest yeshiva in Vilna.

Cahan's reflections on his education strike a responsive chord with readers more than a century later. "If I had studied at a gymnasium or an American public school instead of at cheders and yeshivas I would have known more at eleven than I knew at fourteen," he wrote. But he quickly added that he could not write off the Talmud study he had engaged in from the age of eight. Not only did it make "the most rigorous reasoning required in arithmetic easy," but it clearly left an imprint on his soul. Years later, presiding over a newspaper that ushered generations of immigrants into modern American life, that core of Jewish learning would serve as a touchstone and orient him in an uprooted world.

In his youth, however, Cahan, like many young Jews, turned to speaking and reading Russian. As for piety, Hershka Levinson, a childhood friend, was an atheist and ridiculed the idea of God. But that approach left Cahan unmoved. "I was no longer pious. I had long ago stopped saying the daily prayers; nor did I fear to desecrate the Sabbath," Cahan wrote. "But I had not stopped believing in God."

2

In later life, Cahan remained acutely aware of the painful transition that immigrant Jews made as they passed from youthful piety into a wider world of secular learning. He made his own journey not as an immigrant but while still an adolescent. When he was fourteen, he learned, from students at the Vilna Teachers Training Institute, about the city's free government library. It stood opposite the governor-general's residence, where the czar stayed when he came to Vilna. Its facade announced the building's purpose in large, gleaming gold letters—PUBLIC LIBRARY—and inside, its shelves were well stocked with the complete works of Turgenev, with Ostrovsky's dramas, and with Pisarev's novels.

Not until he was fifteen, however, was Cahan able to overcome his awe and summon the courage to enter the library. He asked the librarian for the first volume of Turgenev's complete works. As he looked for a seat, the librarian insisted he remove his overcoat. Blushing, for the garment was neither a jacket nor an overcoat but the only clothing he wore, he fled the library. Once home, he undertook to have a jacket made, and when it was finished, "I felt as if I had suddenly grown ten times more Gentile than before." He then returned to the library to commence his reading of Turgenev and the vast literary world beyond.

Cahan spent five hours a day in the library, reading voraciously. Decades later he could still recall the smell of the books, the stillness of the reading room, and the feel of the book bindings. "The Vilna Public Library became for me a temple of learning and inspiration," he wrote. It was the sort of experience that, twenty years later and an ocean away, the immigrant readers of Cahan's own paper would know well.

As he plunged ahead in his secular studies of geography and astronomy, Cahan's newfound knowledge shifted his perspective on religion.

"Clearly, there were no mysteries!" he recalled thinking. "There was no God!"

It was not only reading that changed him. During this period Cahan and several cronies took a room in a courtyard where geese were sold. It was called the Goosery. Friends brought girls. They danced the quadrille to their own singing. Their behavior toward the girls was, he wrote, always exemplary; "on rare occasions, however, there would be another kind of young lady." Cahan characterized them as "not street girls" but girls from respectable families, and with them "we spent lusty hours of the sort one does not write about."

Not long before, Cahan had developed an eye infection and had been treated by a *feldsher*, a health practitioner who did not hold a medical degree. The infection lasted weeks and left him cross-eyed, a condition that though he later alleviated it with the local application of cocaine, troubled him for the rest of his life and made him ashamed of his appearance and shy, especially with women. But he was shedding his inhibitions, both social and political.

One day while Cahan and his friends were at the Goosery, a small boy entered their hideaway and handed one of them a printed leaflet. "A Jewish man told me to give you this," the boy said. They ran to the door to see if they could catch the sender, but "no one was in the corridor." The leaflet was a socialist proclamation, written in Yiddish on one side and Russian or Hebrew on the other. Cahan called the leaflet "the first underground, forbidden writing I had ever seen. We were all shaken by it."

This world of mysterious messengers and subversive pamphlets, combined with his intensive reading of Russian literature, constituted Cahan's true education. Still, the Vilna Teachers Training Institute, which he attended from 1878 to 1881, was an enormous step up for him, given his lopsided learning during his early years of religious education. The school—less a university than what today we might call a junior college—consisted of five buildings and a courtyard. The Ministry of Education intended it "to insure that future Jewish teachers of Jews be mentally and physically healthy and alert." It was also an instrument of assimilation. None of the Jewish students spoke Yiddish at the school; to do so would have been to risk severe punishment. But Cahan quickly soured on the institution, which bored him with its rote learning, and on the prospect of becoming a teacher.

Meanwhile the world around him was changing. The relaxation of the laws regarding military service and Alexander II's small steps toward granting Jews rights (including, in some cases, the right to live outside the Pale of Settlement) gave rise to a feeling that the government was moving—haltingly but inexorably—toward the emancipation of its Jewish population. But as Jews began to take a larger part in Russian cultural and professional life, they were accused of polluting the purity of the Russian people. Anti-Semitic attacks rose, gaining in strength after the Russo-Turkish war of 1877–78.

All these pressures took their toll: revolutionaries were increasingly frustrated by the Russian government's autocratic ways, and Jews felt their chances for inclusion in Russian society slipping away. In April 1879 a teacher named Alexander Soloviev fired five shots at Alexander II in a failed assassination attempt. Later that same year a revolutionary group called Narodnaya Volya (People's Will) placed a bomb on the railway tracks from Livadia to Moscow, but it missed the czar's train. In February 1880 a bomb exploded in a room directly below the dining room at the Winter Palace, missing the czar by only minutes. "Each new terrorist deed," Cahan wrote decades later, "received short shrift in the newspapers because the official censor had banned publication of details. However, even these short accounts were enough to inform the public that an effective underground movement was conducting a heroic struggle against the throne."

For several years, Cahan had heard stories of the existence of a secret revolutionary movement. He recalled that on one Passover there was excitement over the arrest of a group of Jewish revolutionaries. One was the "hunchbacked son of a cantor," and he remembered his mother telling him, "In the hunchback's trunk they found a loaf of bread—an outrage during Passover—and a book. And in the book it was written, 'There is no God and we don't need a czar.' " Cahan's comment: "I was already well on my way to atheism so that the declaration about God did not disturb me. But how could the world exist without a czar?"

Down by the railroad tracks, he had noticed that a group of young men and women gathered regularly near a refreshment table that a watchman's wife had set out beside a railroad track. "Even though they dressed and chatted like the others, they had a certain manner that set them apart." Curious, Cahan approached a friend who attended the same school as one of the members of the group. The boy eventually confessed to Cahan that he had been reading underground literature. He "drew from his pocket a forbidden pamphlet and handed it to me," Cahan recalled. Cahan realized that it was published by the group that had tried to blow up Alexander II's train, and he held it with reverence. "The pamphlet came to me from people who lived as brothers, who were willing to face the gallows for freedom."

Cahan joined the revolutionary underground, and "life took on new meaning. . . . All could be equal. All could be brothers." A reading program was organized for him. He became an impassioned believer in socialism, hungering to convert others. "I walked in a daze as one newly in love."

As Cahan fell in deeper with his new friends, his relations with his family suffered. His father worried about his abandonment of religion, and for many weeks father and son sat in silence at the Sabbath table. One evening a relative, seeing a bulge in Cahan's jacket pocket, sought to reach in and pull out what he thought were underground pamphlets. Cahan struck his hand and pushed it away, shouting at his relative. When the relative left, Cahan's mother remonstrated him. "You will bring misfortune on your own head," she said sadly.

On Sunday morning, March 1, 1881, Alexander II was traveling from the Winter Palace to the riding academy to watch a military parade, following a well-known route along the Catherine Canal. The czar sat in a closed, bulletproof carriage, protected by Cossacks. The head of his guards and the chief of police followed closely behind in separate sleighs.

A member of Narodnaya Volya named Nikolai Rysakov approached and threw a small package wrapped in a white handkerchief at the carriage. It landed near the horses' hooves. The bomb exploded, killing one of the Cossacks, but the czar emerged from the carriage, relatively unscathed. Rysakov was quickly apprehended. Just as the guards were urging the czar to leave the scene, another member of Narodnaya Volya, Ignaty Grinevitsky, threw another bomb at him. This one killed him.

Cahan was in a classroom studying botany when a student burst in with the news. The school's director requested that they close their books immediately and assemble in the corridor. The director announced that there would be no classes the following day, saying, "Our czar is dead." Two of Cahan's cronies pinched him, and Cahan sneaked out of the institute at night to make contact with his underground comrades. On March 15 he and his classmates and teachers were taken to a Russian church where they all swore loyalty to the new czar, Alexander III. But Cahan no longer had trouble envisioning a world without a czar. When one of his comrades from his underground group made the sign of a fig instead of saluting their new leader, Cahan had difficulty controlling his laughter.

The plotters were rounded up. In the post-assassination chaos, censorship fell by the wayside, and newspaper headlines trumpeted the newest revelations. Decades later Cahan thrilled at the memory of hurrying to read the daily papers. "Every day the press blazoned a new sensation," he recalled. He and his socialist friends eagerly awaited the next revolutionary step. Even outside Russia, it was expected that great upheavals would follow the assassination. *The New York Herald* rushed a special correspondent to St. Petersburg to cover the stirrings of revolution.

Alexander II's death was a catastrophe for Russian Jews, and pogroms erupted throughout the Pale, as Russians obsessed on the idea that Jews were responsible for the country's troubles. Many Jews felt that nothing good would come from the czar's assassination, but Cahan, at the height of his socialist fervor, took a more positive tone. "Even though the pogrom brought dread into the heart of every Jew," he wrote years later, "I must admit that the members of my group were not disturbed by it. We regarded ourselves as human beings, not as Jews. There was only one remedy to the world's ills, and that was socialism." The phrase "I must admit" suggests that Cahan, looking back decades after the event, had long since come to comprehend the degree to which participation in a "universal" program often required, as the price of admission, the abandonment of concerns about Jewish suffering.

Upon his graduation from the Vilna Teachers Training Institute, Cahan's education, so to speak, accelerated rapidly. He plunged immediately into helping organize an underground press and then traveled, on his summer vacation, to visit a rich uncle in St. Petersburg. His heartbroken father refused to accompany him to the train station. Cahan was thrilled to be in the big city, where Jews had only recently been allowed to settle following Alexander II's easing of residence restrictions. Upon arriving, he asked the driver of his *droshky* to call out names of streets as they passed—Cahan recognized many from newspapers and literature.

His uncle received him warmly, whisking him out by train to his country home and buying him a proper teacher's black frock. At a bookstall, he bought a copy of John Stuart Mill's *Political Economy*, with notes by the translator N. G. Chernyshevsky, the prerevolutionary philosopher who was at the time in prison in Siberia. During that period, books, pamphlets, and ideas could be as dangerous as chemical explosives. Cahan spent three weeks in St. Petersburg, but when he returned to Vilna, he felt as if he had been away for many years.

Cahan's teaching assignment was in the province of Vitebsk (where

Marc Chagall would be born in 1887) in Velizh, near Lubavitch, a center of Hasidism and the seat of the Lubavitcher Rebbe. Cahan said good-bye to his revolutionary comrades as his family fussed over him. He made peace with his father, who agreed to accompany him and the rest of the family on the first fifteen miles of the train ride. The family got off at Vileika, and the parting lasted a minute. "We kissed and embraced, and my mother cried and my aunt cried and the children kept jumping," Cahan recalled. "Finally, I disengaged myself. Then the train began to move. Through the window I could see my mother standing rigid, her face pale. I was in a daze. I pulled myself together. I put on a brave front. I waved my kerchief and managed the pretense of a smile."

3

In Velizh, the tension between Cahan's universalist, radical self and his Jewish self only increased. His entire life, in fact, would be a series of inner battles between these two aspects of his identity. Pious but rationalist Vilna had not prepared him for the lifestyle of the community of Hasidic Jews in Velizh. Here, a man walking in the street followed at a distance behind his wife; walking together would have been considered a sign of moral looseness. Cahan found himself homesick, repelled by the Hasidim but drawn to them at the same time. Soon after his arrival, he decided to attend synagogue, which he justified in his memoir as applying "the principle of the revolutionaries . . . to mingle with the people." He and a friend went to *shul* "fully aware of the fact that in view of the old-fashioned piety of the city our education branded us as Gentiles."

It turned out, however, that when they entered the synagogue, the congregation welcomed them as important guests and offered them seats of honor. They invited Cahan to chant the *haftorah*, a short reading from one of the biblical books of the prophets that follows the weekly Torah reading. It had been eight years since Cahan's bar mitzvah and he was out of practice; he managed the Hebrew well enough, but the tune confused him, and soon he was stumbling over the words as well. "I began to burn with blushing," he wrote, still smarting from the embarrassment decades later. "When it was done I couldn't look anyone in the face."

The synagogue did not reject him; instead, Cahan turned away from it and looked for other ways of meeting people. He struck up friendships with the socialist underground in Velizh and found living quarters with a family that was also involved in prerevolutionary stirrings. He published his first article and encountered, for the first time, a Russian translation of volume one of Marx's *Das Kapital*. But he never felt at home in Velizh and wondered, as he wrote in his memoir, "How can I get out of here?"

The answer came shortly before Purim, when he received a letter from his mother: "Your darkly charming friend who teaches Rivka caught a cold. The funeral has already taken place. He was buried deep, deep, deep. The cold is great; take care of yourself, my son! Do not go outside without your muffler." This was not his mother's usual way of writing, and it was already spring—the cold weather had ended. Cahan understood that his mother was telling him that one of his underground friends had been arrested.

In Cahan's first heady days as a socialist, he had anguished over his sacred duty to love everyone equally. "If I loved my mother more than other women it meant only that I still harbored sentiments from an evil and unjust world," he wrote in his memoir. "But in my heart I continued to feel that I loved her more than all others." He might not yet have been "a fully developed socialist," but his mother's love was, in effect, saving him now.

Soon thereafter a postcard arrived from a Vilna friend containing even more disquieting news: another friend, Stotchick, had been arrested and taken to the political prison in Vilna. (Stotchick, alone in a cell, would later take his own life by hanging himself with a sheet.) Cahan gathered his forbidden reading materials and gave them to his landlord's servant, then returned to his room and fell into "an uneasy sleep." Awakened by the local police, he convinced them that his copy of *Das Kapital* was a book about business. A few days later they showed up at the school where he was teaching. He was searched and marched out of school, held in custody while his apartment was searched again, and then told to appear for further questioning in the evening.

"When the interrogation was ended," Cahan wrote, "I was warned not to leave the city." He was told that he would be kept under surveillance and taken to Vitebsk for further questioning. His landlord's family was placed under house arrest. The surveillance of Cahan was lax, but even though some of his local acquaintances remained friendly, he sensed a change of attitude toward him. He decided to make a run for it and planned an escape by barge. When complications arose, he found a rowboat. A trusted old friend named Meyerson, who aided him, urged him to use an alias. For the time being, he would no longer be Cahan, but Lifshitz. On the appointed night, under a moonlit sky, Lifshitz-Cahan handed Meyerson his elegant, government-issued teacher's hat and replaced it with a cheap, ordinary hat. Then he twisted two strands of hair down the sides of his face. The irony that the fugitive socialist was disguising himself as a Hasidic Jew was not lost on either man.

Cahan made it across the Dnieper River safely. He spent three weeks in a town called Moghilev, where he was astonished to discover the existence of a local Yiddish-language theater, something that had not been permitted in Vilna. (He would become deeply involved with Yiddish theater in New York.) Through friends he made in Moghilev, he heard about a man named Israel Belkind who was looking for young people to go to Palestine. Cahan asked for an introduction immediately.

Why was a socialist/universalist interested in meeting a Zionist emissary? The answer is complex. The pogroms ignited by the assassination of Alexander II and the accession of Alexander III brought home to Russia's Jews the fact that they could no longer live in the Russian Empire. But where could they go? In his memoir Cahan described a student who entered a synagogue in Kiev and stunned the congregation by announcing: "We are your brothers. We are Jews, just as you are. Until now we thought of ourselves as Russians, not as Jews. Now we regret it. The events of these last weeks—the pogroms in Elisavetgrad, in Balta, here in Kiev, and in other cities have shown us how tragic has been our mistake. Yes, we are Jews."

Cahan called the event "the beginning of the nationalist movement among the young Jewish intellectuals in Russia," though the Kiev student group consisted of those "who favored America as the land to which Jews should look for a new home."

The impact of the nationalist idea was so powerful that, Cahan said, some Jews "stopped talking in Russian and began to use only Yiddish."

Many, he wrote, "discarded their Russianized names and assumed their Jewish ones. Yakov became Yankel again and Natasha answered only when addressed as Ethel." The new Jewish nationalists were only a small group, Cahan admitted, as were the Jewish revolutionaries who fell in with the nationalist movement. The reason more revolutionaries did not join the Jewish nationalist movement, Cahan wrote, "may seem unbelievable. Among the Jewish revolutionaries were some who considered the anti-Semitic massacres to be a good omen."

Cahan was discovering a pattern that, over time, has played itself out repeatedly: leftists, in thrall to a fantasy of universal or populist liberation, have sided with their natural enemies in the hope of purging from their own group any particularistic taint. According to these revolutionaries, he wrote, the pogroms "were an instinctive outpouring of the revolutionary anger of the people, driving the Russian masses against their oppressors. . . . Uneducated Russian people knew that the czar, the officials, and the Jews sucked their blood . . . so the Ukrainian peasant attacked the Jews, the 'percentniks.' The revolutionary torch had been lit and would next be applied to the officials and the czar himself." He attributed such reasoning only to some revolutionaries, "Jews and non-Jews."

Cahan quoted from a proclamation addressed to "the Ukrainian pogrom makers" by People's Will that "urged the pogrom makers to continue their revolutionary work," and he noted that one of the members of the group that composed the proclamation was a Jew.* Cahan was slowly coming to agree with those who felt that the Jews had no future in Russia. "Two groups emerged," he wrote. "One believed that a new home for the Jews should be started in America, the land of rich resources and opportunity. The other urged a return to Palestine, the historical home of the Jewish people."

* An editor's footnote to the English-language edition of Cahan's memoir remarks that "the sole Jewish member of the Party's executive committee . . . rushed back to Moscow" to try to get the committee to disavow the proclamation. But it was apparently too late. "The damage was done."

He made the acquaintance of Israel Belkind,* whom he would call "a pioneer of this pro-Palestine movement." Twenty-two-year-old Abraham Cahan realized that he had to think all this through by himself. Belkind, a Zionist recruiter, "carried a book into which he wrote the names of candidates for Palestine." Cahan called him a "doer of deeds, an idealist, almost one of 'ours.' "

But Cahan was not yet ready to throw in his lot with the Zionists. He viewed himself as "first of all a socialist." He felt strongly that it was his duty to try to establish full rights for all citizens of Russia, and he believed that with proper education, the Russian people would abandon pogroms in favor of universal brotherhood. In any event, he was eager to get to Switzerland.

Belkind argued that if Cahan were to go there, all he would be able to work for was to return to Russia as an "illegal," with false papers, and once he'd returned, he would sooner or later be arrested. "And what would he be giving his life for?" Belkind asked him. "For a Russian people who made pogroms on Jews?" But if he went to Palestine, Belkind argued, Cahan "could work for the fulfillment of an ideal of happiness and security for our people and without risking my life."

Then Belkind, the Zionist recruiter, put to Cahan a question that found its mark. "If I was so determined to serve my socialist ideal, why must I go to Switzerland? Why not America? Many socialists were heading for America, where they planned to establish communist colonies." As he thought about it, Cahan "imagined a wonderful communist life in that far-off country, a life without 'mine' and 'thine.' I had thought until now that such a dream of equality could be realized only in the distant future. In America, it could become a reality now." For many Jews, America was the "Golden Land." For Cahan, it existed in his mind's eye as a socialist utopia.

* Belkind was a Zionist pioneer (1861–1929) who was part of the First Aliyah and a founder of BILU, an organization of Russian Zionists who established agricultural settlements in Ottoman Palestine.

He was suddenly on fire with the idea of going to America. "Pro-Palestine Belkind had made a pro-American out of me," he recalled. Thousands of Jewish immigrants were gathering in Brody, Belkind told him, just across the border in Austria-Hungary, with the idea of getting to America. The two men had a warm parting, and Belkind wished him a successful journey.

As he made plans to leave, Cahan wrote, "I paced my room in a fever. America! To go to America! To re-establish the Garden of Eden in that distant land. My spirit soared. All my other plans dissolved. I was for America!"

It took a bit more doing to actually escape from Russia. Cahan acquired a forged passport, adopting a second false name. He worried a great deal about his parents and learned, eleven years later, that during this time they had in fact been visited by the gendarmes. He sent them false word that he had reached Paris safely, and then, on a cold day in 1882, he embarked on the steamer *Marusia*, bound southward for Kiev. En route down the Dnieper, the vessel was boarded by police. At one point, to avoid being identified by his crossed eyes, Cahan hid his face by carrying on his shoulder the trunk of another passenger.

After disembarking in Kiev, he boarded a train that would take him west to Dubno, a Ukrainian town near the Austrian border and near Brody. The train was full of Jews seeking to leave Russia—and he realized that he was part of a historic moment. "On that Saturday night there began the broad stream of Jewish migration that was to continue for almost two generations," he wrote in his memoir. "It was to make America the major center of Jewish population. The course of Jewish history would be changed by it."

As new emigrants boarded at each stop, Cahan's excitement grew. He cut a deal with a smuggler to get a group of them over the Russian border, then took charge of the bribe money. They left the train at Dubno and approached the border by horse-drawn wagon. "We made a strange group, going across the fields and meadows in the night," Cahan recalled. One of their peasant escorts halted them every few minutes, "holding up his finger and pausing to listen for God-knows-what disaster. . . . We went on and on. In the dark, our red-headed smuggler disappeared. Further on, we were joined by a husky, red-haired, clean-shaven Jew who spoke with a strange new accent." Cahan clutched his false passport tightly in his hand, figuring that if they were apprehended, it would be safer simply to throw it away. "We stumbled on endlessly. It seemed as if the border was miles away. Then the peasant straightened up and announced we were already well inside Austria."

During the spring of 1882, thousands of Jewish refugees from Ukraine were arriving in Brody, more than doubling its population of 15,000. Many slept in the streets. During the three weeks Cahan spent there, he got a haircut, bought a hat, and wrote to his family. He was struck by the affection with which Austrian Jews spoke of the emperor, Franz Josef, and by the Austrian government's friendliness to the Jews. Austrian Jews, he marveled, feared neither the military nor the gendarmes, "with their feminine black feathered hats, with swords." At one point at a parade ground he and some other Russian Jews listened as taps was played. "The sad tones touched the sorrowing ears of our people, standing in the lengthening shadows, overcome by longing for their forsaken home and by fear of a homeless future."

He sought to link up with a group of socialists bound for America, about whom Belkind had told him. To do so, he felt he had to demarcate himself from the vast majority of refugees. "I was not just running away like an ordinary immigrant," he wrote. "I was from the underground . . . I had evaded arrest." According to one eyewitness who knew Cahan during this period, he wore "a long coat that was a cross between an overcoat and a Jewish *kapoteh*. . . . He had a beard of five long hairs and at times looked like a damned one." Cahan, this source said, "was trying to get in with the intellectuals. . . . He stood apart and talked to no one." His detachment belied his observational powers. "[He] looked everywhere and listened to all."

Although Cahan would later write that he was "bitterly disappointed" at not finding more socialists during his layover in Brody, he actually did make many socialist friends there. He joined a group of Balta Am Olam, socialists who sought to establish agricultural settlements in the United States. He declared tactlessly (by his own account) that he would teach them socialist principles. ("Who needs you?" was the reply). He smoothed over his relations with his comrades by contributing some of the money his family had sent him for his journey.

Cahan set out for Germany with the Balta Am Olam by train, traveling third class, to the cheers of "Long live freedom in the American republic!" They stopped the next day at Lemberg, arrived in Cracow the following morning, and continued westward on to Breslau, where, Cahan remarked in his memoir, "for the first time I could see the marks of a highly civilized nation." In Germany, it seemed to him that "everyone dressed like a nobleman."

They traveled to Berlin and then arrived in Hamburg, where they boarded a ship going to England. In Liverpool, Cahan purchased a dictionary and began learning English, but the new language was as foreign to him as England's "bicycles, bootblacks, and hansom cabs." Cahan wondered if the mouths of those who spoke English were somehow formed differently than his own. In any case, in May 1882, the committed socialist set sail for America aboard the SS *British Queen.*

Cahan made his emblematic passage at the beginning of the vast wave of eastern European Jewish immigrants to America. Like them, Cahan spent much of the crossing standing at the rail, gazing at the seemingly limitless ocean. He wrote that he had imagined "that all Americans were tall and slender and that all the men wore yellow trousers and high hats." The journey took about two weeks, but the days felt long, and Cahan began to feel as if "the place called America was only a figment of the imagination."

Finally, the *British Queen* entered Delaware Bay, on its way to the port in Philadelphia. As he stood at the rail in the bright June sunshine, looking to spot his first American, he noted that "the water and the sky were blue with the blueness of paradise and all around us the sea gulls hailed us with their cries."

In his novel *The Rise of David Levinsky*, Cahan gives a similarly florid account of Levinsky's arrival in America, albeit intertwined with references to prayer and to God. When Levinsky's vessel reaches Sandy Hook, New Jersey, he is "literally overcome with the beauty of the landscape" and observes that "the immigrant's arrival in his new home is like a second birth to him." The immigrant is like a "new born babe in possession of a fully developed intellect." As Levinsky's ship nears the shore, he recites verses from Psalm 104: "Thou openest thine hand and they are filled with good. Thou hidest thy face, they are troubled; thou takest away their breath, they die." And as he stands at the rail, Levinsky prays that God will not hide His face from him in the new land.

4

Abraham Cahan arrived in America on June 6, 1882, disembarking at Philadelphia, where the U.S. Constitution had been crafted only ninety-five years earlier. Some individuals who had been infants at the time when the political giants were creating America might still have been alive. Before long, however, they would be gone, and in a sense, America was at a historical tipping point. The Civil War had been over for only seventeen years, and the Fourteenth and Fifteenth Amendments to the Constitution had been adopted shortly thereafter, to ensure that the southern states, furious over Reconstruction, would not deny the newly freed slaves their basic civil rights. Industrialization was well under way in cities throughout America, and the machines that were mass-producing men's and women's clothing created factory jobs for the thousands of immigrants arriving at America's shores. Chester A. Arthur, who had become president in 1881 upon the assassination of James A. Garfield, would confound his corrupt political cronies two years later by establishing the landmark Pendleton Civil Service Reform Act. Change was clearly in the air.

With astonishing speed, the ideas of socialism, Marxism, and social democracy—brought to America by European immigrants such as Cahan—would become part of the American political conversation and would revolutionize the relationship between laboring men and women and their employers. With equally surprising speed, Cahan, "greenhorn" though he was, became a part of the emerging reform movement and, through his journalism, rose to a position of unparalleled power and influence within it.

From Philadelphia, Cahan made a beeline for New York, arriving by train and ferry on the morning of June 7, 1882. He was twenty-two years old. At the time, no Statue of Liberty stood guard over the harbor, Ellis Island was a military post, and the Brooklyn Bridge wouldn't be completed for another year. Horse-drawn streetcars and elevated steam railroads served as the primary mode of public transportation, and the tallest building in Manhattan had but ten stories. Immigration officials directed Cahan to the offices of the Hebrew Immigrant Aid Society, where the German-speaking Jew who interviewed him seemed a "heartless bourgeois. . . . He probably suspected that I was a wild Russian." Cahan would later realize that other "Yahudim [German-American Jews] . . . fervently wished to help us stand on our own two feet in the new homeland."

Cahan immediately set out to catch up with his socialist friends from Vilna. They were living in the Brooklyn neighborhood of Greenpoint. His comrades were overjoyed to see him, he wrote later; he considered them "the first Russian-Jewish intellectuals in the United States."

The group had been met with hostility by German Jews, who had begun to arrive in America in the 1840s and had gradually displaced the long-established, assimilated Sephardic Jews as the country's largest and most influential Jewish ethnic group. The Germans "considered us to be atheists and lunatics; we intellectuals thought of them as ignorant, primitive people," Cahan wrote. As socialists, Cahan and his comrades were only a tiny minority even among the recent eastern European immigrants. "The Jewish masses in the old country knew little about socialism," Cahan wrote. "A mere handful of Jewish workers in Vilna had grasped the meaning of socialism—and almost all of this handful had come to America." The new immigrants were a great deal more sophisticated than the Marxist factions who wanted to set up Communist-type farm colonies in the new world. It took all of three days in America for Cahan to realize that starting a communal agricultural colony "was not really my dream." He was drawn to life in the city.

In 1882, when Cahan arrived in New York, the Jewish community was at the beginning of an enormous transformation. The Lower East Side was largely populated by Irish and German immigrants. There were small Jewish-owned shops, but no cafés or restaurants. The arrival of the great numbers of eastern European immigrants in the 1880s swelled the number of Yiddish-speaking residents in the neighborhood. By 1890 the Lower East Side was one of the most densely populated areas in the United States. Irving Howe notes in *World of Our Fathers* that the small neighborhood contained "two dozen Christian churches, a dozen synagogues (most Jewish congregations were storefronts or in tenements), about fifty factories and shops (exclusive of garment establishments, most of which were west of the Bowery or hidden away in cellars and flats), ten large public buildings, twenty public and parochial schools—and one tiny park."

Cahan boarded at the home of a widow on Monroe Street, between Catherine and Market Streets; from his window he could hear the clip-clop of horsecars on the Bowery and the iceman's cries of "Ice! Ice!" on unbearably hot summer days. He paid for his board by teaching his landlady's son to write Yiddish and read Hebrew, even though "I learned more English from him than he learned Hebrew from me." His fellow boarders, who spoke a poor Yiddish that was sprinkled with American words and expressions, furthered his education, however much he may have looked down on them for their bastardization of their mother tongue—"non-Yiddish Yiddish," he called it. Displaying a determination similar to the one he would cultivate years later within the immigrant readership of his newspaper, Cahan diligently studied English at night, relying upon *Appleton's English Grammar*, a textbook specifically for German-speakers who wished to learn English.

He worked in factories by day—first making cigars, then tin. This monotonous work did not come easily to him. "Every hour of work seemed like a year," Cahan wrote. He was not alone in feeling this way. The factories were filled with young, educated Russian Jewish immigrants, like Bernard Weinstein, who was to become secretary of the United Hebrew Trades, a federation of predominantly Jewish trade unions; Cahan converted him to socialism over long hours laboring together in a cigar factory. The same cigar factory employed Samuel

Gompers, the future president of the American Federation of Labor, but on a different floor.

In *The Downtown Jews*, Ronald Sanders points out that the presence of so many educated workers in factories made for a situation that was unique in labor history: factories now "contained a large class of proletarian intellectuals, who brought an articulate class consciousness right into the shops." Cahan described how it felt in his memoir: "The worker was being reduced to a dead tool. These things I had previously read in books on political economy, and now I would say to myself, 'Here I am, a dead tool like the rest.' It fascinated me that the facts were just like the books said they were."

In June 1882, the same month Cahan came to New York, a strike broke out on the waterfront among the longshoremen. Many were immigrants from Ireland and Germany, and they agitated for a raise in pay. The foremen went down to Castle Garden* on the hunt for able-bodied men right off the boats to replace the strikers. They offered jobs to the mostly Polish and Russian Jews—without telling them that they would be crossing a picket line. Isidore Kopeloff, who would later be active in the anarchist movement, was one of the strikebreakers. Several longshoremen came to the newly hired workers, saying "we were scabs who were taking the bread out of the mouths of the strikers' families," Kopeloff recalled. ". . . I couldn't understand what I was doing wrong or what my sin was. Why should I not be permitted to earn my piece of bread? And what was this union, and why were those for it kosher and those against it *treyf*?'"

A group of Jewish intellectuals formed what they called a Jewish socialist propaganda society and handed out leaflets in Yiddish advertising a town hall meeting on Rivington Street. Its goal was to convince fellow immigrants not to cross the picket lines.

On July 7, Eisler's Golden Rule Hall at 127 Rivington Street was packed with several hundred people listening to orators speaking in Russian, the

* New York's port of immigration at the Battery from 1830 to 1892, when Ellis Island replaced it.

language of the radical intellectuals. Using Yiddish to lure people to an event was acceptable, but to fire them up politically, only Russian would do. At the meeting's end, when the floor was thrown open to members of the audience, a man who looked younger than his twenty-two years approached the podium with a "thumping heart." Abraham Cahan had been in America for only a month, yet he was speaking in public for the first time.

When Cahan rose to speak, some people, apparently without time for a newcomer, "started for the door." Speaking in Russian, he declared: "We have come to seek a home in a land that is relatively free. But we must not forget the great struggle for freedom that continues in our old homeland. While we are concerned with our problems, our comrades, our heroes, our martyrs are carrying on the struggle, languishing in Russian prisons, suffering at hard labor in Siberia. There is little we can do at this distance. We can raise money to aid the sacred cause. And we must keep the memory of that struggle fresh in our minds."

His words made him, as he himself put it, the "hero of the day." And he had established a pattern that would pervade all his later writings. For all the posturing of the socialists about being the wave of the future, in practice Cahan was also obsessed with an obligation not to forget the past.

Later in the evening, a friend named Mirovitch told Cahan about the propaganda society, explaining that its aim was to spread socialism among the Jewish immigrants.

"If it is for Jewish immigrants, why are the speeches in Russian and German?" Cahan asked.

"What language do you suggest? What Jew doesn't know Russian?" his friend replied derisively.

"My father," Cahan replied sharply.

Mirovitch, who hailed from cosmopolitan St. Petersburg, didn't speak Yiddish and couldn't fathom the world from which Cahan had come. "Why don't you deliver a speech in Yiddish?" he suggested, laughing.

"Why not?" Cahan replied.

And so was born a career in which the medium of Yiddish became part of the message.

The following Friday night, the propaganda society rented a hall in the back of a German saloon on East Sixth Street. Some four hundred people crammed into it and heard what Cahan called "the first socialist speech in Yiddish to be delivered in America." His topic was Marx's theory of surplus value and "the inevitability of the coming of socialism."

In advance of his next Yiddish speech, on Suffolk Street, he and his friend Bernard Weinstein handed out hundreds of Yiddish leaflets on the streets of the Lower East Side, which Cahan had printed at his own expense. This new hall was much larger, but Cahan still packed them in; some of the audience members were forced to stand. Others stood on tables. One was a dark-haired young woman wearing a pince-nez. Cahan kept glancing at her. His talk "kindled a wave of excitement . . . as if the dumb had begun to speak," Weinstein later recounted. Cahan spoke for three hours, cursing the millionaires "with elaborate Vilna curses" and shouting for workers "to march on Fifth Avenue with their tools and their axes and to seize the palaces and the riches which their labor had produced."

Did Cahan truly envision that the Jewish shirtmakers of Canal Street with their metaphorical axes would storm the upper avenues of Manhattan? Not likely. As Irving Howe explains, such speeches were "typical of the moment, with its mixture of Marxist approximations and anarchist bravado, its verbal radicalism at once innocent and empty. . . . Not everyone was certain as to which he really was, or what the differences amounted to, and some, like Cahan, shifted back and forth between anarchism and socialism before coming to a halt." Cahan himself seemed aware of his ambivalence, even if he didn't publicly acknowledge it. "It is a joke," he wrote to an old Russian friend in 1883. "I debate, I argue, I get excited, I shriek, and in the middle of all this, I remind myself that I am a vacant vessel, an empty man without a shred of knowledge, and I begin to blush. I am ashamed of myself."

Even as he was calling for violent marches, Cahan was being seduced by America. "The anarchists and even the socialists argued that there was no more freedom in American than in Russia," he wrote in his memoir. "But that was just talk, I concluded." There was no czar, "no gendarmes, no political spies." One could say and write whatever one wanted.

What Cahan wanted was to speak in and write English. All that work with *Appleton's English Grammar* was paying off. After but a few months in New York, he began giving English lessons to other immigrants, and soon he was earning enough as a tutor to quit the factory. But remaining one linguistic step ahead of his fellow immigrants was not good enough for him; he wanted to master the new language.

In the fall of 1882 Cahan approached the principal of an elementary school on the corner of Chrystie and Hester Streets, not far from where he lived, with an unusual request. In "careful but tortured English" he explained that although he had been a teacher in his old country, he wanted to be a student in his new one. The principal granted him permission, and for the next three months the twenty-two-year-old Cahan sat in on classes, joining thirteen-year-old boys in their lessons in reading, writing, and geography. He studied his fellow students as well, so as to learn their mannerisms as well as their pronunciation. It was not simply English he wanted to conquer, but *American* English, in all its idiomatic complexity. By winter, he had picked up enough to sail through the American daily newspapers. And soon he was speaking English with only a hint of an accent. In the fall of 1883, he landed a job teaching English at the Young Men's Hebrew Association night school, which left his days free for writing and political activities.

Cahan was spending time with William Frey, né Vladimir Heins, a charismatic Russian nobleman who had come to America intending to join a Communist agricultural society. Frey set up a commune in Oregon, but then became taken with what he called the "religion of humanity" and eventually returned to Russia. With Frey, Cahan attended lectures at Felix Adler's Ethical Culture Society. Frey considered Adler a preacher of progressive morality, but as Cahan wrote in his memoir, "for me the sermons were merely English lessons."

It was during this period that Cahan began to develop an interest in the Yiddish theater, which was just then getting underway in New York; it would be one of his great passions throughout his life. He also spent time in socialist salons—or more often, saloons. He attended a memorial for the German-Jewish socialist Ferdinand Lassalle and another for the Paris Commune. But he also stood a bit aloof from, or above, the fray.

Despite all his activities, Cahan was lonely. As much as he had wished to flee his homeland, he missed it. He dreamed of Vilna and his family, his heart "filled with a crushing longing." Everything in America seemed "strange and contrary. Everything was different from what it had been at home." Still, he *wanted* to fit in, and this ambivalence about his new home would, in years to come, mark not only Cahan but also his immigrant readers.

This is not to understate the headiness of the time for a young Yiddish-speaking exile from Russia. At one point, Cahan related in his memoir, he and his roommate were awakened in the middle of the night by a "determined" knock on the door. In marched the young revolutionary Lev Hartmann. "Only a few years earlier," Cahan related, "the entire world resounded with that name." In 1879 Hartmann had been involved in a plot to blow up the czar's train as it traveled south from Moscow. His wife had famously used her shawl to signal the attack.

The plot had failed. But even with someone as famous as Hartmann, Cahan affected a slightly detached tone, focusing not on Hartmann's subversive activities but on his entrepreneurial, distinctly American ones. Hartmann, who had applied for American citizenship, was apprenticing as an electrician, drawing upon the skills he had picked up as a revolutionary with a taste for explosives. He had invented a tiepin that contained an electric light, and Cahan decided to help him try to interest storekeepers in selling it. But when the storekeepers learned that the user was required to carry a battery in his pocket, the two men were laughed out of the store.

By the end of his first year in America, Cahan was attending socialist meetings held in English. "I call them socialist meetings," he wrote in his memoir, "but in truth every kind of reformer came to them to advance his or her personal cause." At the same time, he was drawn to American democracy and its symbols. When he heard that President Chester Arthur and Governor Grover Cleveland were scheduled to unveil a statue of George Washington in front of Federal Hall, Cahan was among the first on hand. But when the crowd went into a room where Arthur was signing autographs, he held back. "How," he wrote in his memoir, "would it look for a socialist to ask for a souvenir from a capitalist President?"

Still, Cahan couldn't contain his fascination with his new country. Beneath his outbursts of socialist rhetoric, he was developing a journalistic detachment from the events that swirled around him. For the St. Petersburg journal *Viestnik Yevropy*,* he wrote a long piece in Russian about the U.S. presidential election of 1884. He described the candidates and their campaign platforms with true journalistic dispassion, as he tried to understand them and the issues that divided them: the reform-minded Democratic governor of New York, Grover Cleveland; Republican James G. Blaine, a former Speaker of the House, senator, and secretary of state, known as the Plumed Knight, with a history of financial scandal; and the candidate of the populist Greenback Party, Benjamin F. Butler, a former Massachusetts governor, whom the socialists and radicals, Cahan observed, thought too weak in his progressivism.

Much to his horror, political operatives from both major parties were bribing voters. "For Russian socialists, the ballot was a sacred ideal. [Yet here in America] the naive immigrant was being taught to sell it for a few dollars." Cahan spent "almost my entire first presidential election day" walking the streets "watching the politicians operating and the people voting." He was pained by the "ease with which corrupt politicians were able to persuade our uneducated Jews to sell their votes." Russia denied Jews "even the small rights granted to their Gentile neighbors." But in America, "all enjoyed the same rights, Jew or Gentile. And for us the

* European Courier

right to vote should have been even more precious than for our Christian fellow Americans."

Cahan characterized as his "first lesson in American politics" the blunder committed by an ally of Blaine, Reverend Samuel Burchard. The pastor, who had "a greater talent for sophistry than for common sense," jibed that Cleveland stood for "rum, Romanism, and rebellion." One of the most notorious examples of bigotry in American politics, the phrase may have cost Blaine the White House.

Cahan expanded on his theory that there was basically no difference between the two major parties, which were more like competing corporations. He prophesied the death of the two-party system, a notion he later called "juvenile." Following Cleveland's victory,* Cahan gave a speech in which he "criticized the two capitalist parties and explained that they were interested in political power for the purpose of exploiting the workers. . . . 'The days of the Republicans and the Democrats are numbered!' I thundered. The audience consisted entirely of greenhorns. In that entire hall there wasn't a single citizen."

It was in his account of this campaign that Cahan's journalistic instincts emerged. He was paid for the piece, which he "read and reread" when a friend told him the Astor Library had a copy of the journal on file. He was invited to continue submitting articles, but Cahan had a better opportunity. Only two years after arriving in America, he became a writer for one of the greatest newspapers in America.

The first time Cahan submitted an article about the Lower East Side to *The New York Sun*, Erasmus Darwin Beach, the paper's editor, read it with interest. The piece was great, Beach told Cahan; it would run in the paper the following Sunday, and Beach was eager to publish more pieces by the young journalist. Beach had just one question: "You use a word about which I must ask. What is a ghetto?"

As Cahan worked to advance his journalistic career, he began to exhibit

* The only person to serve two nonconsecutive terms in the highest office, Cleveland was the twenty-second and twenty-fourth president.

a skepticism of certain left-wing nostrums. At one socialist meeting he attended—he was often one of the only Russian Jews in attendance— "a woman with a mournfully pious face again took the floor," he wrote, and spoke about monetary reform. If only more money were printed, she said, all would have more money, and poverty would come to an end. "I remember the sorrow in her voice as she cried: 'How long must we tolerate this insanity? So much tears and blood are flowing! Such crushing poverty, such grinding need, and we do nothing! Nothing! Let's march on Washington! Let's demand that they print more money."

When Cahan got up to speak, he pointed out that "minting more money would solve nothing and . . . money cannot be printed without limit." The mournful lady screamed at him that "humanity must continue to endure its suffering because of people like me." An argument ensued, until "a speaker with a German accent began to explain that no matter how much money would be printed the pockets of the poor would remain empty and the money would end up in the hands of the rich." The mournful lady jumped to her feet again, "and when the meeting was adjourned she was still shouting hysterically at this so-called socialist meeting that we were all out to help the Vanderbilts and the Goulds." In other words, more than a decade before he founded the *Forward* and began his career of socialist newspaper work, Cahan was already being described as a shill for the capitalist system.

5

By the mid-1880s, socialist activists were forming educational societies called "unions" for Jewish laborers, sponsoring lectures and debates about political and labor issues facing the working classes. Cahan attended many of their organizing meetings and was a popular and sought-after speaker at their events. In February 1885 he married Anyuta (Anna) Bronstein, the young woman who back in 1882 had perched atop a table to catch, through her pince-nez, a better glimpse of Cahan at his second Yiddish speech. In his memoir Cahan devoted remarkably few words to her, aside from the fact that she came from Kiev, was an educated intellectual, perhaps more so than he, with an interest in both French and Russian literature, and was "much admired for her discriminating intelligence and attractive personality." They set up housekeeping in an apartment in a relatively new tenement building on Division Street, between Clinton and Suffolk Streets. "My intellectual friends considered my three new rooms with brand-new furniture just fine," Cahan recounted.

The year after Cahan was married, he began to advance his plan for publishing his own Yiddish-language socialist newspaper, a project about which he had long dreamed. But he would be involved with several Yiddish newspapers and then spend some time writing for English-language publications before he finally came into his own at the *Forward*.

The first Yiddish socialist paper where Cahan worked was *Di Neie Tzeit*,* which he and his cronies launched in June 1886 ("on Shavuos," Cahan recalled in his memoir). It was written in simple, conversational Yiddish, prompting an immediate outcry from those who were partial to

* "The New Era"

the more florid, German-infused Yiddish vernacular known as Daytshmerish, which was then used in journalism and the theater. Cahan was the chief editor as well as "proofreader, manager, bookkeeper, and advertising agent." The paper, issued weekly, lasted six months, done in by competition from a better-funded Yiddish socialist weekly.

Around this time an event occurred at Chicago that would have strong reverberations throughout the American labor movement and, indeed, the world. On the evening of May 4, 1886, some twelve hundred people gathered in Chicago's Haymarket Square to protest police tactics against workers who had gone on strike for an eight-hour workday, and to show solidarity with the striking workers. The demonstration, organized in part by the editors of an anarchist German-language paper called the *Arbeiter-Zeitung*, was fairly peaceful. Carter Harrison, the mayor of Chicago, who had come by to observe the rally, left early. As the last speaker was finishing, the police appeared and ordered the crowd to disperse. A bomb was thrown at the column of policemen, killing one. Mayhem broke out. In the ensuing violence, six more policemen died and at least four workers were killed. Sixty policemen and at least fifty other people were wounded.

In the aftermath, eight individuals associated with various anarchist movements were arrested, including most of the staff of the *Arbeiter-Zeitung*. There was no proof that any of the accused anarchists had thrown the bomb, but public opinion was certainly not on their side. *The New York Times*, which covered the incident along with much of the American press, described the Haymarket affair as the "bloody fruit" of "the villainous teachings of the Anarchists." All eight defendants were found guilty, and four were sent to the gallows on November 11, 1887. Protest rallies were held around the country, including in New York, where Cahan, perhaps remembering the bodies he had seen swinging from Russian gallows as a young boy, said, "For us, the thirteenth of March was the sacred anniversary of the martyrs of the Russian Revolution, and the eleventh of November was that of the martyrs of the American labor movement."

But as sympathetic as he may have been toward the Chicago radicals,

Cahan was growing skeptical of anarchism as a viable movement. The American political system, in contrast to the Russian, offered possibilities for reform, and the New York mayoral campaign of 1886 was a tantalizing case in point. Henry George, the political economist and author of *Progress and Poverty*, a popular book on economic inequality, ran as the candidate of the United Labor Party, an alliance of the Socialist Labor Party and the Single Taxers Union. George lost to the Tammany Hall–backed Democrat, Abram Stevens Hewitt, but did manage to receive an impressive 68,110 votes to Hewitt's 90,552. A twenty-eight-year-old Republican state assemblyman by the name of Theodore Roosevelt came in third, with 60,435 votes. Cahan was heartened by the fact that socialism could actually make inroads within the American political system. In December 1887, he formally gave up on anarchism and joined the Socialist Labor Party. He became a frequent contributor to the party's English-language weekly, the *Workmen's Advocate.* "When I got my membership card, I felt as if a stone had been lifted from my heart," he later wrote.

By now, Jewish immigrants were pouring into New York City, overcrowding the already cramped tenements and streets of the Lower East Side. If the numbers offered comfort, they provided misery, too; conditions in the sweatshops worsened, and few other jobs were to be had. Sanders writes that the task of organizing the Jewish workers was "both more necessary and more possible than ever." A battle between the generally older anarchists and the younger radical intellectuals, who considered themselves social democrats, was brewing on the Lower East Side, and the issue of unionism brought it to a boil.

In the fall of 1888, several Jewish Social Democrats, inspired by the United German Trades and by the anarchists' competing organization, proposed the formation of a like-minded group of Yiddish-speaking workers. Bernard Weinstein, Cahan's friend from his factory days, and a nineteen-year-old immigrant from Riga who spoke little Yiddish, Morris Hillkowitz, were assigned the task of reporting on the current state of Jewish organized labor. They hit the streets of the Lower East Side, peering into cramped basements and crowded lofts. "There had been, we knew, unions of shirt makers, cloak operators, and bakery workers at one time or another," wrote Hillkowitz, who later took on the moniker Hillquit. "We thought them dormant. We found them dead."

Despite the lack of actual unions to organize, Weinstein, Hillquit, and their colleagues decided to press on. On October 9, 1888, they wrote the charter for the United Hebrew Trades, which grew quickly. In early 1890, the UHT pulled almost 3,000 striking cloak makers (the industry employed more Jewish immigrants than any other) into its fold and won significant increases in wages for its members.

Around this time, the anarchists and the Social Democrats on the East Side were discussing pooling resources and publishing a nonpartisan labor newspaper. Their differences were too great, though, and in January 1890 the Social Democrats struck out on their own. The new Yiddish-language weekly was to be called the *Arbeiter Zeitung*, a tip of the hat to the Haymarket victims. Cahan, who had been writing more and more in English, was invigorated by the thought of a true social democratic newspaper, a venture that would enable him to marry his political interests with his journalistic ones. He was not the paper's inaugural editor, though; Philip Krantz, the former editor of a Jewish weekly in London, served in that capacity.

But from the get-go Cahan, enthusiastic and convinced that he knew better than anyone else (much to Krantz's consternation), attempted to shape editorial policy. He had several pieces in the first issue: a front-page feature juxtaposing New York scenes of wealth and poverty and written in a deliberately lowbrow tone; an account of African cannibalism that he had pulled from the pages of *Scribner's Magazine* (Krantz disliked it and decided to run it only at the last moment, for fear of not having enough material); and a column called "The Proletarian Preacher," which taught socialist lessons cloaked in Jewish tradition. Here is how Cahan introduced the preacher in his first column:

> Me, I'm from the town of Proletarishok. . . . Do you know, folks, where Proletarishok is? Not far from Capitalishok. The two *shtelakh*

> are as near to each other as in New York, for example, Fifth Avenue is to the Pig Market [a derisive nickname for Hester Street].

Subtle he was not. And from a later column:

> Today our biblical portion is about strikes: the cloak-makers still have a little strike to finish up, the shirt-makers are on strike, the pants-makers are striking, even our teacher Moses called a mass meeting to talk about a strike. . . . *Sheyshes yommim te'asseh m'lokhoh*, more than six days a week you shouldn't work for the bosses, the seventh day you shall rest.

It was in "The Proletarian Preacher" and in his column "The Hester Street Reporter," which related the colorful day-to-day events of the Lower East Side, that Cahan found his voice, a winning mix of politics and cultural and religious topics that his fellow immigrants immediately responded to. The *Arbeiter Zeitung* quickly became a success, and its editors and writers, Cahan chief among them, delighted in its rivalry with the anarchists' newspaper. The following year Cahan assumed the editorship of the *Arbeiter Zeitung*, a year that marked another personal milestone as well: on June 8, 1891, less than a decade after landing at Philadelphia, Cahan became an American citizen.

Cahan began to branch out in other directions with his writing as well. He became an admirer of Henry James and William Dean Howells. Anna Cahan insisted that her husband take another stab at reading *Anna Karenina*, which he did and found eye-opening. He turned to Tolstoy's other works as well and began taking his own fictional efforts seriously.

In 1892 Cahan penned his first short story, "Motke Arbel," which ran in the pages of the *Arbeiter Zeitung*. He read the story aloud to an old Russian friend, a man by the name of Zhuk, whose literary opinion he held in great esteem, diligently translating it for him word by word into Russian. The story itself was not a serious work of literature, Zhuk told him, but it showed great promise, and he pressed Cahan to continue writing fiction. This vote of confidence meant much to Cahan. Zhuk lent him a collection of short stories written by Anton Chekhov, an author not particularly well known among émigrés at that time. This book, Cahan later wrote, "caused a revolution in my brain." He went back to *Anna Karenina* for a third time and immersed himself in the work of other Russian writers. Perhaps distance was what Cahan, like so many of his fellow immigrants, required. Only in America, more than a decade after he left Russian soil, did he find himself entranced and consumed by the writers of his homeland.

Cahan might have been thinking and dreaming about literature by night, but by day he had to contend with more pressing, mundane matters. In the mid-1890s, the Socialist Labor Party was riven by the feud between its leader, Daniel De Leon, and a reformist branch led by Morris Hillquit. De Leon was a lawyer and a professor at Columbia University. He had been born in Curaçao to well-off parents of Sephardic Dutch ancestry and had become a socialist during the mayoral campaign of 1886. An uncompromising, doctrinaire Marxist, he was more interested in advancing revolution than in improving the workplace. "Reform is chloroform," De Leon was quoted as saying by one long-time writer for the *Forward*, Augustus "Gus" Tyler. De Leon believed that improving conditions for workers only obfuscated the true problem—capitalism—thereby lulling exploited workers into complacency and postponing the day when they would collectively rise up and dismantle the capitalist system altogether. De Leon's chief rival was Eugene V. Debs, a founder of the American Railway Union who had become a socialist while in jail for obstructing the delivery of the United States mail in connection with the Pullman Strike of 1894.

Hillquit and Cahan eventually left the Socialist Labor Party and joined up with Debs, insisting "that the place of the socialists was within the American Federation of Labor," the union that was winning the contest to become the main representative of organized labor. As Tyler related it, Hillquit and Cahan believed that "although the Federation was non-socialist, even anti-socialist, in time, through the experience gained in a common struggle, the workers would come to realize that the ultimate solution was socialism."

Cahan's biographers have all had to plow through the many political battles that rent his world during this time, and it would be shortsighted to set them down as unimportant. The remarkable thing about these struggles, from the perspective of a century later, is the degree to which they foreshadowed later feuds—between, for example, the New Left and American liberals in the 1960s, and between liberals and neoconservatives in the 1980s. This is particularly true when it comes to the Jewish dimension of the debates, an element that time and again during Cahan's long political metamorphosis emerged as a pivotal issue, one that asserted itself in his fiction, in his newspaper work, and in his engagement in the political struggle.

Just how the "Jewish question" fit into all of this was a subject that began to take on increasing importance as the situation for Jews in Russia continued to deteriorate. It was becoming increasingly apparent that they had to leave the country and go *somewhere*, and more and more immigrant Jews were becoming involved in the various socialist organizations that were springing up in the United States. The question, as Tyler put it, was "how to put an end to the endless persecution of the Jews. To Cahan and others of his political persuasion, the answer was clear: socialism. In a global cooperative commonwealth, without national, religious, or ethnic antagonisms, there would not, there could not, be an economic or political reason for anti-Semitism, a weapon of the capitalist ruling class to 'divide and rule,' to turn worker against worker."

Cahan's chance to test his belief came with his assignment as a delegate of the United Hebrew Trades to the second congress of the Socialist International, to take place at Belgium in August 1891. The socialists were not the only ones obsessed with the Jewish Question. That same year the German Jewish philanthropist Baron Maurice de Hirsch established the Jewish Colonization Association, with the idea of fostering Jewish emigration from Russia to Argentina. And in the same year the noted cultural Zionist writer Ahad Ha'am made his first visit to Palestine and, upon his return to Russia, wrote his landmark essay "Truth from Eretz Yisrael." One hundred thousand Jews left Russia that year, as Jews were being expelled from Moscow, and its Great Synagogue was closed. It was the same year that the German Zionist Max Bodenheimer wrote "Whither Russian Jewry?" Also in 1891, Theodor Herzl, while hiking in the Pyrenees, would receive word from Vienna that the *Neue Freie Presse* was making him its Paris correspondent, in which capacity, three years later, he would attend the trial of Captain Alfred Dreyfus.

Cahan left for Europe in July. According to Ronald Sanders, the United Hebrew Trades had chosen him to represent them because he had become "widely recognized as the most articulate" among the social democrats in New York. Sanders further notes that "nine years of activity among the Yiddish-speaking immigrants had awakened in him the germ of a Jewish nationalist that he once had not imagined to be there." Those years had also tempered his utopianism with pragmatic realism. Advance word of Cahan's trip reached London, and he was invited to stop there en route and give lectures. At one meeting, Cahan took on the anarchists. He asked his audience to imagine that a small village of one hundred people discovers that a stream is poisoned. Sixty of the inhabitants want to solve the problem by filling the stream in with sand, while forty want to build a bridge over it. Under socialist rule, Cahan said, the villagers would vote, and the majority would win the day. Under the anarchists, who preach the freedom of every individual to act independently, the villagers would build the bridge *after* they covered the stream with sand. "He's a clown, a comedian, not a debater," the irate anarchists protested.

Cahan found London to be much like New York. While there, he met and took quite a liking to Karl Marx's daughter, Eleanor, a writer and translator and erstwhile secretary to her father, who had died in 1883. Eleanor had attended the Socialist International's first congress and told Cahan, "We Jews have a special obligation to devote ourselves to the working class." This remark came as a bit of a surprise to Cahan, given the anti-Semitism of her father, whose parents had baptized him as a Lutheran and whose 1844 essay "Zur Judenfrage" (On the Jewish Question) advocated the "emancipation of society from Judaism."

Cahan next went to Paris, which was not at all like New York—it reminded him of Russia. He was, for the first time in nine years, back on continental European soil, and he was hit with an attack of nostalgia. His lodging only compounded the feeling; he stayed in a working-class neighborhood in the home of David Gordon, one of his former classmates from Vilna. Unlike Cahan and his socialist colleagues in New York, Gordon and his wife were living a proletarian life, not simply espousing one. The Gordons seemed not only content but happy. "He was always telling jokes and she was always laughing," Cahan wrote somewhat wistfully. It was not only Gordon and his wife who affected Cahan, but a young woman as well: Eva, Gordon's sister. She lived nearby and served as Cahan's Parisian tour guide. She was "a lively and happy girl [who] usually came in singing," he wrote, a more complimentary description than any he would bestow in print upon his wife in the course of more than fifty years of marriage. With Eva he visited parks and museums; they stood before the Venus de Milo in the Louvre and returned to view it several days in a row. Eva took him to cafés on the Left Bank, where they would talk or visit with her revolutionary friends.

One day in Paris another ghost from Cahan's past appeared: a friend from Vilna named Anton Gnatowski. Cahan learned that in 1887 Gnatowski had taken part in a plot to kill Alexander III with the same kind of bomb that had been used to assassinate Alexander II. The plot had failed, and most of the conspirators had been captured. (One of them was a young chemistry student named Alexander Ulyanov, who went to the gallows. That sent his younger brother Vladimir into the welcoming arms of Alexander's revolutionary comrades, from which he emerged with the nom de guerre Lenin.) But Gnatowski had escaped. Cahan felt his old anarchistic impulses stirring within him: "I had never had such a strong feeling of life passing me by as I did in that moment." While he was in Paris, away from the pressures of trying to fit into his new country, Cahan wrote to his parents for the first time in several years.

Despite his nostalgia for his former life and despite his long-standing universalist beliefs, Cahan was by now indisputably an American. He gave a lecture where, as one attendee, George Leonard, later wrote to him: "Eloquently you spoke of the freedom you found in the United States and contrasted it with what you had gone through in your native land before leaving it for America. The plight of the immigrant worker in the new land of freedom had a prominent place in your speech. But it breathed hope, not despair. I was captivated by your eloquence. I sat so close to you that I allowed no word to escape me. I was moved. So was everybody else in the hall."

Cahan may have felt that much about his new home needed to be improved, but he seems to have had no question that improvement was possible. He was certainly not the first American newspaper editor to spend years criticizing his country at home only to discover, when he went abroad, an urge to proselytize for America's manifest virtues.

Becoming Americanized did not mean abandoning his Jewish identity. In August, at the congress of the Socialist International, he surprised his fellow delegates by submitting an item for discussion on the agenda: "What shall be the stand of the organized workers of all countries concerning the Jewish Question?" The item caused "considerable embarrassment," as Sanders notes. The Jewish Question, after all, "had been a major issue in the classic struggles of European liberalism half a century before, and was thought to have been disposed of."

Cahan, an almost compulsive newspaperman, perceived that the Jewish Question had not, in fact, been disposed of. On the contrary, political parties in Austria, Germany, and France were propagating a new wave of anti-Semitism, this one with a political element. Emancipation and the spread of Enlightenment values might have muted the older, atavistic anti-Semitism, but a backlash against the newly emancipated Jews was under way, as the economic and social success brought about by their emancipation was becoming a source of popular resentment. As Theodor Herzl was to note eloquently only a few years later, the irony of the emancipation of Europe's Jews was that a liberal enterprise had spawned an illiberal backlash.

Socialism was late to concern itself with this dynamic. As Cahan had observed when he was still in Russia, some Jewish socialists had condoned the pogroms in the name of socialist revolution, lumping the Jewish victims of the violence in with the capitalist villains who had been exploiting the masses. Cahan had been disgusted and refused to tolerate such an elision here in Brussels. So he was prepared to embarrass a socialist movement that, precisely because so many Jews were prominent in it, took pains to downplay anything that smacked of Jewish particularity. Both Paul Singer, the head of the German Social Democrats, and Viktor Adler, the Jewish head of the Austrian Socialist Party, let Cahan know that they preferred he not raise the Jewish Question.

Cahan refused to withdraw his proposal. Even the chief rabbi of Brussels tried to get him to back down, but he wouldn't. The matter became part of the conference agenda, and the discussion around it exposed the persistence of old prejudices in the new world order. The French delegation, as Sanders tells it, "were in no way prepared to assume what they thought would seem to their colleagues back home to be a 'philo-Semitic stance.' Eventually, a compromise, face-saving resolution was passed, condemning 'both anti-Semitism and philo-Semitism.' "

The episode served only to strengthen Cahan's attachment to America. Perhaps, as Sanders points out, America "did not permit a heroic and pure-hearted socialism," but neither did it "nourish the kind of powerful and relentless anti-Semitism that was traditional to continental Europe. . . . If it was easier to be a good socialist in Europe, it was easier for a radical like Cahan to be a good Jew in America." Cahan might have objected to that characterization, believing that an anti-Semitic socialism was no socialism at all. But American society and culture certainly played a large role in Cahan's political evolution. Its careful balance between the rights of the individual or of states against a national identity allowed him to understand his Jewishness not as a contradiction of universal values but as an essential precondition of it.

In the summer of 1892, Cahan was invited back to London to lecture in Yiddish. He visited Eleanor Marx and her partner, Edward Aveling (whose infidelities, it is said, would drive her to suicide in 1898). He also went to see Friedrich Engels, to propose a Yiddish translation of his and Marx's *Communist Manifesto*. Eleanor accompanied Cahan to Engels's home, and at one point during their meeting she pushed him into a big leather easy chair that stood in the corner. "She laughed, and Engels smiled happily," Cahan recalled. "That was my father's chair, the chair in which he died," she said by way of explanation. So while sitting in Karl Marx's chair, Cahan met with the coauthor of *The Communist Manifesto*. Two decades later Engels's face and Marx's would be chiseled into the facade of the brand-new *Forward* Building.

Past seventy but still vigorous, Engels was working on finishing volume three of Marx's *Das Kapital*, which had been left incomplete at Marx's death. Engels raised a glass of beer and they drank to "social democracy in the world."

Cahan declined a second drink. "You know, Comrade Engels, the Jews are not drinkers," he explained.

To which Engels retorted, "Yes, that's truly a shame—if the Jews would drink more, they would be even better people."

Engels promised to write an introduction to Cahan's translation of *The Communist Manifesto*, and in parting he gave Cahan six photographs of Marx to share with comrades in America.

It wasn't only European politics that helped Cahan realize that he was finally an American. One evening in 1892, after completing his day's work at the *Arbeiter Zeitung*, he retired to nearby Sussman and Goldstein's Café, the regular hangout of the newspaper's staff. There he found a simple, penciled note waiting for him: "I wanted to have the pleasure of making your acquaintance," signed William Dean Howells.

Some twenty-three years older than Cahan, Howells had begun his literary career several years before Cahan was born. By 1882, when Cahan arrived in America, Howells had been editor of *The Atlantic Monthly* for nearly a decade. In the intervening years, his novels had helped establish the genre of American literary realism, most notably *The Rise of Silas Lapham* (1885) and *A Hazard of New Fortunes* (1890). He was fascinated by the variegated place America was becoming and by the world beyond his purview. He had recently ended a column in *Harper's* with the remark: "I will close with a name, which is the name of the greatest of all literary artists: Tolstoy."

He had heard of the burgeoning Jewish neighborhood on the Lower East Side and had made several trips there. When he learned that a Jewish socialist newspaper was being published in the neighborhood, he resolved to meet its editor and stopped by the *Arbeiter Zeitung*'s offices on Delancey Street. But Cahan hadn't been there. Someone had suggested he try the café, and it was there that Howells left his note.

Cahan, who had read all of Howells's work and greatly admired him, was astounded—he could never have imagined meeting him in the flesh. But he immediately wrote back, and soon he received an invitation to visit Howells at his brownstone on East 17th Street, across from Stuyvesant Park.

Upon his arrival, Cahan, understandably anxious, delivered a little speech about what an inexpressible pleasure it was to make Howell's acquaintance: "I feel so not only as the socialist editor whom you honored with your visit but also, and especially, as one of your most enthusiastic readers and admirers."

"Have you read my work?" Howells asked, apparently surprised that a socialist editor would be knowledgeable about literature in general, let alone his own work.

Cahan replied that he had read everything Howells had written. They ended up discussing Russian and English literature, and the socialist movement. This meeting must have given Cahan a new confidence; not only was a great American novelist interested in his world, but Cahan, still very much a Russian intellectual, had something to offer Howells as well. Immersed in his work at the *Arbeiter Zeitung* and myriad socialist activities, however, Cahan's own literary work took a backseat.

In December 1893 Cahan serialized a portion of Howells's recently published novel about a utopian island, *A Traveler from Altruria*, which he had translated himself. Howells had by this time moved uptown, to

59th Street, near Central Park, and now frequented a nearby shop to buy stationery supplies. As it happened, the owner of the shop was Jewish and an *Arbeiter Zeitung* reader. When he came across the Yiddish translation of Howells's novel, he read sections of it aloud to his customer. Howells replied that he had met and been impressed by Cahan, an observation that eventually got back to Cahan.

Cahan applied himself anew to his writing, and in 1895 placed "A Providential Match," in *Short Stories* magazine. One day Howells's wife, while waiting on the elevated platform for a train, glanced at the titles on the newsstand and spied Cahan's name on the magazine cover. She purchased a copy and brought it home to Howells, who, after reading it, invited Cahan for another visit.

It was at this meeting that Howells really got down to business. "I have read your story in *Short Stories*," he told Cahan. "Of course, it's not a serious thing. But it shows me that you must write. It is your duty to write."

"Imagine then what an effect the compliment of the 'Dean of American Literature' had on me," Cahan later wrote. It made him realize that his writings about the Jewish immigrant experience would have an American readership far beyond the world in which they were set. That insight set in motion the creative frenzy that in 1896 produced Cahan's first novel, *Yekl: A Tale of the New York Ghetto*. But the reverberations of this meeting went well beyond Cahan himself. William Dean Howells, a consummately American writer and a supporter of Mark Twain, was now encouraging a writer who was chiefly a portraitist of the Lower East Side. The immigrant Jewish enterprise was entering American life and becoming a much more central element.

Despite their amateurish tone, Cahan's early stories have moments of poignant beauty. In "A Providential Match," an unattractive, pockmarked immigrant Russian Jew pays a matchmaker to convince a young woman from back home to come to New York to marry him. He rushes to meet the boat on which she has arrived, only to discover her on the arm of a young "collegian" with whom she has fallen in love during the crossing. When he shouts that he wants his hundred and fifty dollars back and will call for a "politzman," a burly runner for an immigrant hotel, who has been observing the proceedings, shoves him aside, then escorts the couple away.

In "A Sweat-Shop Romance," Beile, a finisher, is berated by the boss's wife. Her coworker and beau, the machine-operator Heyman, silently sits by. But David, a baster in the shop, sticks up for Beile, and they are both fired. He thereafter pursues her with persistence and humor. Here is an excerpt:

> He found work for her and for himself in the same shop; saw her home every evening; regularly came after supper to take her out for a walk, in the course of which he would treat her to candy and invite her to a coffee saloon—a thing which Heyman had never done; kept her chuckling over his jokes; and while sitting by her side in Central Park one night, he said, in reply to her remark that it was so dark that she knew not where she was, "I'll tell you where you are—guess."
>
> "Where?"
>
> "Here, in my heart, and keeping me awake nights, too. Say, Beile, what have I ever done to you to have my rest disturbed by you in that manner?"
>
> Her heart was beating like a sledge hammer. She tried to laugh as she returned: "I don't know—You can never stop making fun, can you?"
>
> "Fun? Do you want me to cry? I will, gladly, if I only know that you will agree to have an engagement party," he rejoined, deeply blushing under cover of the darkness.
>
> "When?" she questioned, the word crossing her lips before she knew it.

In Cahan's life, immigrant melodrama was not confined to his fiction. One day in October 1892, at the Jewish Labor Lyceum—a two-story building on Delancey Street—he met two friends who had with them a young man with red hair. He looked to be about nineteen years old. Cahan had no idea who the boy was until one of the men introduced him as Isaac Cahan. He was Abraham Cahan's only sibling, whom he hadn't seen for eleven years. Cahan wept and resolved to do right by his brother. Isaac, who had been working since he was a young boy, was not as educated as his brother, and Cahan decided that Isaac would now learn English well, quickly. He became his personal tutor.

Despite Cahan's voluminous writings about his own life, he says little else about his brother, or about his parents for that matter. But in August 1893, when he traveled to Europe to attend the third congress of the Socialist International in Zurich he made arrangements to meet his parents at Vienna; it was still too dangerous for him to return to Russia. He described the meeting in his memoir:

> I rang the bell and heard sounds inside. The door opened all the way and I saw an old lady. At first glance she did not look familiar to me, but I realized right away that this was my mother. I threw myself towards her and she towards me.
>
> "My son, I don't recognize you!" she wailed without tears. I forgot about my resolve to be calm. I was confused and nervous.

Cahan had changed irrevocably, they all realized. He described for his parents his journalistic and speaking career in America. His father confessed that he didn't like the sound of it; his mother offered no such judgment but constantly touched him and begged him to take good care of Isaac. Cahan spent eleven days with his parents then and never saw them again.

It is something on which to reflect. His memory of his childhood was so acute that he could recall in detail the condition of a couch upon which he stood as a toddler; and he was obsessed with creating a career using the language of his parents. Yet after he left home, he failed to maintain contact with them or even, if direct contact was deemed too dangerous, to send word back to them through a third party. When he finally did see them again, for what would most assuredly be the last time, he could barely speak to them, much less offer to bring them to America. Such behavior suggests that Cahan's character included a degree of self-control and self-regard that enabled him to keep an emotional distance from radicals, Communists, office schemers, and even his wife, leaving himself free to pursue his enormous ambitions. It also captures something of the immigrant ethos, which would become essential to Cahan in the creation of his own persona and in achieving his other goals in America.

The *Arbeiter Zeitung* to which Cahan returned had a circulation of about 10,000, and its principal backer, the United Hebrew Trades, had about a quarter-million members. It must have been a kind of paradise for a writer-editor like Cahan. He could, and did, publish news, editorials, feuilletons, fiction, and even poetry, at a time when significant feuds roiled the socialist movement, the labor movement, and the literary world, and when the trend toward realism in American fiction was on the rise and was influencing Cahan's writing. At the same time, the work environment at the paper was deteriorating. Power was shifting to a management board that wanted more say in running the paper; Cahan chafed at having to answer to an outside bureaucratic entity. For a world-class journalist like him, it must have been a kind of hell.

For a while Cahan thought he could live with the situation at the *Arbeiter Zeitung*, but eventually he and a colleague, a fellow Lithuanian Jew named Louis Miller, began laying plans for a new newspaper. Adding fuel to the fire was a showdown he had with Daniel De Leon over the direction of the Socialist Labor Party.

The economic crisis of 1893 would have a far-reaching effect on Cahan and his socialist colleagues. After a period of feverish growth and expansion, the American economy took a nosedive, culminating in the economic depression known as the Panic of 1893. The rush to build railroads across America had created a bubble that eventually burst, fueling bank runs, credit crunches, and bank failures. Unemployment soared.

The presidential election of 1896 was fought over economic issues, as William McKinley headed the pro-gold, high-tariff Republican ticket and William Jennings Bryan led the pro-silver, populist Democrats. McKinley's victory meant the Gilded Age was nearing its end, and the Progressive Era was about to begin. Thereupon the Socialist Labor Party came into its own in America. Dominated since its birth in 1876 by German-speaking immigrants, the SLP regarded it as a coup when Daniel De Leon, an urbane intellectual fluent in seven languages, joined the party in 1890 and became editor of its newspaper, *The People.*

De Leon's zeal and dogmatism were polarizing, and when he abandoned his academic career and turned his full attention to the SLP, he became intent on defeating rivals by any means possible. He once called Samuel Gompers, the legendary leader of American Federation of Labor, "an entrapped swindler." Cahan, for his part, once referred to De Leon as "a Bolshevik before there were Bolsheviks, a Leninist before Lenin." De Leon anathematized small, incremental efforts to improve the workers' conditions, especially if those efforts came about through cooperation with nonsocialist labor leaders. Such "labor fakers" were deluding the workers into believing that the capitalist system could somehow be reformed from within. De Leon, determined to work only with unions that specifically supported socialism, embraced the tactic of "dual unionism": breaking an existing union and developing another in its stead. Many within the SLP, including Cahan, considered this tactic destructive and strenuously opposed it. In *World of Our Fathers*, Irving Howe describes the battle:

> Though led by men who regarded themselves as socialists, the unions had to fight for immediate reforms which the De Leonists scorned, had to work out peaceable relations with nonsocialist union leaders whom the De Leonists abused, and had to respond with sympathy to the Jewish sentiments of their members, which the De Leonists dismissed. De Leon was an ideologue most comfortable in the seclusion of the sect, and as long as he practiced a kind of "dual

unionism," that recurrent curse of the American left, his leadership could only be a disaster.

Cahan's quarrels with De Leon are illuminating because they disclose his ability to judge character, an ability that he had by now keenly developed. One time, according to one biographer of Cahan, Theodore Pollock, Cahan was in the audience when De Leon was lecturing. A man named Goldenstick contested one of De Leon's points, and the audience "was startled to hear the lecturer reply by addressing him as 'Mr. Goldenstink.'" One of the listeners, an elderly man, thought De Leon had "simply made a mistake," Cahan recalled, "and corrected him. De Leon laughed, and then proceeded to mispronounce the name again, this time in a different way." Cahan was shocked at this rude behavior, and his dislike of De Leon intensified, over and above his disagreement with the strategy of dual unionism.

The battle between the two factions of the Socialist Labor Party was bitter and broadly waged, involving not only the SLP but the staff of the *Arbeiter Zeitung* and members of the United Hebrew Trades. Eventually the newspaper's management board decided to reduce the *Arbeiter Zeitung* to a weekly supplement to the evening paper, the *Abend Blatt*. The board was prepared to leave Cahan as editor of the supplement, but it complained that he was "nervous and extremely temperamental." So Cahan quit and published his account of the controversy in the SLP-sponsored magazine *Die Zukunft*, characterizing the management board as a "House of Lords" and calling instead for a "House of Commons."

Louis Miller, on his return from a trip to Europe, brokered an attempt at a compromise. It brought a period of detente during which Cahan wouldn't go to the office but sent in his weekly column by messenger. But De Leon continued to gain ground with members of the management board. Miller, Cahan, and another member of the SLP named Morris Winchevsky attempted to stage a coup at a meeting of the *Arbeiter Zeitung* publishing association in early 1897, but once again De Leon outmaneuvered them. So their faction retreated to the basement in a nearby hall and laid plans to launch a new Yiddish newspaper.

The response from those in the hall was immediate and favorable. Cahan and another editor "went about with hats in our hands, and people threw ten-dollar, five-dollar, two-dollar bills and silver coins into them. Off came rings and watches and all were thrown into the hats. . . . I remember how my hat became so heavy that I had to support it with my other hand lest it rip." One enthusiastic supporter felt so buoyed that he pawned his own suit to give money to the cause.

Emboldened, Cahan and his colleagues called a meeting of their allies among the socialist and union leaders. On January 30, 1897, representatives of nearly two dozen organizations from cities as far away as Philadelphia, Baltimore, and New Haven descended on Walhalla Hall on Orchard Street, where they created a new organization called the Press Association. The association declared that it would "hold high the flag of international class conflict" and "work with all its might for the Socialist Labor Party." It was delinked from the United Hebrew Trades, though its sympathies were with the labor movement generally. It was Louis Miller who proposed naming the association's newspaper the *Forvertz*, or *Forward*, after the *Vorwärts*, the official newspaper of the Social Democratic Party in Germany.

6

The founding of the *Forward* was but one of three events that took place in 1897 and that changed the course of Jewish history. In August of that year, Theodor Herzl attended the First Zionist Congress in Switzerland, later writing in his diary, "Were I to sum up the Basel Congress in a word—which I shall guard against pronouncing publicly—it would be this: At Basel, I founded the Jewish State." In Vilna, a band of socialists met in secret to unite Jewish workers across the far-flung Russian Empire and, in October, founded the General Association of Jewish Workers, which came to be known simply as the Bund. Its goal was to create an educated Jewish proletariat that could partner with other social democratic organizations in Russia and throughout the world. One Russian Marxist referred to them as "Zionists with seasickness." Over the succeeding decades, Cahan would cover both movements for the *Forward*'s readers. The efforts of the Zionist pioneers gave rise to the State of Israel. The Bund would emerge as a powerful force in Poland, only to split into Communist and social democratic factions whose masses would be murdered by the Nazis and its remnant leaders by the Communists. With Cahan's creation of the *Forward* in April, three movements that would have a profound effect on world Jewry—Zionism, international socialism, and an activist, democratic American Judaism as exemplified by the *Forward*—can trace their origins to this momentous year.

As the American economy began to recover from the Panic of 1893, Cahan's adopted hometown boomed. New York had become, if not the official capital of America, its cultural and economic heart and a city to be reckoned with internationally as well. In 1898 the five boroughs united into one municipality, to become the city we know today. A record-breaking number of press rooms were set up to cover local, national, and international news. Some fifty-eight dailies in New York alone jostled for attention; two of the best known, William Randolph Hearst's *New York Journal* and Joseph Pulitzer's *World*, engaged in a bruising war for readers, lowering their newsstand prices to one cent and raiding each other's staff. From Pulitzer's newsroom, Hearst grabbed Stephen Crane, the journalist and author of the novella *Maggie: A Girl of the Streets* (1893) and the novel *The Red Badge of Courage* (1895). Crane was a writer whom Cahan greatly admired and to whom he had already been compared.

In the race for readers, these newspapers refashioned themselves into crusading advocates of social reform; commissioned crowd-pleasing, gossipy feature articles; and often sensationalized the stories they covered, sometimes making them up out of whole cloth. They tried to lure readers with huge, screaming headlines and offered games and contests in their pages. They instituted cartoons and eye-popping graphics using the latest technologies. Typewriters were installed in the city rooms, though some old-timers hated the clattering noise. The first halftone photograph in a mass-circulation newspaper was published in 1897, in the *New-York Tribune.*

In short, there was little subtle or quaint about "yellow journalism," as more staid publications called it, and its influence in the public sphere was enormous. Hearst in particular took great pride in his paper's activism, going so far as to help stage the jailbreak of a young female political prisoner in Havana. The venerable *New York Sun*, for which Cahan had freelanced, played a prominent role in the struggle for free Cuba. The leader of the movement, José Martí, kept his office in the *Sun*'s newsroom. Martí was mocked by *The New York Times*, which Adolph Ochs had acquired in 1896. It began printing its famous motto "All the News That's Fit to Print" at the top of its front page in 1897, as a not-so-subtle response to the lurid reporting of its competitors. The *New-York Commercial Advertiser*, a musty paper that had been founded in 1793 by Noah Webster as the *American Minerva*, sought to breathe new life into its pages by appointing as its city editor in 1897 a crusading young western journalist by the name of Lincoln Steffens.

On April 22, 1897, the *Forward* jumped into this mix in full Marxist regalia, with the slogan "Workers of the World Unite!" at the top of its front page. The headlines of that first issue included "Blood Runs in Civilized Europe" (on the Turkish-Greek war), "Bravo, Cubans!" (supporting the island's resistance to Spain), and "From the Class Struggle: Locked-out Steamfitters are Holding Fast." The paper's headquarters were on one floor of a warehouse on Duane Street in downtown Manhattan. The loft had been newly divided with unfinished planks of lumber into three distinct areas housing the paper's writers, editor, and typesetters, and the smell of fresh wood filled the air. Cahan shared his narrow office with a staff writer and a rising playwright named Jacob Gordin, who had already written several plays and would go on to become one of the most successful writers for the Yiddish theater. Cahan had written a critical review of Gordin's work in another publication, and relations between the two men were cool; they would grow infamously strained in the years to come.

The *Forward*'s first Sunday edition, produced in a tabloid format, featured an illustration of a sword-carrying woman labeled "Social Democracy" under the headline "Eight-Hour Working Day." The woman was depicted as attacking the fort of Capitalism, out of which burst forth angry rich men shaking their fists. Inside the paper, following the model of the *Arbeiter Zeitung*, were popular science pieces, political columns, literary essays (Cahan wrote an early one praising Thomas Hardy as "the only good novelist in England"), short stories (Anna Cahan translated some Russian tales), and poems.

Despite the initial excitement and enthusiasm, as the months wore on it became clear that neither the SLP nor the labor movement was ready to let an editor of Cahan's caliber operate outside party or union discipline. Was Cahan himself ready? He was, after all, a promising writer of fiction who was being tugged at by the world of belles lettres; and he had never really worked on staff for a general interest daily newspaper with a mass audience.

From the start, Cahan opposed using the *Forward* to carry on the feud with De Leon, though an internal faction felt otherwise. As the most seasoned newspaperman among his colleagues, he had strong ideas about what the paper should be: a freewheeling press that would reflect the richness and complexities of life on the Lower East Side. He was certainly no fan of De Leon, but spilling too much ink over their battles in order to take him down, he contended, would simply alienate readers. "People love a fight," Cahan later conceded. "When two men fight, passersby stop and look. But that is no solid basis for a newspaper."

De Leon, meanwhile, was not content to sit back. He viewed the *Forward* supporters as traitors to the SLP and succeeded in ousting hundreds of them from the party. But they would soon find another, more companionable home. In 1897 Eugene V. Debs, fresh out of prison, founded a political party that he called the Social Democracy of America, which a few years later, after some splits and mergers, would become simply the Socialist Party of America. In the summer of 1897, a convention of socialist press associations, including the *Forward*, voted to sign on with Debs and affiliate with his party.

Many *Forward* staffers remained incensed at De Leon and grew increasingly angry at Cahan for imperiously stifling their view that the newspaper should polemicize against him. Several accounts of the period suggest that Anna Cahan wasn't terribly enthusiastic about the idea of her husband as a career Yiddish newspaperman and was encouraging Cahan* to continue to write fiction and pursue a more literary career. By August 1897, Cahan had enough. He left the *Forward*, intending never to come back.

Anna Cahan's ambitions for her husband were not without merit. Cahan had been simultaneously developing his talents as a Yiddish-language newspaperman and as an English-language novelist. In the summer of 1895 he had finished writing his first novel, *Yankel the Yankee.*

It tells the story of an ambitious young Russian Jewish blacksmith

* Cahan biographer Theodore Pollock calls Anna, during these years, "the more voracious and penetrating reader," though he notes she had more time on her hands.

who leaves his wife and child behind and arrives in America determined to shed all trappings of Jewish identity and become a thoroughly assimilated "Yankee." He takes up with a more Americanized fellow immigrant and promises her marriage. The novel concludes with Yankel divorcing his traditional, pious wife. But the social realist Cahan was not going to give his readers a happily-ever-after ending: riding off with his paramour after the divorce proceedings, Yankel realizes that he is "painfully reluctant to part with his long-coveted freedom so soon after it had at last been attained, and before he had had time to relish it." His ex-wife, by contrast, plans to marry a religious scholar who was their boarder.

After Cahan completed the manuscript in the summer of 1895, he had delivered it to Howells, who promptly invited him to dinner. Cahan, nervous again when he arrived at the Howellses' residence, dined with the novelist, his wife, and their daughter, all of whom were exceedingly polite but silent on the subject of the manuscript. After the meal, Cahan and Howells went into Howells's study, where the dean of American literature showered him with praise—so much so that Cahan "grew shy and could not say a word," as he later wrote. Howells remembered "almost every line of the novel" and "expressed joy" that American literature would have "an important power added to it."

Howells, who was also a great editor, thought the title ought to be changed—*Yankel the Yankee* seemed more suited to vaudeville. So Cahan began throwing out names. When Howells heard "Yekl," he fixed on it immediately. "Not *Yekl the Yankee*," he said—"*Yekl*." It was an inspired suggestion—a simple Jewish name crowning an American novel. Howells offered to help Cahan place the manuscript, suggesting that he try for magazine serialization before shopping it around in book form. But it wouldn't be easy. "Our editors have their own notions about literature," Howells said, in Cahan's recollection. "They can't be blamed. They must keep the reading public in mind, and the taste of the great masses is not the same as yours or mine."

That night Howells also showed Cahan, with evident pride, a letter he had received from the Russian master Ivan Turgenev, praising Howells for his work. In any event, he was true to his word; he submitted Cahan's manuscript to *Harper's Magazine*, where he had been writing a literary column since 1886. But his pessimism was also on target: Cahan's book was rejected on the grounds that Jewish life on the Lower East Side held little appeal for American readers. At a second magazine, the editor's wife signed the rejection. "You know, dear Mr. Howells, that our readers want to have stories about richly dressed ladies and gentlemen," she explained. "How can they be interested by a story about a Jewish immigrant?"

When the manuscript was sent over to *McClure's Magazine*, Cahan asked to see the editor, John S. Phillips, to receive his answer in person. "You describe only Jews," Phillips said. "Someone who reads your novel is likely to think that there are no other kinds of people in America than Jews." The purpose of art, he said, was to capture beauty; what was the appeal in Cahan's factories and teeming streets? Cahan protested, citing examples from Russia's literary masters who wrote beautifully about peasants, but to no avail. Phillips told him his work showed undeniable talent; it was his subject matter that needed changing.

Cahan despaired of ever publishing his novel in English, so he translated it into Yiddish and, when Howells was out of town, published it in the *Arbeiter Zeitung* as *Yankel the Yankee*, under the pseudonym Socius.* The *Arbeiter Zeitung*'s readers loved it. Letters poured in, complimenting the book and wanting to know who Yankel really was. Some of the letter writers were uncomfortable with the title character: Yankel wasn't the most sympathetic or likable person. Couldn't the novelist have painted a more flattering portrait of a Jew?

When Howells returned to New York, he wasn't happy to hear about *Yankel*'s appearance in the Yiddish press. Finally, he sent the manuscript to his own editor, Ripley Hitchcock, at R. Appleton. A year earlier Hitchcock had taken on another Howells protégé, a twenty-three-year-old journalist named Stephen Crane. So Howells had a bit of a track

* Latin for "comrade"

record with his publisher in recognizing new talent. Hitchcock liked Cahan's novel and agreed to publish it. And so in July 1896, Cahan's first novel, *Yekl: A Tale of the New York Ghetto*, was brought out by the publisher of the famous grammar book that he had used to learn English only fourteen years earlier.

Social realist writer that he was, Cahan made sure that his characters sounded the way immigrant Jews on the Lower East Side actually sounded. No one in American fiction had ever spoken that way. "You can betch you' bootsh!" the Yankee Yekl says to one of his friends. "An' dot'sh ull!"

The critics were flummoxed. The *Commercial Advertiser*, in an unsigned review, described the story as being written in "the most hideous jargon" and complained that "we are asked to give it a place in literature because it represents still another dialect alleged to be spoken on the east side. . . . There is not a thrill of human sympathy from cover to cover." In a review in the literary journal *The Bookman*, the author Nancy Huston Banks declared that "from beginning to end throughout the work there is not a gleam of spirituality, unselfishness, or nobility. . . . Are such books ever worthwhile? Do they add anything to literature? Above all, *are* they literature?" But some readers comprehended it. The *New York Times* reviewer who concluded that *Yekl* "and his fellow-personages and the life they live are vividly depicted with graphic descriptive skill, with a keen sense of humor, and not a hint of preachiness." Howells, writing in *The World*, hailed Cahan as a "new star of realism" and put him on the same plane as Stephen Crane.

Cahan now realized that he could do more than serve as a guide to America for arriving immigrants; he could also be a guide to the burgeoning immigrant Jewish community for non-Jewish Americans, who were only just becoming aware of its existence. How all of this would translate into earning a living, however, was unclear. *Yekl's* sales were tepid at best. This was not due to anti-Semitism, according to the historian Moses Rischin, who has written trenchantly about Cahan's life. "Novels dealing with the Irish were equally unsuccessful," he notes. The readers of novels were largely women who "desired to read about aristocrats." Also taboo, Rischin noted, "were literary intimations about the less romantic aspects of the relations between the sexes."

Cahan's financial situation was becoming problematic. Not only had he walked out on the *Forward*, but the New York City Board of Education, which had taken over the Young Men's Hebrew Association night school, had fired him from his job teaching English to immigrants because, as he was later told, he had been spotted giving a socialist speech in the street. Cahan no longer had an income. Desperate for cash and unable to rely on his fiction for financial support, he hustled for freelance journalism work and once again submitted articles to the *Sun*. He also decided to try his luck with the *New-York Evening Post* and headed over to the paper's offices, in an old residence on Fulton Street in lower Manhattan, carrying an article he had written.

Cahan handed his manuscript to the office boy and took a seat—a ritual that was familiar and no doubt wearying to him. But a door soon opened, and a young man emerged who proceeded to shake Cahan's hand with warmth and enthusiasm, telling him what a fine novelist he was and that he had read *Yekl* with great pleasure.

The young man was Lincoln Steffens, who in the early fall of 1897 was serving as assistant city editor of the *Evening Post*. Six years younger than the thirty-seven-year-old Cahan, Steffens would prove to have, like Cahan, a talent for leadership and would go on to become a progenitor of the genre of reform-oriented investigative journalism known as muckraking. A Californian by birth and the son of a wealthy businessman, he had graduated from the University of California, then spent time studying in France and Germany. He returned to America as a worldly and idealistic young man.

Steffens quickly arranged for the *Evening Post* to publish Cahan's article, then invited him for a walk. They talked about literature, Stephen Crane, and William Dean Howells, and before they knew it they had arrived at Steffens's home on West 56th Street. Steffens invited him inside and introduced him to his family. The immigrant Cahan had acquired another influential friend in America's Protestant literary establishment, as well as a deeper appreciation of the possibilities that his new home held out to even its newest citizens.

The *Evening Post* published only a few of Cahan's articles, and he remained on the lookout for more assignments. Steffens steered him to more work at the city's oldest newspaper, the *Commercial Advertiser*, a paper rarely read on the Lower East Side. Steffens would shortly follow Cahan there to be his editor, creating one of those magical newsrooms that come together only once in a while and that are remembered and talked about for years to come. The *Commercial Advertiser* was then one of the smaller papers in the city, with a circulation of just 2,500. But it had a lineage as a conservative voice. At one point Thurlow Weed, an anti-Mason politician, had edited it. When Cahan got there, its proprietor was the railroad magnate Collis Huntington, who sustained the money-losing paper "for its influence, the resultant prestige accruing to the family name, and as a hobby." Steffens got Cahan the work through one of the *Advertiser*'s drama critics, Norman Hapgood, who, decades later, writing for a Hearst publication, played a part in exposing the anti-Semitism of Henry Ford.

Cahan's five years at the *Commercial Advertiser*, from 1897 to 1902, are sometimes overlooked, being overshadowed by his fifty years at the *Forward*. But it was there that the young socialist ideologue and labor activist became a newspaperman. Cahan's first editor was Henry J. Wright, who gave him his first lesson in classical newspaper reporting: he sent him to cover a rally for Benjamin V. Tracey, the Republican nominee in the first New York mayoral election in which the victor would be the chief executive of all five boroughs. Cahan tried to get out of the assignment on the grounds that he was a socialist and could not possibly write about a member of the bourgeoisie. Wright told Cahan he just wanted a straightforward report on Tracey's speech and appearance and on the response from the crowd; once that was done, Cahan could write his conscience. Cahan covered the rally and wrote up the story, complete with his unfavorable opinion of Tracey. Wright rejected it. "Belles lettres is one thing and newspaper writing is another," he explained.

That November Steffens came on board as city editor, with a mandate to make the paper more lively and position it somewhere between the sensationalism of the *Journal* and *The World* and the dry, just-the-facts approach of *The New York Times*. Steffens promptly cleaned house, firing two-thirds of the reporters. In their place he hired young Ivy League graduates who had little newspaper experience but grand literary ambitions; he planned to mentor them along with the fiery Russian already on his staff.

"'We' had use for anyone who, openly or secretly, hoped to be a poet, a novelist, or an essayist," Steffens wrote in his autobiography. "I could not pay them much in money, but as an offset I promised to give them opportunities to see life as it happened in all the news varieties. . . . When a reporter no longer saw red at a fire, when he was so used to police news that a murder was not a human tragedy but only a crime, he could not write police news for us. We preferred the fresh staring eyes to the informed mind and the blunted pencil." Before long Steffens felt his experiment was working. "We are doing some things that were never done in journalism before," he wrote to his father in March 1898.

It was a perfect fit for Cahan. He loved pontificating to his bright-eyed young colleagues, and they were in awe of the older Russian socialist who had accomplished things of which they only dreamed—and who was a published novelist to boot. In the afternoon, after the paper had been put to bed, they would gather around a long table in the newsroom, where Cahan would hold forth on the higher virtues of Tolstoy and Chekov. "I love you . . . clever good fellows, but you are children in the fields of art," he told them.

When Steffens asked Cahan what he would like to write about, he replied, "Give me assignments that will bring me in close contact with life." So Steffens assigned him to the police headquarters, then located on Mulberry Street, near Houston. All the dailies had reporters there. Cahan loved the assignment, which gave him the education in American urban living for which he longed. "The duties of a police reporter had a two-fold character: One part of the work was connected to the police itself—to the 'politics' among the officials," he wrote in his memoir. "The second part of the work consists of paying attention to the police bulletins and reporting the various sensational events announced in them: a murder or another major crime, a suicide, a tragedy, a fire. . . . Chiefly, the second part of the work interested me, but the first part did also. Everything interested me."

There Cahan met one of the greatest reporters in the city, the Danish-born Jacob Riis of the *Sun*, the leading muckraker in America and an ardent advocate for the poor.

> Riis was not a tall man, and not a fat one either. He was in his forties, with a blond moustache and glasses. He spoke with a slight Danish accent. Steffens introduced me to him as a writer, the author of *Yekl* and a man "with ideas." We spent about half an hour together, and we didn't like each other. To me, Riis seemed like a person with outdated notions. . . . I saw that he didn't like my socialism much, and even less my low opinion of certain American writers. I felt that he considered me a pretentious young man. But he treated me courteously, and he showed me and explained everything related to my work. He introduced me to the reporters from the other newspapers and to all the officials at Police Headquarters, from the Chief of Police to some of the clerks.

On this first day at the police headquarters, Cahan experienced another rite of American passage: he used, for the first time, a telephone. After a meeting of the police board, Cahan needed to write up the story, and Riis told him that he didn't have enough time physically to bring his copy to the office. "You have to call it in," Riis said.

"At the words 'call it in' I got hot and cold flashes," Cahan recalled. "Up to that time I had never held a telephone in my hand. . . . In my last year at the Vilna Teachers' Institute, in 1881, I learned about the telephone in a new physics textbook. Only when I came to New York did I see a real telephone. . . . I don't think I would exaggerate by saying that in the whole Lower East Side then there were only a few telephones."

Cahan managed to find a phone in a drugstore on Houston Street, a few blocks from Mulberry. But

> I did not trust my own abilities on the instrument. In despair, I asked the druggist to speak for me. The druggist was friendly, but he was an Italian (the area was already at that time a part of the Italian quarter), and he had a real Italian accent, with hard "r"s that cut me like dull knives. Some of his English words I could barely understand. But every second was precious. . . . In short, I dictated my report to him word for word and he repeated it into the phone. He was so excited about the job that he pronounced the words resoundingly in a loud voice. In this way we took turns "singing" for about ten minutes—for a third of a column.

Cahan's time at the *Commercial Advertiser* greatly broadened his horizons—he was entranced by the great variety of people he encountered. At the same time his colleagues were particularly interested in his Russian Jewish background. He had more than his share of cronies at the paper. He had lunch with Steffens nearly every day and took long walks with him. Another was Hutchins Hapgood, younger brother of the drama critic Norman Hapgood, who was fascinated with the religious life in the "Jewish quarter." According to Moses Rischin, author of a marvelous monograph on Cahan's years at the *Advertiser*, when Hapgood's fascination became evident, Cahan "would act as his liaison agent and interpreter, introducing him to some of his friends and acquaintances." Steffens shared his interest. "I had become as infatuated with the Ghetto as eastern boys were with the wild west," the editor recalled. He even put up a mezuza on the door to his office.

Steffens was pleased to give space to articles that highlighted the vibrancy of the Lower East Side, regardless of what others thought of it. While he was at the *Evening Post*, he received a letter from "a socially prominent Jewish lady [who] had written to the editor asking why so much space was given to the ridiculous performances of the ignorant, foreign East Side Jews, and none to the uptown Hebrews. . . . I had the satisfaction of telling her about the comparative beauty, significance, and character of the uptown and downtown Jews. I must have talked well, for she threatened and tried to have me fired, as she put it."

Rischin quotes a description by Hapgood of one Eliakim Zunser, a "jester and folk-poet" to whom he had been introduced by Cahan.

> As he chanted his poems he seemed to gather up into himself the dignity and pathos of his serious and suffering race, but as one who had gone beyond the suffering and lived only with the eternities. His wife and children bent over him as he recited, and their bodies kept time with his rhythm. One of the two visitors was a Jew, whose childhood had been spent in Russia, and when Zunser read a dirge which he had composed in Russia twenty-five years ago at the death by cholera of his first wife and children—a dirge that is now chanted daily in thousands of homes in Russia—the visitor joined in, altho he had not heard it in many years. Tears came to his eyes as memories of his childhood were brought up by Zunser's famous lines; his body swayed to and fro in sympathy with that of Zunser and those of the poet's second wife and her children; and to the Anglo-Saxon present, this little group of Jewish exiles moved by rhythm, pathos, and the memory of a far-away land conveyed a strange emotion.

The weeping visitor was, of course, Abraham Cahan, and the description became part of Hapgood's famous compilation *The Spirit of the Ghetto*.

Another friend of Cahan at the newspaper was Carl Hovey, who went on to become editor of *Metropolitan Magazine*, (which would send John Reed south of the border in 1910 to cover the Mexican Revolution). Cahan introduced Hovey to Russian novelists, and the literary group at the *Commercial Advertiser* became something of a newsroom aristocracy. Some of the reporters asked Cahan to read their stories before they submitted them to the paper. Cahan became friends with the financial reporter, Edwin Lefèvre, and with the paper's war correspondent, Pitts

Duffield, who came from one of the wealthiest families in Ohio. Hapgood and Hovey, both Harvard alumni, would on occasion bring Cahan along for an evening at their alma mater's club on West 44th Street.

During his years at the *Commercial Advertiser*, Cahan interviewed President William McKinley on a ferryboat, had lunch with William "Buffalo Bill" Cody, and strolled down Fifth Avenue with the financier Russell Sage, no doubt getting a different perspective on capitalism from a master. Cahan was at the *Advertiser* when Theodore Roosevelt came to visit Steffens. They'd known one another from Roosevelt's days as New York's commissioner of police. Cahan became friends with Samuel Gompers after covering a debate between the legendary president of the American Federation of Labor and Harvard professor Edward Atkinson, whom, Rischin notes, Cahan characterized as the court economist to "King Capitalism."

If Cahan was getting an education in American culture, the *Advertiser* and its readers were learning about the immigrant world flourishing in their midst. The *Advertiser* gave considerable space to features about the Lower East Side Jews. Almost every week its Saturday supplement contained an article on the East Side "Jewish quarter," with such titles as "Yiddish Comedy," "Literature of the Slums," "Ghetto War Spirit," "Zangwill in the Ghetto," "Researches of a Rabbi," and "Hamlet in the Bowery." Some of the coverage was written by Cahan, and some by others.

The *Commercial Advertiser* was by no means the only newspaper that covered the Jewish neighborhood, but it was the one that had Abraham Cahan, who could describe the area and teach others how to do so better than anyone else. According to Steffens, Cahan would take his coworkers to the Yiddish theater, where they observed with fascination the ongoing battle between advocates of realism and romanticism.

> Cahan took us, as he could get us, one by one or in groups, to the cafés where the debate was on at every table and to the theaters where the audience divided: the realist party hissing a romantic play,

> the romanticists fighting for it with clapping hands and sometimes with fists or nails. A remarkable phenomenon it was, a community of thousands of people fighting over an art question as savagely as other people had fought over political or religious questions, dividing families, setting brother against brother, breaking up business firms, and finally, actually forcing the organization of a rival theater with a company pledged to realism against the old theater, which would play any good piece.

In the five years he spent at the *Commercial Advertiser*, Cahan produced a thick file of astonishingly eloquent and wide-ranging feature writing. It would serve as the basis for a lush anthology, compiled by Moses Rischin and published in 1985 as *Grandma Never Lived in America: The New Journalism of Abraham Cahan*.* The book opens with Cahan's description of a visit to a café in 1898, where conversation centered on the recent explosion of the USS *Maine* in Havana Harbor under mysterious circumstances. Some argued in favor of declaring war on Spain over the incident; a Hungarian insisted that the time for imperialistic colonies was gone. The only person who offered a counterargument "was a dark-eyed young woman of thirty, the wife of one of the gathering. 'You men cannot do without bloodshed. If you were mothers, you would not be in such a hurry about sending your children, the flower of the population, to the battlefield.' Whereupon the champion of liberty bowed deeply, and with a broad smile of gallantry supplanting the look of martial enthusiasm on his bewhiskered face, he said: 'Madam, love is the vocation of your sex. I may feel like remarking that it is for the sake of love that I advocate war, but who dares oppose you?' " The anthology closes with Cahan's paean to the great nineteenth-century Russian novelists whom he loved and in whose ranks, under a different set of political circumstances, he might have found himself.

* The title implies, and Rischin notes in his introduction, that Cahan's immigrant feature writing anticipated the "new journalism" of the 1960s and 1970s.

The camaraderie of the *Commercial Advertiser* staff would not last indefinitely; bigger publications came calling. Norman Hapgood was the first to go, in 1901, taking a job at the popular magazine *Collier's Weekly*. Steffens left shortly thereafter, joining *McClure's Magazine*. Cahan quit at the end of 1901, but not before, in the late summer, he and Anna took a vacation, his first holiday ever. They went to the Catskill Mountains, where the young newspaperman took up bird-watching. He'd awaken as dawn was breaking at five a.m. to study them until breakfast, then return to observe them in the afternoon until darkness fell. Not surprisingly, according to his biographer Theodore Pollock, Cahan infused his new leisure-time pursuit with "the same penetrating intensity he had come to lavish upon men."

This idyll was brought abruptly to a close on September 6, when an anarchist named Leon Czolgosz shot President McKinley at the Pan-American Exposition in Buffalo, New York. Cahan raced back to New York to cover the story. Eight days later the president died. Czolgosz told authorities that he had attended a number of anarchist lectures, including some by Emma Goldman. Goldman was arrested, and the grief-stricken country vented its ire on its immigrant community. Goldman was later released, but Congress passed legislation to allow for the exclusion or deportation of anyone "who disbelieves in or who is opposed to all organized government, or who is a member of or affiliated with any organization entertaining or teaching such disbelief." In years to come, this anti-immigrant feeling would have catastrophic results for refugees seeking a haven in the United States.

One day that fall Cahan was walking on Broadway when someone came up from behind and clapped his hands over his eyes. It turned out to be Steffens, who had by then begun, for *McClure's*, the muckraking journalism that would make him one of the most famous newspapermen in American history. His exposés would be collected in the groundbreaking 1904 book *The Shame of the Cities*. "The deeper you probe into corruption," Steffens had told Cahan, "the more convinced you become that capitalism is the source of all evil." In any case, that day Cahan ended up at Steffens's home, where the talk was of how a group from *McClure's* was now founding another muckraking periodical, *The American Magazine*. Cahan wanted to hear about its literary policies, but Steffens brushed him aside, saying "Oh, let's rather talk about socialism."

In reply, Cahan reminded Steffens "of a similar but exactly opposite answer that he used to give a few years back, when I tried to talk to him about socialism. He used to stop me and say: 'Oh, let's rather talk about literature.' " It was a split consciousness Cahan understood well from his own life. In some sense it was a fruitful tension, never wholly resolved, one that would make Cahan's journalism, once he returned to the *Forward*, encompass both art and politics.

7

During Cahan's years at the *Commercial Advertiser*, he churned out not only hard news and feature stories but also short fiction. In 1898 Houghton Mifflin brought out a collection of Cahan's stories entitled *The Imported Bridegroom and Other Stories of the New York Ghetto.* In addition to the title story, the volume included "A Providential Match," "A Sweat-Shop Romance," "A Ghetto Wedding," and "Circumstances." Between 1899 and 1901, Cahan also published stories in popular American magazines, including *The Atlantic Monthly*, *Cosmopolitan*, and *Scribner's*: "The Apostate of Chego-Chegg," "Rabbi Eleizer's Christmas," "The Daughter of Avrom Leib," "A Marriage by Proxy," "Dumitru and Sigrid," and "Tzinchadzi of the Catskills." By now he was well on his way to establishing himself as the master of immigrant narrative fiction. His stories illuminated both the pain and the wonder of the greenhorn experience, the romantic dilemmas, the retreat from religion, the attraction of personal freedom, and paradoxically, the undeniable yearning for the old world.

In 1900, while still employed by the *Commercial Advertiser*, Cahan found himself gravitating to Herrick's Café, at 141 Division Street, where the tables were often crowded with members of the *Forward* staff, whose offices were just a few doors away. The congenial atmosphere of the café helped to ease whatever lingering resentments existed between Cahan and his former staff, and he soon began contributing freelance articles to the paper.

A lively series of fictional sketches penned by Cahan for the *Forward* in the winter of 1900-1 stands out as a sign of his mind-set. As Sanders writes in *The Downtown Jews*, the series focuses on the generational differences between family members, but what fuels their conflicts is not religion but politics. "Socialism occupies the place of religion," Cahan scribbled in a note to himself. This was simply a reflection of what was happening in the real world. The socialist movement in America was in a state of disorder. The Socialist Labor Party, under De Leon's autocratic leadership, lay in tatters. Eugene Debs was inspiriting the two-year-old Social Democratic Party (with which the *Forward* was affiliated), but it hadn't yet muscled its way past the SLP. Cahan was becoming convinced that a realistic, pragmatic approach to implementing social change, and not the uncompromising, doctrinaire views of the movement's orthodox wing, was the best way to achieve socialist goals.

This belief is reflected in the sketches in Cahan's *Forward* series. In one story Dr. Bunimowitz, a former socialist, now has a booming medical practice as well as real estate holdings. A good and generous person, he is also an unapologetic capitalist. "When I was a fool, a socialist, I used to talk a lot and do nothing," Bunimowitz says. "But now I don't tell stories, and I know full well how much good I do—and so do the hundreds of people I help." These sketches were popular among *Forward* readers, and buoyed by their success, Cahan began contributing even more to the paper. After he left the *Commercial Advertiser* at the end of 1901, some *Forward* staffers floated the idea of Cahan returning to the paper.

One afternoon in early March 1902, as Cahan was walking on East Broadway, heading toward the paper's offices, he spotted two advertising agents for the *Forward*, William Lief and Albert Feller. The three chatted about the difficulty the paper was encountering in gaining the custom of the big retailers, and about the stagnant circulation numbers, which just couldn't seem to push past 6,000. Some at the paper feared it was on the brink of closing. Both ad men believed that a new, forceful editor might be able to turn the paper around by moving it toward a more colorful and lively format. Cahan, Lief and Feller declared, was just the man.

Cahan considered their offer. He would need assurances that he would have a free hand—"absolutely no interference with my editorship" was how he put it—and that he would be occupied for no more than two hours a day by the paper. His plan was to get the edition on course in the morning and then head home to work on his fiction.

The assassination of Czar Alexander II by members of Narodnaya Volya on March 1, 1881, was followed by pogroms throughout the Pale, but it stirred in Abraham Cahan hopes for a Russia without Romanov rule.

Cahan (below, left, in 1883) was twenty-one years old when, in the crackdown on revolutionaries following the assassination of Alexander II, he fled Russia, one step ahead of the police. (*Forward Association*)

After arriving at America in 1882, Cahan taught school and began writing not only for socialist journals but also for the general press. (*Library of Congress, Prints & Photographs Division, George Grantham Bain Collection*)

Lincoln Steffens (above, left), who brought Cahan to the *New-York Commercial Advertiser.* "'We' had use," he wrote, "for anyone who, openly or secretly, hoped to be a poet, a novelist, or an essayist." (*Library of Congress, Prints & Photographs Division, George Grantham Bain Collection*)

William Dean Howells helped establish the genre of American literary realism and took Cahan under his wing. It was Howells who seized upon the name that became the title of Cahan's first novel: *Yekl.* (*Library of Congress, Prints & Photographs Division*)

H. L. Mencken, the sage of Baltimore, at the *Evening Sun* in 1913. He corresponded with Cahan, and the two dined together, agreeing that Mencken's derogatory references to Jews were, as Mencken wrote, "only a small part of a discussion that was generally favorable to them." (*Reprinted by permission of The Baltimore Sun Media Group, the estate of H. L. Mencken, and the Enoch Pratt Free Library of Baltimore, in accordance with the terms of the will of H. L. Mencken. All Rights Reserved. Photograph courtesy of the Yale Collection of American Literature, Beinecke Rare Book and Manuscript Library, Yale University*)

Jacob Riis, celebrated reporter of his day, rose to fame at *The New York Sun* and showed a young Abraham Cahan how to make his first telephone call, telling him at the New York Police Department's press room, "You have to call it in." (*Library of Congress, Prints & Photographs Division, Frances Benjamin Johnston Collection*)

Samuel Gompers, future president of the American Federation of Labor, worked in the same New York City cigar factory as Cahan at a time when organized labor was starting to stir throughout America, including on the Lower East Side. (*Library of Congress, Prints & Photographs Division*)

Cahan's use of the techniques of yellow journalism, learned from his contemporaries William Randolph Hearst and Joseph Pulitzer, kept the *Forward*'s circulation climbing and required a small army of newsboys. "300 People Burned in a Theater"; "Pittsburgh Millionaire, Bachelor, Gets 2 Wives After Death"; "8 Bandits Ravish Girl in Mid-day on Washington Street"; "70-Year-Old-Worker Takes Job and Drops Dead"; and "She Burned Out Her Husband's Eye with Carbolic Acid" were typical *Forward* headlines. (*Library of Congress, Prints & Photographs Division*)

The *Forward* Building housed not only the editorial offices but also, on the top floor, the composing room, where mechanical mastodons formed hot lead into lines of type. The lower floors had space for a meeting hall with a thousand-person capacity and for the headquarters of several unions and fraternal organizations. (*Forward Association*)

Twenty-three-year-old Clara Lemlich helped instigate a strike in the garment industry in 1909, when she stood up at a meeting of the Ladies' Waist Makers Union and declared, "I'm tired of listening to speakers who talk in general terms . . . I offer a resolution that a general strike be declared—now." She later betrayed the garment workers, joining the communists. *(Courtesy of the Catherwood Library Kheel Center at Cornell University)*

"For No Reason, a Savage Mass Murder Has Occurred" was the headline in the *Forward* two days after a fire broke out on March 25, 1911, at The Triangle Shirtwaist Company. One hundred and forty-six persons perished, mostly young women. Wrote Cahan in an editorial: "Who is the Angel of Death? Who is the thug? Who is the mass murderer? Must we again say it is that gluttonous ravager of humans—capital?!" *(Forward Association)*

Forward 113,800 Vorwarts

פארווערטס

VOL. XIV. No. 4687 NEW YORK MONDAY, MARCH 27, 1911 PRICE ONE CENT.

נים קיין סיבה, נור א ווילדער מאסענמארד איז דאס געווען.

וויניג פייער-עסקייפס, פערמאכטע טהירען, קרומע, שמאלע טרעפ, א שאפ אנגעפאקט מיט מאשינען זיינען סימנים פון א קרימינעלע נאכלעסיגקייט, וועלכע האט בערויבט 144 ארבייטער פון זייערע יונגע לעבענס.

ארום דיעזע בילדער גיעסען זיך טרעהרען. יעדעס בילד רעפרעזענטירט מיט זיך א בעזונדערע הערצרייסענדע טראגעדיע.

לויות אנשטאט חופות. — היסטערישער געוויין אנשטאט מוזיק. — צוריסענע גליקען. — טויזענדער צובראכענע הערצער.

Cahan and his wife, Anna, on their return to New York from a trip overseas in the late 1920s. The two were married for more than sixty years, until Anna's death in 1947. (*Forward Association*)

The *Forward*'s headquarters at 173–75 East Broadway was a ten-story Beaux Arts building that one historian described as seeming "to bestride the Lower East Side like a colossus." On the front of the building, just above the second floor, a series of reliefs depicted Karl Marx, Friedrich Engels, Ferdinand Lassalle, and Friedrich Adler. (*Forward Association*)

ART SECTION, JUNE 16, 1929

OUR BEAUTY AND CHARM CONTEST

Cahan moved the *Forward* into rotogravure printing, which enabled newspapers to reproduce photographs on newsprint. The rotogravure section became one of the *Forward*'s most popular features by carrying scenes of Jewish life throughout the world. It was but one of the reasons Oswald Garrison Villard, the longtime editor of *The Nation*, wrote, "Which is the most vital, the most interesting, the most democratic of New York's daily journals? . . . In my judgment it is the *Forward*."

"Our Beauty and Charm Contest." From the *Forward*'s rotogravure section, June 16, 1929. (*Forward Association*)

ART SECTION, AUGUST 3, 1294

PICTURES OF JEWISH LIFE AND CHARACTERS

A MARKET SCENE IN THE OLDEST SECTION OF WARSAW.—This exceptional photograph was taken especially for the FORWARD, by A.Kacyzne.

"Pictures of Jewish Life and Characters." From the *Forward*'s rotogravure section, August 3, 1924. (*Forward Association*)

V. I. Lenin (top, left, in 1920) received Cahan at Cracow, Poland, in 1912 and presented him with copies of *Pravda*, which he was editing. (*Library of Congress, Prints & Photographs Division*)

Alfred Dreyfus, by then cleared of treason, received Cahan at Paris in 1912 and spent two hours with him. (*Library of Congress, Prints & Photographs Division, George Grantham Bain Collection*)

Rabbi Yissachar Dov Rokeach, head of the Belzer Hasidic dynasty, received Cahan at Belz, Poland, in 1912. The sage spoke admiringly of Theodore Roosevelt, but dismissed Zionism, unions, and newspapers.

Eleanor Marx, daughter of Karl, received Cahan at London in 1892. "We Jews have a special obligation to devote ourselves to the working class," she told him.

Friedrich Engels, father of Marxist theory, was finishing volume three of *Das Kapital* when Cahan visited him at London in 1892. "If the Jews would drink more, they would be even better people," he told the abstemious editor.

Not a problem, both men said. The paper was put to bed by two p.m. every day; it would be easy for Cahan to leave by then.

Cahan thought about it as they continued down East Broadway. "I'm afraid you're making a mistake, Lief," Cahan finally said. "The comrades are the same as they were, but I am not. I have been in the outside world, I have discovered that we, the socialists, have no patent on honesty and knowledge. The outside world is more tolerant of us than we are of it." He said socialists of the Lower East Side needed to know something about the world beyond their own. "It's as important to teach people to carry a handkerchief in their pockets as it is to carry a union card. And it's as important to respect the opinions of others as it is to have opinions of one's own."

"I'm not the one making a mistake, Comrade Cahan. You are," Lief answered. "We don't quite know how to give expression to our inner aspirations. . . . What we need is, precisely, someone who can put it all into words for us." They were by now standing in front of the *Forward*'s offices.

"I want to think about it," Cahan finally said. "An editor should have unlimited authority."

He walked home to East 7th Street, his mind awhirl. Could he really return to the *Forward*? Hadn't he left the parochial world of the Yiddish press far behind? But what if he could apply to the *Forward* the lessons he had learned at the *Commercial Advertiser*? What if he could truly create the paper of his dreams, "a living novel," as Steffens used to call it, *and* continue his fiction writing as well?

Anna argued against it. "Have you forgotten the Party frictions and how they embittered your life?" she warned him, adding that the conflicts would be "worse than the pot-boilers" he was writing. He had acquired a name in the literary world; he was assured a fine future and peace of mind. Her advice was to "serve the Socialist Party as an ordinary member and devote yourself to literature."

At the next meeting of the *Forward* Press Association, Cahan's name was put forth as editor. All his demands had been met, including the most difficult, given the paper's precarious economic state: the *Forward* would be expanded from six pages to eight.

Cahan couldn't resist—he returned to the *Forward*. His first issue was scheduled for Sunday, March 16, 1902. From the start he made his ambitions abundantly clear. "There will be much more to read than there has been so far," he wrote in an announcement to readers that appeared in the paper the day before he officially came aboard. "The news and all the articles will be written in pure, plain *Yiddishe Yiddish*, and we hope that every line will be interesting to all Yiddish-speaking people, big and little."

The paper he inherited had employed a serious, dry tone, "a kind of highbrow Yiddish with a lot of Hebrew and German and Russian terms that only the educated man could understand," Cahan later told an interviewer. Its editorial cornerstone had been the daily "lead article," which was not a news story but generally an essay filled with theoretical arguments about socialist ideas.

For that first issue, Cahan wrote many of the articles himself, working late into the night (so much for leaving the office at two p.m.). In place of the usual leading essay on socialist theory, he ran a human interest story. A translation of a piece he'd written for the *Commercial Advertiser*, it was headlined "In Love with *Yiddishe Kinder*" and told lively tales of young Gentile men and women who had fallen in love with Jews and in some instances married them. *Forward* readers weren't used to reading about domestic relationships in their paper, let alone frowned-upon ones.

"Send your children to college if you can, but don't let them become disloyal to their own parents and brothers!" admonished the headline of Cahan's inaugural editorial. Instead of a theoretical discussion or a political statement, the piece began with the simple details of working life in the city: "On Second Avenue, after 8:00 a.m. each morning, one can see hundreds of Jewish boys—from fourteen to eighteen or nineteen years old—walking with books under their arms. They're going uptown from Houston or Christie Street. They travel in pairs, or in great companies, chattering happily amongst themselves. Their clothes are for the most part old. . . . These are Jewish college boys, children of immigrants."

The editorial was a paean to the compulsion of Jewish immigrants to put the education of their children ahead of all other matters. It also lamented "saddening examples . . . here in this land of hoo-hah and dollars and sense" in which hard-working immigrants produce a "poor Jewish boy who flatters the rich and crawls to the politicians who are enemies of the people." It called such boys "traitors to their parents." The Proletarian Preacher was back.

Another change in that first issue was a slight softening of the *Forward*'s fervently antireligious stance. In an opinion column, Cahan described "the three stages in the life of a free-thinker: (1) when he passes a synagogue and gnashes his teeth; (2) when he passes a synagogue and smiles; (3) when he passes a synagogue and, though inclined to sigh because the world is still in such a state of ignorance, nevertheless finds himself taking an interest in such moments as these, when men stand together immersed in a feeling that has nothing to do with the egoistic life."

Readers responded to the new *Forward* immediately. An avalanche of letters arrived at the paper's offices, most laudatory, some disapproving. Nearly all expressed, in some form or another, surprise, if not bewilderment: Why was the socialist *Forward* concerning itself with such popular matters? Cahan was delighted. It didn't matter if they loved his paper or hated it, as long as they kept reading it.

The changes continued. Cahan pushed aside the long dissertations on socialism and ran human interest stories on marriage, divorce, and jealousy. He opened the paper to nonsocialists. He wrote a series on tolerance. As Hearst and Pulitzer had done before him, he added pictures and banner headlines and ran contests—asking, for example, for the best definition of luck (the winner: "*Mazel* is somebody else's *schlimazel* [bad luck]") or the best account of "how I rid myself of superstition." More and more letters poured in, often containing details of the readers' personal lives. The *Forward* was becoming more than just a paper of record; to the legions of recent immigrants devouring its pages, it was a sympathetic, seasoned voice, an enlightened cousin who had been in America just that much longer and could serve as a guide to the country's strange ways.

Circulation shot up, tripling within four months of Cahan's return. By midsummer, 19,000 copies of the *Forward* were being sold every day. Cahan, his veins now coursing with news black, took to the streets of the Lower East Side, spending hours each Sunday eavesdropping on conversations in barbershops and cafés, chatting with the owners of newspaper stands and their customers. "I wanted to know what sort of impression the new *Forverts* was making on the public," he wrote later, "how they reacted to the various articles; what was good, what had to be changed, and what sort of other news it would be advisable to introduce. That was mainly my 'job' late Sunday morning. You can sit and listen to the conversations, and sometimes you can slip in a few questions yourself."

There were so many new immigrants in the neighborhood that Cahan could often do this reconnaissance work anonymously. But he was bursting with pride and enthusiasm for his new journalistic enterprise. "Sometimes somebody did recognize me," he recalled. "But that also wasn't so bad." He was, at heart, still a reporter. "Several times I got up very early to see what was going on in the Jewish neighborhood at that hour—how the stores were opened, how the market on Hester Street took shape, how poor people searched through garbage barrels, how tailors ran to work at six in the morning. In this way I used to put together articles that appealed to our readers—often in a deeper and more delicate way than what usually interests them in a newspaper."

Cahan's fiction writing took a backseat. The *Forward* was becoming his great American Jewish novel, a kind of epic in itself—entertaining, dramatic, and didactic.

Some of his fellow newspapermen were horrified: they thought he was transforming their beloved *Forward* into a lowbrow, crass publication, watering down its socialist ideals, "lower[ing] himself to the masses instead of lifting them up." Cahan, in a favorite reply, would say. "If you want to pick a child up from the ground, you first have to bend down to him. If you don't, how will you reach him?"

As the *Forward* grew, the cost of putting it out skyrocketed as well. It desperately needed more advertising. Then at the end of the summer of

1902, workers at the American Tobacco Company, a big advertiser in the *Forward*, organized a strike. In solidarity, the paper refused to carry the company's ads. The gesture put the paper even further in the red.

Help arrived. Some "kangaroos," people disillusioned with De Leon who hopped from one socialist party to another, had cash on hand from a failed attempt to start a new Yiddish paper. They agreed to bring their money to the *Forward* with one significant condition: the paper had to become "more socialistic." This Cahan refused to do. He quit instead.

After this resignation, Cahan had no exciting new venture to focus on. The *Forward* had commanded his full attention. Anna, who still viewed him as a serious fiction writer, urged him to return to his typewriter. Whether because of this disagreement or one of a more personal nature, they decided it was best if they lived separately for a while. Anna remained in the city, moving from their relatively pricy apartment to a simple furnished room to save on expenses, while Cahan decamped to the country. He had long wanted to give rural life a try, ever since his fleeting fantasy, upon his arrival in America, of living with the agricultural settlers of the Balta Am Olam.

He chose Woodbine, New Jersey, a small town in Cape May County, at the state's southernmost tip. Woodbine had been settled by eastern European Jews in 1891 as an agricultural community, with financial assistance from Baron Maurice de Hirsch. Cahan had always wanted to investigate the settlement, and now he began writing about it for the *Commercial Advertiser.* After a visit from some apologetic members of the Forward Association, he began contributing articles to the *Forward* as well. In April 1903, he moved to New Milford, Connecticut, and threw himself into such avid bird-watching that the locals called him the "bird-man."

"In the bird manual you would read (and see the picture) of types of birds that you had never seen in reality. . . . When you recognized one of these birds [outside], your heart would pound with joy," Cahan wrote. This was something he had neither the time nor the inclination for in Russia, but here it made him feel more connected to his new home—to its very land as well as its people. "In my native land the birds had been strange to me. I knew their names from Russian literature, but how this or that one looked or what kind of songs they sang—of this I had no idea."

It was the Kishinev massacre that brought Cahan back to the *Forward*. On April 6–7, 1903, forty-five Jews were murdered and more than one thousand injured in a pogrom in the provincial capital of Moldova. It was the worst violence against the Russian Jewish population in more than twenty years. Upon learning of it, Cahan jumped on a train to New York and headed straight for his old office on Division Street, where he contributed to a series of editorials on the pogrom that ran in the *Forward*. The editorial on April 30 asserted that what happened at Kishinev was of a scale beyond anything the Jews had previously experienced and said a march was planned for May 1.

"In the march on the first of May," the editorial said, "lies the honest hope, the only hope, that there will come a time when no pogrom will exist in Russia any more. . . . For every evil Christian who has spilled Jewish blood in Kishinev, hundreds of Christian revolutionaries stand ready to let their own blood be shed in the struggle against the darkest force of all dark forces."

It is unclear whether Cahan was the author of this editorial, but the sentiments were unrealistic, as others understood. Theodor Herzl, born the same year as Cahan, was about to convene the Sixth Zionist Congress. His belief in the necessity of a Jewish homeland was years ahead of Cahan's thinking, and it would be nearly fifty years before Cahan fully accepted Herzl's view.

Working furiously, Cahan remained in New York for a few more days, then returned to New Milford, where Anna joined him several weeks later. There they stayed for the spring and summer. In the weeks after the pogrom, Cahan published a long, detailed account of the event in the July issue of *The North American Review*, a prestigious Boston-based literary magazine. He described the vast scale of the anti-Jewish riots and how they had spread from district to district, and he highlighted the role of the Russian authorities in enabling the killings. He linked the violence against the Jews to "the stupendous growth of the revolutionary movement," which had begun in the late 1870s, flared in the early 1880s with the assassination of Alexander II, and appeared to be gathering steam with every passing decade. He concluded:

> Russia seems to be on the eve of important events, and the danger of the present situation does not lie "in a society made up of a handful of people," as M. von Plehve assured the correspondent of a Paris newspaper, but in a state of things under which, to borrow a phrase from an "underground" Russian leaflet, "Cossack whips are snapping, and unsheathed sabers are gleaming at every turn"; in a state of things under which the white terror of the knout, the prison cell, and the gallows gives birth to the red terror of the pistol and the dynamite bomb. It is one of those situations, in fact, to which apply the words of Emerson: "Of no use are the men who study to do exactly as was done before, who can never understand that today is a new day."

Typically for a Cahan piece, it sketches a broad picture and takes a forward-looking stance in favor of revolution—and explains it, in language suited to a sophisticated public journal, by citing, of all people, the transcendentalist philosopher Ralph Waldo Emerson. For Cahan, this revolution would be an American one as much as a Russian one.

In the fall of 1903, the Cahans moved back to New York. He was immediately besieged by requests that he return as editor of the *Forward*, and he gave it careful consideration. His fiction writing had stalled, and his finances were in a mess. Writing about the Kishinev pogrom had reawakened both his ideological and journalistic passions. Moreover, in the past year, he had discovered that guiding a paper like the *Forward* was just as creative a project as writing a novel. This was a time when writers such as Cahan were using their literary powers for other purposes. Herzl had been diverted from playwriting to become a dramaturge of history. Cahan, in the process of leaving journalism, was called back to it because of a pogrom. Jewish destiny, American journalism, and the literary impulse were coming together. Once he was assured that he would have the control he wanted, he allowed his name to be put forth as a candidate for editor. His election was unanimous. At forty-three, Cahan once again took the helm of the *Forward*. He would stay there for the rest of his life.

On the heels of the Kishinev pogrom, the failed revolution of 1905, and the Russo-Japanese War, Russian Jews arrived in America in record numbers. By 1905 New York was home to one million Jews; it had the biggest Jewish population of any city in the world. These immigrants, some active in the Jewish Labor Bund, swelled the membership of labor unions sponsored by the *Forward*. Flush with revenue, the *Forward* purchased a three-story building on East Broadway. The revolution of 1905 had been abortive, but it was fodder for the *Forward*, whose circulation soared.

These turn-of-the-century greenhorns were quite different from those who had arrived in the first great wave of eastern European immigration in the early 1880s. Sanders points out that those earlier immigrants were by and large young single men, more often than not radicals who were uninterested in religion. Or as one character remarks in *The Rise of David Levinsky*, "Judaism [had] not much of a chance." Those arriving at the turn of the century, however, came as families, and some brought their religious practices with them. These were Cahan's new readers, and he well understood that the *Forward* had to reflect their concerns and interests as well.

Soon after he returned to his desk at the *Forward*, Cahan learned that his mother had died, toward the end of 1903; he found out about it in a letter from his father. Cahan went with his brother, Isaac, to synagogue and "stood mutely by his side as the younger Cahan intoned Kaddish." Another connection to his life in Europe had been severed. How he felt about it, we just don't know. In a five-volume autobiography filled with details about his schooling, his political activism, and his socialist comrades, his family is rarely mentioned.

Cahan was now focused on turning the *Forward* into a publication that would teach his new readers how to become Americans and embolden them to embrace their new country's modernity. He defended America and its freedoms to die-hard socialists, all while denouncing capitalist exploitation of the laboring masses and advocating socialist solutions to the problem. He wrote articles about table manners, matrimonial difficulties, and baseball, the last of which was motivated by a letter he received in the summer of 1903 from a father who asked for advice in dealing with a son who wanted to play this peculiar American game. Teaching a youngster to play chess or checkers is one thing—at least that sharpens the mind. "But what kind of purpose can such a crazy game as baseball have?" the man asked. The *Forward* came out in favor of baseball, so long as the youngster stayed out of trouble and pursued his studies. In his article addressing the issue, Cahan cited the example of a recent Jewish Rhodes scholar. "We should especially not raise our children so that they will grow up to be foreigners in their own birthplace. An American who is not swift and strong with his hands, feet and his entire body is not considered to be an American at all."

Letters such as these, sent by immigrants puzzled by American life to the newspaper that they relied upon as their guide to the manners and mores of their new home, led in 1906 to the emergence of the most famous of all columns in the *Forward*, the *Bintel Brief* ("bundle of letters"). The column might not have gotten off the ground if it hadn't been for newspaper competition.

In 1905 Louis Miller, a founding member of the *Forward* staff, wrote a vigorous defense of a play by Jacob Gordin, called *Taharas Hamishpocha* (Family Purity). The play criticized the Orthodox newspaper *Tageblatt* and its readers for religious hypocrisy. Cahan disliked the play and refused to publish Miller's defense of it. So in November Miller left the paper and helped launch a new Yiddish daily, the *Warheit* (Truth), which seemed to have one mission: to oppose the *Forward.* By then Yiddish readers could also pick up the *Morgen Journal* (Morning Journal), a spirited paper that was aimed at Orthodox readers.

Cahan felt the competition nipping at his heels and was on the hunt for new features to pull in more readers. As a fiction writer, taken with Steffens's notion of the "living novel," he had asked readers to send in autobiographical stories for publication in the newspaper: "Send us interesting true novels," the *Forward* implored its readers in December 1903. But the few that the paper received were not sufficiently compelling.

In December 1905, Louis Miller, who might have disagreed with Cahan on certain points of socialist theory but shared a journalistic instinct, received a letter at the *Warheit* from a recent immigrant. The man was worried that when he could finally afford to bring his wife over from Russia, he would discover that he no longer loved her. Miller ran the letter as a feature article under the headline "Broken Heart," and a subhead that proclaimed "Not an invented one, but a *real* tragedy from real life." He invited readers to respond with suggestions for the man. They did, in droves. Soon Miller was gleefully running as a regular feature letters from readers asking for advice, together with selected reader responses.

One can only imagine Cahan's reaction to Miller's success. The personal was, after all, *his* bailiwick. A few weeks later, he responded with a variation on Miller's theme. Leon Gottlieb, the editorial secretary at the *Forward*, brought Cahan two letters to the editor "which didn't seem suited for any particular department," as Cahan recalled, because they were of a "personal nature rather than a communal one." Cahan, as Gottlieb recalled, said, "It's a Godsend." One letter was from a "poor working woman" who believed that a neighbor had stolen her deaf son's watch and pawned it; she had written a letter to the neighbor and asked that the *Forward* print it, anonymously, in hopes that it would shame the woman into giving her the pawn ticket. "I'll go on being the same good friend to you that I've been the whole three years we've lived on the same floor—only mail the pawn-ticket to me!" she wrote. "Give me back my bread." The other letter was from a man who had asked another man with whom he was eating breakfast to say the Grace After Meals on behalf of both of them, "because he had a beard and was a pious Jew." The man replied that he'd be happy to do so—for a payment of three cents, a symbolic purchase of the man's matzoh that remained on the table. "Now I ask you," the letter concluded, "what kind of man is that?" A third letter had come from a woman looking for advice on how to help her son stop stammering. These were just what Cahan had been looking for—true human interest stories about the lives of ordinary working people that could have come from the pages of a novel.

Unlike Miller, Cahan decided to respond to the letters himself, rather than leave it to his readers. The letters and Cahan's replies were printed on January 20, 1906, with the editorial note, "Among the letters the *Forward* receives . . . there are many which have a general 'human interest,' as American critics call it. Starting today we will select these and print them separately, with or without comments, under the name *A Bintel Brief*." In response to the letter from the woman about the stolen watch, he wrote an impassioned statement about the tragic living conditions of the working class: "What a picture of workers' misery is to be seen in this letter!" To the man who had to pay for his Grace After Meals, he expressed his hope that the "pious Jew" was simply a practical joker. And to the mother with the stammering son, he gave practical advice, for which the *Bintel Brief* would soon become legendary: "There are special methods for dealing with this, and specialists who concern themselves with them. But we'll have to write in greater detail about this another time."

By the end of the month, Cahan was receiving enough mail to run the *Bintel Brief* feature daily. Not all the letters concerned domestic issues. One early letter seems almost to have been written by a young Abraham Cahan:

> Permit me to convey my shattered feelings in our workers' paper. I'm still a greenhorn in America . . . and now I can't forgive myself for being here. My head and heart grow numb whenever I read in your paper that thousands of workers are standing on the barricades in Russia fighting for their lives. . . . I know that I've committed a crime, that I'm a deserter, that I've run away from the field of battle. Oh, how I would like to stand alongside my brothers again in the

war! . . . But the great ocean does not permit us to hurry to the scene without a ticket . . . and I have no money for the journey. . . . I beg of you, dear editor, answer me, what should I do?

Cahan's reply was succinct: "Well, we can give no better advice than to fight right here in America for a social order in which a man wouldn't have to work like a mule for five dollars a week." The young Cahan had been so bedazzled by revolutionary socialism that he "walked in a daze as one newly in love"; he was now becoming a social democrat. Whatever struggles were going on within Cahan, in the *Bintel Brief* column he was crisp and to the point: the important struggle today was for unionization here in America, not for revolution on the Russian barricades.

Many of the *Bintel Brief* letters came from Jewish mothers and wives who sounded thrilled to know that the paper they trusted would offer them advice on deeply personal issues that they couldn't discuss with their friends. "I must write to you about my situation because I see no other way than through your newspaper," begins one typical letter. "I am one of those women whose husbands spend less time with them than they spend hanging around in the barber shop. I am certainly not the kind who stays in the grocery store all day."

Readers rushed to read about themselves and their neighbors in the paper, and the *Bintel Brief* quickly became the newspaper's most-read and best-known column. The circulation of the *Forward* soared to more than 52,000 by the end of 1906. But the letters were more than a circulation-driving stunt. They gave the paper an organic life, a collaborative interactivity that anticipated by just about a century the phenomenon of social media, in which new content is created by people who started out as readers of existing content. The column also performed an important public service, and occasionally created some high drama. Through the *Bintel Brief*, mothers were able to locate children whom they hadn't seen for more than twenty years. Twice, engaged couples discovered through the *Bintel Brief* that they were, in fact, sister and brother. "Many of these encounters took place in the *Forverts* editorial offices," Cahan recalled.

"And often, when the readers knew in advance that a mother and son who had not seen each other for many years were to be reunited, a crowd would be waiting on the street near our building in order to watch the happy mother with her newly found child."

In May 1906, at a conference of Jewish socialist organizations, those who opposed Cahan's editorial direction confronted him on it. Three hundred people crammed into a basement hall on East Fourth Street to hear the criticism and to hear Cahan defend the new *Forward.* Having a big crowd played to his strengths; warming up, he poked fun at his rivals, calling them pedestrian and uninspired, "comparing their litany to the tune of a Salvation Army Band." The audience laughed, and no one seemed surprised when the resolution condemning Cahan's policies didn't muster enough votes to pass. Cahan refused to be intimidated, but throughout his career he was dogged by charges that he had diluted his socialist principles for the tawdry and the titillating. In one cartoon that appeared in a competing paper, Cahan calls Karl Marx an old geezer and forces him to carry off his socialist cornerstone, which is then replaced by boxes filled with *Bintel Briefs.*

8

Even as Cahan was flush with the success of the *Forward*, he felt the pull of fiction. He had planned a vast novel—which he had intended to call *The Chasm*—about the exodus of the Jews from Russia to America and the gulf between them and the German Jews who had arrived decades earlier. Two anonymous columns in *The Bookman* noted Cahan's plans, but nothing materialized. Cahan did, during this period, bring out his longest book to date. *The White Terror and the Red: A Novel of Revolutionary Russia*, which was published in 1905 by A. S. Barnes & Company and ran to 430 pages, was set in Russia during the years leading up to the assassination of Alexander II; it imagines a young Russian prince who falls in love with a Jewish revolutionary and joins the cause. The two protagonists are last seen, or heard, tapping notes to each other on the walls of the prison into which the czarist government has cast them.

The *Times*, in a favorable review, concluded that Cahan hadn't intended to tell a story so much as to "draw a graphic picture of conditions." Cahan had given a long, detailed narration of a pogrom, ending it with a bitter, sardonic paragraph of Jewish shame. He described the moonlight over the ransacked Jewish quarter, where the occasional house that remained standing belonged to a Christian. Officers on horseback "were moving about musingly, the hoofs of their horses silenced by layers of down" from the gutted quilts of the ghetto. "Seated on empty boxes and barrels, their fingers gripping new accordions, their eyes raised to the moon, a company of rioters on Little Market were playing and singing a melancholy, doleful tune. The Jews were in their hiding places."

Although Cahan had great insight into the concerns and needs of his fellow Russian Jewish immigrants, he was not without a capacity for error. On July 9, 1904, five days after the death of Theodor Herzl, the founder of political Zionism, the *Forward* published an editorial that was certainly respectful of Dr. Herzl but was also condescending toward and dismissive of the Zionist cause. "Does the Zionist idea have any reality to it?" the editorial asked. "Can one agree with them while they have a blunt, impractical idea?" The editorial asserted that such questions were "outside our sphere here." The question "is not if their idea is *our* idea, but if they are serious, if they hold this idea of theirs dear." The *Forward* opined that they did, however tragically wrongheaded they were. "We deplore how some pure inspiration is spent on such empty things, but the inspired themselves we love and respect."

The *Forward* noted that Zionists themselves had often criticized Herzl. "About socialists," it added, "there is nothing to say, because the entire concept of Zionism is child's play to them. . . . We, the socialists, doff our hats as the coffin passes by, with respect to the departed as a person, as a devoted leader of a movement, regardless of what we feel and think of the movement itself."

Cahan would eventually change his opinion about Zionism, but in the first decade of the twentieth century, his attention was largely focused on local politics and the effort to elect a Socialist to Congress. In 1904 the *Forward* had supported Eugene V. Debs for president on the Socialist Party ticket. Debs received more than 400,000 votes, which was almost 3 percent of the votes cast. In 1906 Cahan threw the newspaper into the effort to elect the socialist Morris Hillquit to Congress from New York's ninth district, which included the heavily Jewish Lower East Side. Hillquit, whom Cahan knew from his union-organizing days (he had helped establish the United Hebrew Trades), had cofounded the Socialist Party of America with Debs in 1901. On election night, by one account, 60,000 people jammed into Seward Park in front of the *Forward* Building to watch the election results be projected onto a white sheet via a stereopticon from inside the newspaper's offices. Throughout the evening, updated information was interspersed with anti–Tammany Hall cartoons that, Cahan biographer Theodore Pollock noted, were "lustily applauded." But this enthusiasm did not translate into electoral victory.

Hillquit received only 3,616 votes, fewer than half of the 7,265 cast for Tammany Hall's candidate, Henry Goldfogle. The Republican candidate came in a distant third, with 2,733 votes.

While the ideas and ideals of socialism were popular among Jewish immigrants, the party itself remained organizationally and institutionally weak. Jewish laborers often had to exert herculean efforts just to hold down a job and put food on the table; they seldom had time left over to devote to party politics and neighborhood organizing. And there were larger issues as well. "Modern Jewish life has been characterized by a mixture of idealism and skepticism," Irving Howe wrote in *World of Our Fathers*. "The fervor for socialist revolution could be very high among some of the immigrants, yet this fervor was often undercut by a nagging pessimism as to the possibilities of *any* Jewish politics. Even if the entire Jewish working class were converted to socialism tomorrow, how would that change anything fundamentally in the country?"

Anti-Semitism, however muted, still lurked as an issue for the Socialist Party. In 1901 the labor historian John Commons posed the question of whether Jews were constitutionally disinclined to unionism. "The Jew's conception of a labor organization is that of a tradesman rather than that of a workman," he wrote in that year's Industrial Commission report.

Many Socialists were at pains to distance themselves from the particularities of the Lower East Side and ally themselves with the movement at large. When Hillquit ran again for Congress in 1908, he declared at a rally, "The interests of the workingmen of the Ninth District are entirely identical with those of the workingmen of the rest of the country, and if elected to Congress, I will not consider myself the special representative of the alleged special interests of this district, but the representative of the Socialist Party." Gradually the Socialist Party began to gain traction, particularly in New York and Milwaukee, where, in 1910, Victor Berger was the first Socialist to be elected to Congress. In 1900 fewer than 100,000 votes had been cast for the Socialist presidential candidate Eugene V. Debs; a dozen years later, almost one million people voted for him, representing 6 percent of all votes cast.

Hillquit's and Debs's repeated defeats did not dampen Cahan's enthusiasm for the Socialist Party and only increased his scorn for the major parties and their candidates. "They don't begin to ask, 'What is better for the people?'" he wrote during the presidential campaign of 1908, which pitted the incumbent Republican William Howard Taft against the populist Democrat William Jennings Bryan. "The supreme question with them is: 'How will we win most quickly.'" Bryan's formal nomination by the Democratic Party—the third time the party ran him for president—elicited from Cahan a comment that dripped with sarcasm. "Thank God!" he wrote. "A stone has been rolled off our hearts."

In one article, Cahan described a concession in a Broadway theater in which two wax figures, one of Taft, the other of Bryan, were hooked up to devices that played their voices. As one left the theater with their words ricocheting in one's brain, Cahan wrote, "your mind's eye travels to the West, where a third presidential candidate travels from town to town. . . . His words come from a human heart . . . words of light, truth and hope! The name of this third man is Eugene V. Debs." For all that, however, Debs did only marginally better in 1908 than he had done in 1904. So the *Forward*'s election coverage stressed gains made by Socialists in local elections in New York.

Cahan's controversial introduction of the techniques of yellow journalism, which he had learned from his contemporaries William Randolph Hearst and Joseph Pulitzer, kept the *Forward*'s circulation numbers climbing. "300 People Burned in a Theater"; "Pittsburgh Millionaire, Bachelor, Gets 2 Wives After Death"; "8 Bandits Ravish Girl in Midday on Washington Street"; "70-Year-Old-Worker Takes Job and Drops Dead"; "Wife and Mother Blamed in His Suicide"; "She Burned Out Her Husband's Eye with Carbolic Acid" were typical *Forward* headlines from that period.

If the yellow streak in Cahan's journalism brought him much criticism in socialist circles, he ran these stories alongside serious, thought-provoking editorials, including one extolling Abraham Lincoln's ideas on labor (which were later emblazoned on a wall in the lobby of the Amalgamated Bank, a labor-backed institution on Union Square), and another dilating on Charles Darwin's contributions to the study of nature, sociology, and philosophy. Cahan also brought the world of literature to his readers, publishing fiction by, among others, Sholem Asch and Avrom Reisen, two leading Yiddish writers.

In 1921 Cahan would hire Israel Joshua Singer as his Warsaw correspondent and later send him east to report firsthand on life in the Soviet Union. Though he is overshadowed today by his famous younger brother, Isaac Bashevis Singer, I. J. Singer was the better-known sibling during his short life.* His wildly popular novel *The Brothers Ashkenazi* was first serialized in the *Forward* and was published in English by Alfred A. Knopf in 1936, soaring onto the same *New York Times* best-seller list as *Gone with the Wind.* I. J. Singer joined the staff of the *Forward* when he arrived in America in 1934, and when his brother arrived in 1935, he helped him get a job there, too. In 1978 Isaac Bashevis Singer would win the Nobel Prize in Literature for work that first appeared in the *Forward*'s pages.

While Cahan was proud of the literary fiction he published, the overall tone of the *Forward* was intentionally folksy and colloquial. He instructed his writers to write the way they spoke, even if that meant including the English words (such as *boy* or the popular diminutive *boychick*) that Lower East Side residents used in Yiddish conversation. Like those who spoke and read the language, Yiddish was being assimilated into the English-speaking culture. His openness to English words left Cahan open to the charge, throughout his career, that although he created the most successful Yiddish newspaper in history, he simultaneously killed the language.

Adolph Held, a *Forward* business manager who doubled for a time as news editor, described editing copy during World War I.

> We used to write that one side had advanced ten kilometers and another retreated ten kilometers. One day Cahan came in and said

* I. J. Singer died in 1944, at age fifty.

> to me, "Held, does your mother know what kilometers are?" I answered, "I doubt it, my father has to read the paper aloud to her."
>
> "All right," he said, "so when you write about kilometers and they come to that line, she can't go any further. . . . From now on I'll come in every day and write a column of war news without all those hard words, so your mother can understand what's happening in the world."

Cahan could be ruthless with his blue pencil, excising language he didn't like and people with whom he was feuding. In the fall of 1907 he relaunched his public battle with the playwright Jacob Gordin, criticizing his latest theatrical effort in the *Forward*. Gordin in turn denounced Cahan from the stage. Then Cahan decided to run a several-week-long series in the *Forward* titled "Gordin's Place as a Yiddish Playwright," attacking his plays, accusing him of plagiarism, and reprinting anti-Gordin articles from European newspapers. It was almost as though Cahan had some sort of personal vendetta against the man. His timing was spectacularly bad: unknown to most, Gordin was dying of cancer. When the playwright died in April 1909, Cahan ran a respectful front-page obituary bordered in black, but his attacks on Gordin were not soon forgotten.

While Cahan's personal style sometimes left much to be desired, it didn't seem to affect the fortunes of his newspaper. His formula for running a successful Yiddish newspaper, as articulated in a 1920 advertising flyer, was "Jewish in WORD—American in THOUGHT." It seemed to be working. Within a decade of Cahan's assuming the editorship, the *Forward* emerged as the largest Jewish newspaper in the world. In May 1909 it announced on its front page that it had reached a circulation of 83,474, which was well above English-language newspapers such as the *Baltimore American* and the Cleveland *Plain Dealer*. In the same issue, Cahan wrote an editorial with the headline "Our One-Quarter-of-a-Million Readers," claiming that because each copy of the *Forward* was read, on average, by three people, the true circulation could be considered about a quarter of a million.

The *Forward*'s manager, Benjamin Schlesinger, was a shrewd businessman in addition to being a labor leader. He had been one of the founders and was a former president of the International Ladies' Garment Workers' Union, and his position at the *Forward* strengthened the ties between the paper and the labor movement. It was Schlesinger's idea to attract new subscribers by offering premiums. The first was a Yiddish-English dictionary, compiled by Alexander Harkavy, a well-known lexicographer. The uptick of subscriptions made the dictionaries disappear quickly. For the second premium, Schlesinger convinced Cahan that a Yiddish-language history of the United States was in order, adding that Cahan was just the man to write it.

Around this time, the Socialist Party sent out a survey to its members. The *Forward* published some of the results, including the answer to the question "How did you become a socialist?" The largest number of respondents, 39 percent, attributed their political awakening to one source: newspapers. Cahan's critics might say what they wished about his so-called watered-down socialism, but it was working to popularize the idea.

In January 1909 Cahan received a letter from Colorado with the news that his brother, Isaac, had succumbed to tuberculosis. In his autobiography, Cahan mentions the death of his sole living relative almost in passing. It's difficult to know what effect it had on him or how hard he worked to shut out the past. It would have been easy enough to bury himself in work. The *Forward* was covering—and in many cases, leading or mediating—strikes by unions of bakers, children's jacket makers, pants makers, retail clerks, ladies' shirtwaist (blouse) makers, and cap makers. Cahan exhorted his readers to fulfill their "holy duty" and tell their grocers that they should not attempt to "swindle" them by selling them "scab bread for union bread." One bakery after another capitulated, and by February 1910 there were only one hundred nonunion bakers in the city.

A strike called by the Ladies' Waist Makers' Union, which began on November 23, 1909, set off a wave of further strikes and galvanized the

Lower East Side. At a meeting the night before at Cooper Union, where shirtwaist makers gathered to decide whether to strike, one worker, Clara Lemlich, a small thin woman who looked younger than her twenty-three years, stood up and declared, "I'm tired of listening to speakers who talk in general terms. . . . I offer a resolution that a general strike be declared—now." The hall erupted in raucous agreement, the audience rising to its feet. "Do you mean this?" asked the meeting's chairman, Benjamin Feigenbaum, a frequent contributor to the *Forward*. He tried to quiet the crowd as he raised his right hand. "Will you take the old Jewish oath?" About two thousand hands shot up in agreement, and two thousand voices swore: "If turn traitor to the cause I now pledge, may this hand wither from the arm I now raise."*

Within days, 20,000 workers, mostly young women and predominantly Jewish, were on the picket lines. Their uprising captured the imagination of the city and even the world. A judge ordered the women back to work, avowing, "You are on strike against God and nature." The Women's Trade League sent the judge's words to George Bernard Shaw, asking for his reaction. "Delightful," the playwright cabled back. "Medieval America always in the intimate personal confidence of the Almighty."

A reporter covering the strike for *The New York Sun* filed this description of one of the picket lines: "The girls, headed by teenage Clara Lemlich, described by union organizers as a 'pint of trouble for the bosses,' began singing Italian and Russian working-class songs as they paced in twos before the factory door. Of a sudden, around the corner came a dozen tough-looking customers, for whom the union label 'gorillas' seemed well-chosen. 'Stand fast, girls,' called Clara, and then the thugs rushed the line, knocking Clara to her knees."

The strike dragged on for months, until a settlement was finally reached in February 1910. The union didn't get all it wanted—and some shops had already settled on their own—but it had won a moral vic-

* A contemporary variant on the famous verse from Psalms 137: "If I forget thee, O Jerusalem, let my right hand lose its power."

tory. As the *Forward* put it: "Stay firmly together, sisters and brothers! Respect all the union signs and labels as you do the eyes in your head. . . . Hurrah for our victorious gigantic army of the multitudes!" Whatever questions there had been about the viability of Jewish-dominated unions were now largely erased.*

Next came the cloak makers' strike, which lasted ten weeks, between July and September 1910, during which 50,000 cloak makers, nearly all men, went out on strike. The *Forward* emerged as the strikers' defender and launched a fund for them. The paper itself donated $2,000 and by mid-August it announced that contributions pouring in from throughout the country had increased the pot to $16,000. The Manufacturers Association signed a nineteen-point contract, negotiated by the Boston attorney Louis Brandeis, that made the union representative, attorney Meyer London, who had twice run unsuccessfully for Congress, one of the most famous socialists in America. Among the improved working conditions that the union won were a six-day workweek and paid holidays. The *Forward* proudly proclaimed (it was actually evident to all) that it had played a central role in the cloak makers' victory. The Protocols of Peace, as the agreement was known, was the biggest achievement to date for the New York labor movement, and it would serve as a model for labor contracts for years to come. Hundreds of thousands joined in a victory march from Washington Square all the way up to Columbus Circle.

Two months later, on November 12, 1910, the *Forward* threw Cahan a belated fiftieth birthday party at Carnegie Hall. The paper's circulation had passed the 100,000 mark, and there was plenty to celebrate. The hall was packed. The *Forward* reported that thousands had to be turned away. Cahan was escorted in not only by Morris Hillquit and Lincoln Steffens but also by Charles Edward Russell, who had just run on the Socialist Party line for governor of New York, and by the lexicographer Alex-

* Clara Lemlich eventually betrayed the free labor union movement and joined the Communists.

ander Harkavy. When Cahan was presented to the crowd, a forty-piece orchestra launched into *La Marseillaise*, the French national anthem that had become over time the anthem of the international revolutionary movement as well. The audience leaped to its feet to give him a standing ovation.

Many speeches extolled the honoree, including one by Hillquit:

> At his birth Nature said to Cahan: "I have given you the ability to speak, to write, to be active. If you choose, you can be rich, you can become a businessman." . . . But Cahan replied: "Wealth means to live without effort, from the hard labor of others. That is not for me. I want a life of activity, a life of spiritual work, a life of dedication to the oppressed masses, a life of truly useful work for my fellow man." And Cahan kept his word.

"A fifty-year-old smiling public man" is how Ronald Sanders describes Cahan at this point in his life (a play on William Butler Yeats's description of himself as "a sixty-year-old smiling public man"*), a poet turned politician full of private longing and outward calm. Cahan's "outer life had become the expression of two generations of Jewish immigrants in America, their beacon and guide," Sanders continues. "Who could deny that this destiny was the projection of something that had risen from deep within himself? And yet something remained locked within, as ineradicable as it was inexpressible, which insisted that all this activity, all this success, all this mastery of an American reality, was false, a violation of its own hidden truth."

The day after the big event at Carnegie Hall, the *Forward* began advertising Cahan's new history of the United States—the subscription premium that he and Schlessinger had cooked up several years earlier. Two volumes were eventually published, covering Columbus's voyage and the early years of European presence on the North American continent, seeing them through a Marxist prism that strikes the contemporary reader

* Yeats's line is from his poem "Among School Children."

as rather quaint. What is significant about Cahan's historical account is how it reflects his enthusiasm for the idea of America and what it stands for. As Leon Wexelstein* wrote about Cahan in H. L. Mencken's *American Mercury:* "Above all, he kept pounding into the minds of his readers the fact that Americans were perfectly human. . . . Constantly he admonished Jewish mothers to steer clear of any fright that their children might become Americanized. There was nothing to fear, he said, for it was a good thing."

Only four months later, at approximately 4:40 p.m. on Saturday, March 25, 1911, some five hundred employees, mostly young women ranging in age from midteens to midtwenties and from Jewish and Italian immigrant families, were preparing to leave the Triangle Shirtwaist Company, one of the city's largest sweatshops. The company had refused to sign on to the agreement that ended the Ladies' Waist Makers' Union strike of 1909. It occupied the top three floors of a relatively new ten-story building at the northwest corner of Greene Street and Washington Place, one block east of Washington Square Park in Greenwich Village. As hundreds of young workers were collecting their belongings and getting into their coats, a fire broke out on the eighth floor, quickly setting the wood-frame interior and masses of fabric ablaze and turning that floor and the two above it into an inferno. Some workers were able to make it down the stairs and the elevators, but the elevators quickly stopped functioning because of the heat and flames, and some stairways, which the owners had locked as a way to guard against employee theft, were inaccessible. The single fire escape buckled from the crush of workers and the heat of the fire. Firemen arrived, but their hoses reached only to the seventh floor; their ladders, only to the sixth. By the time the fire was brought under control, 146 workers—129 women and 17 men—had been either burned or suffocated to death, or had jumped out of the windows to their deaths in a desperate attempt to save themselves.

"One girl after another fell, like shot birds, from above, from the burn-

* Leon Wexelstein was the father of the late Minnesota senator Paul Wellstone.

ing floors," the poet Morris Rosenfeld wrote in the *Forward*'s special edition, published that night.

> The men held out a longer time, enveloped in flames. And when they could hold out no longer, they jumped, too. Below, horrified and weeping, stood thousands of workers from the surrounding factories. They watched moving, terrible, unforgettable scenes. At one window on the eighth floor appeared a young man with a girl. He was holding her tightly by the hand. Behind them the red flames could be seen. The young man lovingly wrapped his arms around the girl and held her to him a moment, kissed her, and then let her go. . . . A moment later he leaped after her, and his body landed next to hers. Both were dead. . . .
>
> It took a whole hour before the firemen could enter the burning building, and by then it was all over. The sidewalks were full of dead and wounded, and no one could be seen at the windows any longer.

"The Morgue Is Full of Our Dead," read the *Forward*'s banner headline. But it was Cahan's words, published in the *Forward* two days after the fire, that seared: "The entire neighborhood is sitting shiva. Every heart is torn in mourning. Who is the Angel of Death? Who is the thug? Who is the mass murderer? Must we again say it is that gluttonous ravager of humans—capital?! . . . The blood of our victims screams out at all of us. The souls of our burned ones demand we must compel our cloistered government to fulfill its duty."

A mass funeral was held a week later, on April 5. "Come and pay your last respects to our dead," the *Forward* wrote. "Every union man with his trade, with his union." One hundred thousand people did so, taking to the streets of the Lower East Side in the rain.

9

On April 28, 1912, Cahan and Anna sailed for Europe aboard the SS *George Washington.** The ostensible reason for their trip was that Cahan wished to consult a physician in Vienna for an ulcer that had become almost unbearably painful. But he had other plans for their European trip as well. He had just laid the cornerstone for the *Forward*'s new home at 173–75 East Broadway, a ten-story Beaux Arts building that Sanders described as seeming "to bestride the Lower East Side like a colossus." It would house not only the editorial offices but also, on the top floor, the composing room, where the linotype machines and the printing presses churned out the paper every day. The bottom floors had space for a meeting hall with a thousand-person capacity and for the headquarters of several unions and fraternal organizations. On the front of the building, just above the second floor, a series of reliefs featured the likenesses of Karl Marx, Friedrich Engels, Ferdinand Lassalle, and Friedrich Adler. At the top of the building, in large letters, the paper's name appeared, an advertisement that could be seen from blocks away and that would capture the imagination of American Jews for generations thereafter. Alfred Kazin, in his memoir *A Walker in the City*, writes about crossing the Brooklyn Bridge into Manhattan as a young man, where "only the electric sign of the *Jewish Daily Forward*, burning high over the tenements of the East Side, suddenly stilled the riot in my heart."

At around this time the *Forward*'s circulation hit 120,000. The socialist newspaper devoted to the interests of working-class American Jews

* It was the third largest vessel in the world. Two weeks before the Cahans left for Europe, the *George Washington* had radioed from the North Atlantic a warning about an enormous iceberg. Another vessel, the *Titanic*, which was passing through the icy seas, failed to heed it and struck the iceberg and sank on April 15, 1912.

had succeeded beyond Cahan's most optimistic dreams, and he arrived in Europe as a journalistic celebrity, with access to the most notable figures of the day, whom he planned to interview for his readers. Today, when the Internet allows anyone to post information online, it's difficult to imagine a time when newspaper journalism mattered and when those who produced it were well known not only in their own countries but also across the globe. It was a world brimming with ideas and energy, a vital, complicated world that within just a few years would be thrown into the turmoil of World War I, the Russian Revolution, and the civil war between Red and White Russians.

Cahan was thrilled to discover that the Paris that had so charmed him nineteen years earlier as a delegate to the Socialist International had maintained its allure. He met with many old friends and made some new ones, notably the French Socialist leader Jean Jaurès, who had been, as editor of *La Petite République*, one of the defenders of Captain Alfred Dreyfus, the Alsatian Jewish artillery officer who had been framed by anti-Semitic fellow officers, falsely accused of offering military secrets to the German embassy in Paris, court-martialed, convicted of treason, and, in 1895, publicly humiliated.

Through Jaurès, Cahan arranged to meet with Dreyfus himself. Ever the newspaperman, he clearly comprehended the possibilities for the interview. Dreyfus had spent almost five years in prison on Devil's Island in French Guiana before he was pardoned in 1899, after a huge public outcry, and he had not been fully exonerated until 1906. The Dreyfus affair—which included the public battles between those who contended that Dreyfus was innocent and those who blamed him and the Jews for France's ills—had torn the country apart and received worldwide attention.

Cahan had been at the *Commercial Advertiser* when the verdict was brought in. Writing about it years later in the *Forward*, he recalled sitting, "restless and unsettled," near the telegraph editor. "Finally, one of the two telegraph operators gave the telegraph editor a yellow piece of paper upon which he had typed out the last of the dispatches from Rennes. The telegraph editor read it over and with an empathic expression passed me the piece of paper. The verdict was 'guilty,' but with a recommendation for 'mercy,' and the sentence was ten years imprisonment."

Most of Cahan's Gentile coworkers knew little of the trial, Cahan recalled, but for Jews it was a watershed event, a kind of public martyrdom. "'You probably want to be with your Jewish friends,' Steffens said to me. I left for Herrick's Café at 141 Division Street, where our comrades gathered." Now, thirteen years later, Cahan would be meeting the man at the center of the storm, a hero to millions of Jews around the world.

Cahan was "inexplicably nervous," he recalled, when he showed up at the door of the second-floor apartment in which Dreyfus, who had been reinstated as a major in the French army in 1906 and was by this time a colonel, lived. The gray-haired gentleman who greeted him looked nothing like the serious young officer depicted in the famous 1894 portrait. He was warm and friendly in person, and a "pleasant, almost childish smile" appeared on his face as he and Cahan conversed in German. Dreyfus "viewed himself as merely a symbol," Theodore Pollock writes in his biography of Cahan. "The important victory in his vindication, he said, had been the separation of Church and State in France." He felt there was "less anti-Semitism in the France of 1912 than in the other European countries." A dazzled Cahan spent two hours with Dreyfus, who was happy to provide him with the autographed picture he requested. The visit was a classic example of an aspect of newspaper life that Cahan had come to enjoy.

Cahan had by this time become a great editor, though his great struggle against Communism lay in the future. At the same time he was already becoming something of an anachronism, for he had not yet grasped the real meaning of the Dreyfus affair. The one who had was Theodor Herzl, the newspaperman who had witnessed Dreyfus's public humiliation by the French military back in 1895, following his conviction. By the time Cahan met Dreyfus, Herzl had been dead for eight years, having launched the greatest movement in the history of postbiblical Judaism.

III

In Vienna, Cahan looked up Victor Adler, the founder of Austria's socialist movement, who was then in the midst of challenging a proposal by the government to enlarge the army. From Vienna, Anna traveled alone to visit her family in Kiev, while Cahan went to Budapest and then back to Vienna, where he managed to glimpse Leon Trotsky, from a distance, sitting in a café. The two men would not actually meet until Trotsky visited New York in 1917 and paid him a courtesy call. Cahan did meet with Israel Zangwill, the British writer whose play *The Melting Pot* had been a great success in America a few years earlier. Zangwill was also politically active in Jewish issues, a supporter of Theodor Herzl but far from a pure Zionist. In 1905, two years after the Kishinev pogrom, feeling that the need for a Jewish homeland had become urgent, Zangwill had cofounded the Jewish Territorial Organization, whose purpose was to find land outside Palestine on which to establish a self-governing Jewish colony. Between 1907 and 1914, ten thousand Jews immigrated to Texas as part of the organization's Galveston Plan, largely funded by the American industrialist Jacob Schiff. Cahan met Zangwill in Vienna, where the writer was attending a conference of territorialists. There Cahan also met the doctor he'd come to Europe to consult. The doctor found nothing seriously wrong with him but indicated that a trip to the baths at Karlsbad wouldn't hurt.

From Vienna, Cahan went alone to Cracow, where, he had heard, Lenin was living incognito on the outskirts of town. Cahan was quickly able to set up a visit and soon found himself in the presence of the revolutionary leader. He was surprised that a man known for ruthlessness had such an outwardly kind appearance. Lenin knew a great deal about the American economy, but Cahan filled him in on the social and political scene, and Lenin urged him to send the latest American census figures once he returned to New York. In parting, Lenin presented Cahan with copies of *Pravda*, which he had just started editing from Crakow—one editor proudly showing off his product to another.

Cahan's next stop was Lemberg, near Brody, where he had stayed for three weeks before his fateful departure from Russia thirty years earlier.

He was startled by the signs of progress, including new buildings, that he found in Brody. He located his old quarters but not the family of his landlady. "When I had immigrated to America," he wrote in his memoir, "I pictured a fifty-two-year-old as an old man, and thirty years appeared to be an eternity. Here I was—the old man!" Stricken with homesickness, he realized that "home" was now America.

There was one last visit to be made: to Belz, to interview the most renowned Hasidic figure of the time, the Belzer Rebbe. When Cahan arrived at the rebbe's home, the entrance to his study was crowded with Hasidim who had been waiting for hours for a brief word with the rebbe, or even just a quick glimpse of the sage, but Cahan was ushered right in. The editor pressed the rebbe on political questions and found him better informed than he had expected. The rebbe was dismissive of political Zionism: he did not believe that the Zionists could be sufficiently pious, and he opposed their attempts to recruit the Jews of Austria-Hungary to their cause, which only stirred them up. "Today," he told Cahan, "our politics is that Jews must hold their heads bowed." The rebbe was interested in America and praised former president Theodore Roosevelt, well known as a philo-semite, as a "righteous man," but he worried aloud about the state of Jewish souls in the United States, fearing that they were not being religiously nurtured. Cahan brought up the subject of unions, trying to gauge the rebbe's reaction to their rise in America, but he deftly evaded the subject. The Rebbe spoke dismissively of newspapers, gesturing to his bookcases filled with religious works and telling Cahan that "when whole days are spent on such difficult subjects, the lesser things have no value." According to Pollock, Cahan felt himself in the presence of a great personality; after spending an hour with the rebbe, the editor had to elbow his way out the door, just as he had had to elbow his way in.

Whatever Cahan's blind spots, it is hard to imagine another editor who could have sailed through Europe meeting, on the same trip, with Dreyfus, Lenin, and the Belzer Rebbe, filing warm and illuminating copy about each, only to return to America and pursue his own agenda. Cahan had emerged, at age fifty-one, as a newspaper editor in the grand mode, a personage in his own right but also genuinely inquisitive, broadly sourced, and widely sympathetic.

Following his doctor's advice, Cahan did stop at Karlsbad, where Anna joined him, and they enjoyed the elegant resort city. For a while Cahan felt better and a physician found him to be "as healthy as a brick building," but then the stomach pains returned, which ended the remarkable journey on a rather sour note. The Cahans briefly visited Berlin, where they found the German socialists divided and the *Vorwärts* confronting the same circulation problems Cahan had been brought in to fix a decade earlier at the *Forward.* He and Anna left for New York at the end of August and reached home on September 4. By then the new *Forward* Building was towering over the Lower East Side, and Cahan's new offices were ready for him to resume editing and begin covering the presidential election of 1912.

The resounding defeat of incumbent president William Howard Taft and Progressive Party candidate Theodore Roosevelt by the Democratic governor of New Jersey, Woodrow Wilson, was quite a news story. For *Forward* readers, though, the big news was that Socialist Party candidate Eugene V. Debs received more than double the number of votes he had received in the 1908 presidential election—901,551, or 6 percent of total votes cast. The unlikely coalition of Yiddish-speaking immigrants, midwestern idealists, and hard-core leftists, a party that had been cobbled together in less than a decade, was making its mark in the American political arena.

Not two months later the organized labor movement became embroiled in another crisis when the United Garment Workers Union called for a strike in an effort to win for the workers in the men's garment–manufacturing industry the same workplace improvements that the workers who made ladies' garments had won years before. "Tailors on Brink of a Complete Victory," the *Forward* declared on February 16, 1913, but its prognostication was more optimistic than accurate. Only the small shops had settled; none of the big manufacturers were yet on board. Pressure was growing for a settlement, and the union feared the workers couldn't stay on the picket line much longer. Two UGW leaders (one of whom, Max Pine, was also a *Forward* staffer) came to Cahan's office a few weeks later and told him that the union wanted to settle. It wouldn't, however, without the *Forward*'s support.

The next morning's paper carried Cahan's response. "The Great Tailors' Strike Settled," the five-column headline read. "The settlement is not as good as it might have been, but for the future destiny of the tailors it is very good. The great tailors' union has been formed." The *Forward* endorsed a compromise that provided for a maximum workweek of fifty-four hours and a one-dollar increase in weekly wages.

The rank and file were not pleased. The morning after the settlement was announced, a large crowd gathered in front of the *Forward* Building to protest the *Forward*'s support of the unacceptable compromise. Then someone yelled, "To the *Warheit*!" The offices of the progressive but moderate newspaper that was the *Forward*'s great competitor were located just a few doors away, at 153 East Broadway. The crowd moved down the block. There Louis Hollander, a leader of a radical, breakaway union known as the United Brotherhood of Tailors and a Jacob Gordin supporter who disliked Cahan intensely, emerged and exhorted the crowd to keep striking. After he spoke, the angry crowd returned to the *Forward* Building. Who was responsible for their misery if not Cahan's paper? They rushed inside and began smashing windows. *Forward* staffers called Cahan, who was home at his Upper East Side apartment, but by the time he arrived, the mob had decamped.

"The *Warheit*, the Center of the Revolution," Louis Miller's paper crowed the following morning. "Don't Go to Work!" The United Garment Workers Union gave in and called for the strike to resume. It was eventually settled a few weeks later through the efforts of two young labor lawyers: Meyer London, who would go on to become the second Socialist congressman elected to the House of Representatives, and Fiorello La Guardia, who would go on to become the mayor of New York City.

The *Forward* held fast. The incident threw into sharp relief the split within the union between workers from the settled shops and those hungry and tired on the picket line. "The hungry expressed satisfaction with the settlement," Cahan contended. Later, at a union meeting held in the *Forward* Building, he described as "unruly children" the restive employees who had caused the damage. "Why didn't they break the windows of other editorial offices?" he asked. "Because those others are strange to them, whereas the *Forward* is their own. It's like their mother, and one makes demands upon a mother, whether they are just or not. And when a bad boy gets unruly and starts breaking dishes, it doesn't matter. A mother forgets." Those in attendance applauded.

The incident, however, took a toll on Cahan. It aggravated what turned out to be a duodenal ulcer, for which he underwent surgery in March 1913. After the operation, he went to Lakewood, New Jersey, to convalesce. His recovery took several weeks, after which he "felt years younger and took juvenile pleasure out of running up the stairs two at a time." The interval gave him an opportunity to reflect on what he had achieved. The *Forward* was now the third-largest morning newspaper in the city in any language, with a circulation of nearly 140,000. The same large companies that advertised in general-interest English-language newspapers—Gulden's Mustard, White Rose Tea, the Public Bank of America, and the Atlantic Talking Machine—took out ads in the *Forward*, too. Pulitzer's *World* and Hearst's *Journal* were ahead of him in circulation, but the causes into which Cahan threw himself were his own.

The next cause, as it turned out, involved the twenty-nine-year-old superintendent of the National Pencil Factory in Atlanta, Georgia. His name was Leo Frank. While Cahan was in New Jersey recovering from his operation, Frank was arrested for the rape and murder of a thirteen-year-old employee of the company named Mary Phagan. The crime took place in the factory building on Saturday, April 26, 1913, sometime after Phagan had picked up the envelope with her week's wages from Frank. Her body was discovered in the factory basement the next day, in what one historian characterized as "a condition which provided grist for the sensation-seeking press of the city." The case became a national sensation. Frank was arrested, and during his trial nothing more than circumstantial evidence was presented and testimony was given that was later found to be perjured. Nonetheless he was convicted on August 25 by a jury that had deliberated in a room outside of which a mob was shouting for Frank's blood. He was sentenced to hang on October 10, which was delayed to April 17, 1914, and then delayed again as the appeal process went forward.

The *Forward* threw everything it had into the Frank story. Cahan went to Atlanta and personally interviewed Frank, filing from Georgia an editorial on anti-Semitism in the South. "We believe the reasons there are the same as those that have recently developed an anti-Semitic spirit among French Canadians. They are the same circumstances responsible for the present boycott of the Jews in Poland." Jewish success in business in the South, he argued, had humiliated a class of former plantation owners who'd grown rich off slavery and now couldn't compete. Frank, to Cahan, had expounded a different theory, having to do with the politics and pressures on the prosecutor. In some ways, Frank, a gentle soul, seemed as he sat in his cell to echo the behavior of Dreyfus, "trying harder to understand his position than to fight it," according to Pollock's account.

Appeals to Georgia's higher courts and to the U.S. Supreme Court were unsuccessful. Faced nonetheless with the overwhelming evidence that Frank's conviction was a gross miscarriage of justice and with a national outcry against the verdict, Georgia governor John M. Slaton on June 21, 1915 commuted his sentence to life in prison. On the night of August 16, a lynch mob kidnapped Frank from the state prison in Milledgeville and hanged him from a tree in a small town about two hundred miles away.

Cahan, in an editorial, blamed Frank's killing on "irrational race hatred; fanatic, ingrained enmity to everything that is 'strange'; barbaric customs of quondam slave-owners who spare no human life; in addition, corrupt police, corrupt administrations, corrupt courts." All, he wrote, had "conspired to rob the life of a human being." He asserted that "in no other country in the world will it be understood how Frank's death was possible." Long a defender of the idea that America was freer and more welcoming to Jews than other countries, and personally thanked in a note by Frank for his "many kindnesses," Cahan was devastated by Frank's conviction and the murder. He devoted more than two hundred pages to the Frank case in his memoir, and it clearly haunted him for the rest of his career.

The tragedy also haunted Adolph Ochs, the publisher of *The New York Times*. Reluctant at first to speak out about the trial, Ochs had been persuaded by Albert Lasker, the Jewish advertising giant, to launch a defense of Frank. The inability of the *Times* to affect the outcome of the trial and the appeals dismayed Ochs; Cahan also felt this sense of powerlessness. And Ochs was appalled by the fact that his newspaper's involvement in the case had enraged many in the South and most likely contributed to Frank's lynching. He retreated into a certain quietude regarding Jewish issues that would extend for much of the rest of the twentieth century, in marked contrast to Cahan and the *Forward*.

During the years the *Forward* had spent covering the Frank case, dramatic events were convulsing Europe. The heady optimism among European socialists that Cahan had witnessed during his 1912 visit had evaporated; the continent was at war. Jean Jaurès, the former newspaperman and French Socialist leader who had introduced Cahan to Dreyfus, had been killed, murdered by a French nationalist who accused him of wanting peace with Germany.

The Great War had not yet reached America, and in the fall of 1914, the big story for the *Forward* was the election of Socialist Party candidate Meyer London, after several failed attempts, to Congress from the Lower East Side's newly reconfigured twelfth congressional district. When the news of his victory was announced to the crowd of 40,000 gathered in front of the *Forward* Building, a band played "La Marseillaise" and, according to the editorial in the *Forward* on November 4, 1914, "people fell on each other's necks and kissed each other with tears of joy." Both Cahan and London made speeches to the cheering crowd.*

A young Yiddish journalist, Melech Epstein, described the scene:

> Stories of Tammany violence and fraud were flooding the neighborhood. At dusk, crowds had been moving toward Rutgers Square, facing the *Forward* Building. They filled Seward Park and the side streets, waiting impatiently for the election returns to be flashed on the screen in front of the *Forward*. About eleven o'clock the Orthodox *Tageblatt*, a few doors from the *Forward*, published an extra announcing the victory of Henry M. Goldfogle, the Tammany candidate. The crowd refused to accept the finality of this announcement, and thousands remained in the square waiting hopefully. At about 2:00 a.m., after much bickering, Tammany leaders conceded London's election. . . . London was brought to the square at 4:00 a.m. to head an impromptu demonstration. . . . Marchers carried out straw brooms to symbolize that Tammany's rule would be swept out.

A few days later voters filled Madison Square Garden to celebrate. "I do not expect to work wonders in Congress," London said at the event. "I shall, however, say a new word and I shall accomplish one thing that is not in the platform of the Socialist Party. I hope that my presence will represent an entirely different type of Jew from the kind Congress is accustomed to see." This was in marked contrast to Hillquit, who in his 1908 campaign made clear that he would principally represent the Socialist Party and would not be "the special representative of the alleged special interests of this district"—which is to say, the Jews of the Lower East Side.

London's victory was soon overshadowed by the groundswell of international events. World War I was about to shatter Europe, and it would make America a great world power. The war would dwarf the local and national issues that concerned the Lower East Side residents of the

* Meyer London's portrait still hangs in the offices of the *Forward*.

twelfth congressional district; it would also push to the side Cahan's passions for the spread of socialism throughout the world. The war presented American Jews, and the *Forward*, with a peculiar challenge. Americans generally sympathized with the Allies (led by Britain, France, Russia, and Italy), while American Jews tended to be more sympathetic to the Central Powers (led by Germany and Austria-Hungary). It was in Germany that Cahan, as his train passed through Breslau back in 1882, felt that "for the first time I could see the marks of a highly civilized nation." And Germany was, after all, the enemy of the Russian czar. The socialists were generally opposed to any American involvement in the war, but they were also tugged in the direction of Germany, which was, as Pollock puts it, the "fountainhead of socialist thought and doctrine. . . . Even when Germany invaded Belgium and bombed Antwerp, these aggressive acts were overshadowed in Jewish minds by the Russian threat to devour Galicia, with its large Jewish population."

In his semiautobiographical novel *Mercy of a Rude Stream*, Henry Roth captures this sentiment in the scene where Ira Stigman's immigrant mother reacts to news of the outbreak of war and reports of German brutality:

> The Great War came closer. The Huns impaled babies on their bayonets—though Mom ridiculed stories of German atrocities. "What, the Russ is better? *Czar kolki iz a feiner mensch?* [The bullet czar is a better person?] Who in all the world is more benighted than the Russian *mujik* [peasant]? Who doesn't remember their pogroms, the Kishinev pogroms, in 1903? . . . More likely the Russ impaled the infant on his bayonet."

Cahan was neutral at first, and in this editorial, which ran in the *Forward* on September 3, 1914, under the headline "Barbary," his typical condescension and literary histrionics were on full display:

> The blood curdles, the brain splits, the heart grows paralyzed from the shameful barbarism occurring in the war! The tongue turns

to leather, the lips grow numb, when only one-thousandths of the shames are pronounced. Good heavens, what's going on? Is the word "humanity" entirely a mistake? . . . Here in America, we cry more than anything over the barbarism of the Germans, because America is against Germany more than anything. The truth is that the worst crimes are attributed to the Germans not because they, as Germans, are the worst barbarians in nature—but because until now they have been the strongest in the war. But no side is better!

Over time he became less neutral and eventually came out four square for the defeat of Russia, stating flatly:

> I am convinced that in the interests of progress generally and Jews specifically, a Russian defeat would be fortunate: I am convinced that it would be fortunate for all of Europe and for the entire Jewish population if Germany would take all Poland and Lithuania too, from Russia.

The sentiment was reckless, given the support of the majority of the American public for the Allies. But no doubt reflecting his inner turmoil, Cahan was perfectly capable of issuing quite contradictory statements, as in this editorial published in late August 1914:

> If this were only a war between Germany and Russia, certainly not one socialist in the world would not desire Germany to win. Unfortunately, however, England, Belgium, and France are fighting against Germany. A German victory would weaken despotism in Russia, but would strengthen despotism as directed against Belgium, France, and England.

Germany certainly did its best to woo American Jewry, playing on fears about the fate of Galician Jews in Austria-Hungary should they find themselves overrun by Russia. It also hoped to win the support of an imaginary consortium of international Jewish bankers. The German campaign met with some success. A New York lawyer and notable Francophile named Maurice Leon lamented, in a letter to the prominent American Reform rabbi and Zionist leader Stephen Wise:

> Nearly all the public expressions that have come from the Jews in this country have been anti-Russian. That seems to be the Jewish way of being pro-German. Practically the entire Jewish press of the United States has adopted that policy. The leaders in that movement have for the most part more or less avowed German sympathies. All that the Jews have in the way of liberty they owe to the influence of France and England. Yet I have looked in vain for any expressions from prominent Jews in this country laying emphasis on their pro-English and pro-French sympathies. With few, very few exceptions they have all adopted the watchword given out by the international German-Jewish Money Trust, "Anti-Russian."

Astonishing as it may seem to us today, as late as 1915, one year into the war, Cahan accepted an invitation from the German Press Office to lead a delegation of journalists to Germany, from which he sent back favorable dispatches to the *Forward*'s readers. Cosponsor of the junket was Philipp Scheidemann, a leader of the German Social Democratic Party and a regular contributor to the *Forward*.* When Cahan returned home from the "Mecca of socialism," he told a meeting of the International Ladies' Garment Workers' Union that, whatever one might say with respect to German militarism, German socialism was the hope of the world.

As the war in Europe intensified and spread, it rent the Lower East Side. Louis Miller threw the *Warheit*'s support behind England and France, only to have his furious readers burn piles of the newspaper in

* When the Kaiser abdicated on November 9, 1918, Scheidemann would announce the formation of the German republic; he would become its second chancellor as part of the Weimar Coalition in 1919. He would leave Germany when Adolf Hitler became chancellor in 1933.

the streets. By 1915 Miller was forced out of the *Warheit*, replaced by an ex-staffer of the *Forward*, Isaac Gonikman, who was prepared to place the *Warheit* firmly behind Germany.

The *Forward* had started out in the pro-German camp. Even after a German U-boat sank the British ocean liner RMS *Lusitania* in May 1915, Cahan hung on, hectoring President Wilson to "adopt Germany's proposal that he forbid Americans to travel on vessels carrying munitions." He acknowledged that "the principle of freedom of the seas would suffer. But a human life is more important than anything else. Man was not created for a principle; principles were created for men."

Cahan's quixotic pro-German campaign was brought to a halt early in 1917, with America on the verge of entering the war on the side of the Allies. He received a letter from the office of the U.S. Postmaster General saying that if the *Forward* continued to criticize the government's support for the Allies, it would lose its second-class postage rates. Cahan unrepentantly replied that though the paper would "not renounce its convictions," it "would desist from publishing them." Socialists, he declared, "obey the law even if they disagree with it."

For all his experience, sagacity, and idealism, events in Europe were converging to make Cahan and the international socialist movement look like fools. In England, Belgium, Russia, Austria, and France, the socialists swung behind their governments' nationalistic policies and acted firmly in their countries' national interests. In an interview Cahan gave to *The New York Call*, he reflected ruefully on this phenomenon.

> It is a fact, and we may as well look it full in the face, that the French socialist is, in the horrifying circumstances of the war, a Frenchman first and a Socialist afterwards, if at all, just as the German Socialist is a German first. In time of peace many of these men, animated by their class feeling at home, were Socialists to the core and capable of dying for their ideals. But no sooner did they hear the bugle call and scented danger for their country than their Socialist sentiments were suspended and they became Frenchmen or German like their

> fellow countrymen of the dominating classes. There is no such thing as class consciousness in the trenches.

Pollock insists that "at no time could Cahan's motives be suspect" and quotes Cahan as having written, in late 1914: "If there should be an actual threat of a European monarchy attacking the United States we all would fight for America with our hearts and soul . . . because America has the freest institutions in the world. That would be a real struggle for freedom."

Cahan was by no means the only great editor to be made to seem naïve by the war; nor was it only editors of leftist publications who had this experience. On August 2, 1914, the *Chicago Tribune*, owned by Colonel Robert McCormick, issued one of the most famous editorials of all time, "The Twilight of the Kings," suggesting that the ordinary man had no stake in this war:

> Before establishing hell on earth, the pietistic kings commend their subjects to God. Seek the Lord's sanction for the devil's work.
>
> "And now I commend you to God," said the Kaiser from his balcony to the people in the street. "Go to church and kneel before God and pray for his help for your gallant army."
>
> Pray that a farmer dragged from a Saxon field shall be speedier with a bayonet thrust than a winemaker taken from his vines in the Aube; that a Berlin lawyer shall be steadier with a rifle than a Moscow merchant; that a machine gun manned by Heidelberg students shall not jam and that one worked by Paris carpenters shall.
>
> Pray that a Bavarian hop grower, armed in a quarrel in which he has no heat, shall outmarch a wheat grower from Poltava; that Cossacks from the Don shall be lured into barbed wire entanglements and caught by masked guns; that an innkeeper of Salzburg shall blow the head off a baker from the Loire.
>
> "Go to church and pray for help"—that the hell shall be hotter in innocent Ardennes than it is in equally innocent Hessen; that it shall be hotter in innocent Kovno than in equally innocent Posen.

The editorial saw the villains as monarchies, rather than capitalists, and ended with the famous peroration, "This is the twilight of the kings. Western Europe of the people may be caught in this debacle, but never again. Eastern Europe of the kings will be remade and the name of God shall not give grace to a hundred square miles of broken bodies. . . . The republic marches east."

What finally brought American socialists, including Cahan, into the Allied camp was the February Revolution, which took place in Russia in March 1917. It resulted in the abdication of Czar Nicholas II, the end of the Romanov dynasty, and the establishment of a Provisional Government by a coalition of liberals and socialists led by Alexander Kerensky, a Socialist member of the Russian Duma. "That which has long been awaited has finally come," the *Forward* joyously proclaimed on March 16. "A free Russian people, a free Jewish people in Russia! Is this a dream?" Once the revolution broke out, the newspaper's position on the war underwent an immediate, 180-degree change. "As if by magic," wrote *Forward* columnist "B. Razman" (Ben-Zion Hoffman),

> the debates and discussions on the Jewish street regarding whom the Jews should sympathize with in the present war have disappeared. There is nothing more to discuss. It is now clear where sympathies lie. Feelings dictate, reason dictates that a victory for present-day Germany would be a threat to the Russian Revolution and dangerous for democracy in Europe.

In fact, there was one more thing to discuss in 1917. On November 2 of that year, the British foreign secretary, Lord Arthur James Balfour, sent a letter to Baron Walter Rothschild, which Rothschild would send on to the Zionist Federation of Great Britain and Ireland. It famously stated that "His Majesty's Government view with favor the establishment in Palestine of a national home for the Jewish people." The declaration was partly the result of the genuine Christian Zionism of men like Balfour and Britain's prime minister, David Lloyd George, who found the notion of a Jewish return to their historic, biblical homeland religiously stirring.* But it was also the result of shrewd diplomacy by Chaim Weizmann, the Russian-born British Zionist and chemist who had helped the British war effort by coming up with an efficient way of producing acetone, a key ingredient in the cordite explosives essential to the British war effort. The British, and to a lesser extent the Germans, saw numerous advantages in promising the Jewish people a return to their ancient homeland. By making a declaration in favor of the Zionist movement, Balfour argued, "we should be able to carry on extremely useful propaganda both in Russia and America." Sir Mark Sykes insisted that "the friendship of the Jews of the World" was critical to winning the war, and that "with Great Jewry against us, there's no possibility" of victory. Weizmann was perfectly happy to encourage the British in this belief.

The Balfour Declaration, as it came to be known, was the most important letter in modern history supporting the Jews as a people. Yet it was not without controversy within Jewish communities throughout the world. Many, including Cahan, failed to grasp its moral dimension and the practical possibilities that it opened up. He greeted it with an editorial that was full of condescension. Entitled "The 'Victory' of Zionism and the Socialist Enlightenment of the Masses," it asserted that the "mighty change that socialist enlightenment has brought about in the psychology of the Jewish masses" has "protected them from the mass hysteria" that such expectations as the Zionist dream had "created in their souls for thousands of years."

The editorial did contain at least a slight bow to changing times. It noted that the *Forward* had "already remarked"—some two years earlier, on July 3, 1915—that "the time is now such that 'one can speak no more of the impossibility of realizing the Zionist ideal.'" But the 1915 editorial went on to say:

* Simon Sebag-Montefiore argues that the "Declaration should really be named for Lloyd George, not Balfour. It was he who had already decided that Britain had to possess Palestine—'oh, we must grab that!' he said—and this was a precondition for any Jewish homeland." Later in 1917, as British forces entered Palestine, Lloyd George "demanded the capture of Jerusalem 'as a Christmas present for the British nation.'"

> This changes none of our problems: to organize the masses of Jewish workers in the 'diaspora'; to lead their class-struggle; and to work toward the goal that they can live in peace with the masses where they are. Then they, the millions and millions of Jewish workers who find themselves in all countries, will remain there side by side with non-Jews, even if there should be a Jewish state in the land of Israel.

The 1917 editorial quoted a particularly condescending line from the 1915 editorial:

> Economic interests will ensure that millions and millions of Jews will, when Jews will have their own state, still follow the old Jewish saying, "One should lie among Jews in the grave but make a living among *goyim*." . . . And they will have to struggle about exchange among non-Jews, and they will have to search for justice and equality and brotherhood among non-Jews. . . . All left-wing Zionists are in accord with us in this, and this is also the current instinct of the wider Jewish masses. They are not taking part in messianic hysteria as they once would have. This is a victory of the socialist enlightenment."

It turned out, however, that the "wider Jewish masses" had their own ideas about the Jewish state. They found the Zionist vision extraordinarily inspiring, and in retrospect, the response of Cahan and his newspaper to the Balfour Declaration would be seen as a blunder that revealed how out of touch Cahan was with the residents of the Lower East Side and the voters in the twelfth congressional district. Cahan began to appreciate this when, in the closing weeks of the war, he went to Europe as a reporter of the *Forward* and, more generally, as an advocate for the Jewish community in America. He was in Paris for the negotiations that produced the Treaty of Versailles in 1919. While he was there, he interviewed Chaim Weizmann and Stephen Wise, who were part of a prestigious international committee of Jews advocating for a Jewish state, and pronounced himself "personally . . . sympathetic to the movement for a fully independent Jewish home" but worried that the Zionist agitators would endanger "the attainment of equal rights for Jews in their true homes in the European lands."

That Jews back home were now thinking differently about Zionism from Cahan and his movement was underscored by the fate of Meyer London, who during his second congressional term was asked to introduce a resolution endorsing the Balfour Declaration. Even though he represented a district with thousands of Jewish voters, London demurred, with a remark that echoed the *Forward*'s dismissive editorial: "Let us stop pretending about the Jewish past and let us stop making fools of ourselves about the Jewish future." This was certainly one of the contributing factors to London's loss of his seat in the 1918 election. He did manage to get returned to Congress in the election of 1920, but when another congressman introduced the resolution in September 1922, London voted against it. He was not reelected that November. It would be too much to suggest that London's failure to get behind the idea of the Jewish state was the sole source of his political troubles, but it would not be too much to suggest that both he and Cahan had fallen well behind the curve of sentiment among American Jews with respect to Zionism. After making two trips to Palestine, Cahan would eventually come around. We cannot know if London would have had a similar evolution: on Sunday, June 6, 1926, he was struck by a car while crossing Second Avenue at 15th Street and died later that day of his injuries, at the age of fifty-four.

By then, fate had taken things in hand. Whatever else the Balfour Declaration represented, it was at least in part an effort to gain wider support for the Allied cause in World War I. Even as Eugene Debs went to prison for his opposition to the American war effort, the *Forward* emerged as a supporter. Not that Cahan was turning on Debs; in December 1921, when President Warren Harding commuted Debs's sentence to time served, Cahan would be present at the White House when Debs visited. But it would not be unreasonable to imagine that behind Cahan's austere and autocratic exterior a good bit of introspection—perhaps even an awakening—was going on, and the question is where to find it. Could it be in his relationship to an individual who did not in fact exist, except in Cahan's own imagination?

10

In 1933 a mountain climber named Frank Smythe was attempting a conquest of Mount Everest. But the stress was too great, and although he came within one thousand feet, he failed to reach the summit. On his descent, according to an account in *The Wall Street Journal*, Smythe stopped "to eat a mint cake." In the course of the meal, he did something strange: he cut the cake in half, to share it with "someone who wasn't there but who had seemed to be his partner all day." It turned out to be an example of a phenomenon known as the "third man," the sensation, during extremely stressful situations, of the presence of another person.

It would be too much to suggest that the character Abraham Cahan created during the most turbulent years of his life is an example of this famous phenomenon. But it is no doubt more than a coincidence that during his period of great stress, Abraham Cahan created, in David Levinsky, a literary character who seems so real as to be almost uncanny and who casts a cynical eye on everything for which Cahan ostensibly stood.

Cahan had started writing—or at least thinking about—*The Rise of David Levinsky* in 1912. Years later, when writing his memoir, he never laid out the story of how he had created *Levinsky*, and so the best account we have is the one in Pollock's unpublished biography. *McClure's Magazine*, the famous muckraking periodical, had assigned Cahan to write two articles on Jewish immigrants' success in the rapidly expanding garment trade, something that Cahan had already been thinking about. He wrote the first piece just before he became involved in the United Garment Workers strike, as a fictional "autobiography" of a Russian Jewish immigrant, and it was published in *McClure's* in April 1913. He wrote the second piece just as he was being hospitalized for his ulcer surgery in March

1913, and it appeared in *McClure's* in May. *The Autobiography of an American Jew: The Rise of David Levinsky* was so well received that *McClure's* requested two more pieces. Cahan wrote the third while recovering from his surgery—he dictated it to a stenographer—in Lakewood. And he wrote the fourth after he returned to New York; they were published in the magazine in June and July.

McClure's appears to have conceived of the series as a way to expose the ascent of Jews in American commercial life—in a not particularly complimentary fashion.* Cahan, however, seems to have grasped early on the possibility of achieving something transcendent. One has to wonder, as he was recovering from his surgery and from the wounds to his reputation from the stoning of the *Forward* Building by Yiddish-speaking union members: Did he sense error in his life? Did he intimate what lay ahead? In the following decade he and his comrades would not only be challenged on the labor front but would be proved wrong in respect of the world war, the Russian Revolution, and Zionism.

Cahan clearly realized, while recovering in Lakewood, the possibilities that the *McClure's* assignment had opened for him. Over the next few years, he reworked and expanded the stories into a novel about a poor Jew from Russia who falls away from religion, comes to America, and triumphs in the secular world, only to lose his soul—or at least to feel lonely, isolated, and profoundly sorry for himself. *The Rise of David Levinsky* was published by Harper & Brothers in September 1917, one month before the Bolshevik Revolution.

David Levinsky was born in the fictional town of Antomir, in northwestern Russia, and was raised, after the death of his father, by his deeply religious mother. His early life is not dissimilar to Cahan's. As a young yeshiva student, he is traumatized by the murder of his mother as she defends him against harassing Gentiles. He loses interest in his

* As a warm-up to Cahan's pieces, the March 1913 issue of *McClure's* contained an article by Burton J. Hendrick, the magazine's associate editor, entitled "The Jewish Invasion of America."

Leo Frank was arrested in 1913, at Atlanta, for the rape and murder of a fourteen-year-old employee of the National Pencil Factory, where Frank was superintendent. The *Forward* threw everything it had into covering the story. Cahan himself traveled to Atlanta, where he interviewed Frank, who had been convicted on perjured testimony from the actual murderer. Frank was lynched in 1915 by a mob who had kidnapped him from prison. "In no other country in the world," Cahan wrote, "will it be understood how Frank's death was possible." (*Library of Congress, Prints & Photographs Division, George Grantham Bain Collection*)

In 1914 Meyer London (center, addressing striking Brooklyn streetcar workers in 1916) became the second socialist to be elected to the United States Congress. When the news was announced to a crowd of forty thousand gathered in front of the *Forward* Building, a band played *La Marseillaise* and "people fell on each other's necks and kissed each other with tears of joy." London mocked the Balfour Declaration that would lead to a Jewish state, saying, "Let us stop making fools of ourselves about the Jewish future." (*Library of Congress, Prints & Photographs Division, George Grantham Bain Collection*)

Vera Figner (pictured here in 1880) had once conspired against Alexander II, but years later was driven into silence by the Soviet dictatorship. When Cahan visited Russia in 1927, she gave him whispered warnings about the true nature of the Soviet regime and introduced him, sotto voce, to survivin members of Narodnaya Volya as “one of us.” Cahan called his meeting with Figner “one o the most moving moments” in his life.

Eugene V. Debs founded the Socialist Party America and would receive one million vote as its presidential candidate in 1912. “His wo come from a human heart,” Cahan effused, “words of light, truth, and hope!” Debs was jailed in 1919 for his opposition to America’s entry into World War I, but his sentence was commuted by President Warren Harding in December 1921. On his way home from prison he and Cahan visited Harding at the White House (pictured here). *(Library of Congress, Prints & Photographs Division, George Grantha Bain Collection)*

David Ben-Gurion and his wife, Paula, in 1918. When Cahan made his first visit to Palestine in 1925, the future founding prime minister of Israel spent hours with the editor. "The great public draws its ideas mainly from the *Forward*," Ben-Gurion had written in his diary. *(Government Press Office, State of Israel)*

Palestine in 1924, photographed by the Polish photographer Alter Kacyzne, whose images of Jewish life in Eastern Europe and Palestine were popular with readers of the *Forward*. *(Alter Kacyzne/Forward Association)*

Abraham Cahan was lampooned in the satirical paper *Der Groyser Kundes* (The Big Stick) for exploiting his writers at the *Forward* (*YIVO Institute for Jewish Research*) and in the communist daily *Freiheit* as a scourge hectoring his readers from atop the *Forward* Building. (*Courtesy of The Library of the Jewish Theological Seminary/NC1429.G7 A5 1927*)

Vladimir Jabotinsky, leader of Revisionist Zionism, looks out the window of a train at Split, Croatia, in 1937, three years before he delivered, at the Manhattan Opera House, the speech that Cahan would ridicule for its call to evacuate six million Jews to Palestine from Europe. A few months later the *Forward* called Jabotinsky's death "in the true sense of the word, a national catastrophe." (*Courtesy of the Jabotinsky Institute, Israel*)

David Shub (far right), one of Cahan's closest deputies at the *Forward*, wrote of his editor: "Cahan until his last breath remained a convinced Social Democrat. But in the last few decades he would put the accent on the last word—democrat. He put political and spiritual freedom of the person in first place." Standing between Cahan and Shub are the economists Wladimir and Emma Woytinsky (he was one of the architects of Franklin Delano Roosevelt's Social Security policy) and Lazar Fogelman (next to Shub), who edited the *Forward* between 1962 and 1968. (*Forward Association*)

Jay Lovestone, who quit the Communist Party after a feud with Stalin in 1929 and vowed to bring down the Soviet Union, was given a cubicle at the office of the International Ladies' Garment Workers Union, the *Forward*'s arm in the labor movement. From there he helped organize an international movement of free trade unions with which there affiliated a little-known trade union in Gdansk, Poland, called Solidarity, which rose up to crack Soviet rule in the Eastern Bloc. (*Jay Lovestone Papers, Envelope E, Hoover Institution Archives*)

Sholem Asch, in his day the *Forward*'s most famous writer. Asch's novel *The Nazarene* was rejected by Cahan, who erupted in fury over its blurring of the differences between Judaism and Christianity. (*Library of Congress, Prints & Photographs Division*)

Isaac Bashevis Singer won the Nobel Prize in Literature in 1978 for stories that first appeared in the *Forward*. His brother, Israel Joshua Singer, who had been hired by Cahan in 1921 to serve as the paper's Warsaw correspondent, was the better-known sibling prior to his death in 1944. (*Forward Association*)

Cahan in the late 1930s, when the *Forward* maintained a clear-eyed view of Nazism, calling the 1938 Munich Agreement a "shameful document" and referring to Hitler as the "Fascist devil" who had "made a fool of his terrified opponents, of the democratic countries, and of the whole civilized world." (*Library of Congress, Prints & Photographs Division*)

Some twenty thousand readers and friends packed Madison Square Garden on May 25, 1947, to pay tribute to the *Forward* on its fiftieth anniversary. By then the glory days of Yiddish newspaperdom were past. (*Forward Association*)

Talmudic studies, and as word of pogroms in neighboring towns spreads through Antomir, he dreams of joining the exodus of Russian Jews to America. Falling ill, he is taken in by one of the better-off families in Antomir and falls in love with their daughter, Mathilda, and discovers the power of sexual allure. Well-educated, Russian-speaking Mathilda teases the shy yeshiva boy by trying to tuck his sidelocks behind his ears, and he angrily demands that she stop— only to yield to her advances as she encourages him to learn Russian and become an educated man. Eventually she pays his way to America, and he vows to become a success and make himself worthy of her.

In America, by using guile, evoking pity, and trading up, he soon becomes a peddler. When another peddler warns him that his beard makes him look like a greenhorn, he commits the "heinous sin" of shaving. He makes passes at various landladies and falls into a period of dissolution that he calls "unrestrained misconduct," in which he is "intoxicated by the novelty of yielding to Satan." He goes through months of "debauchery and self-disgust." The "underworld women I met, the humdrum filth of their life, and their matter-of-fact, business-like attitude toward it never ceased to shock and repel me. I never left a creature of this kind without abominating her and myself, yet I would soon, sometimes during the very same evening, call on her again or on some other woman of her class."

Like Cahan, Levinsky enrolls in a public night school and undergoes the tortures of learning English grammar. He reads Dickens while living in the basement of a dance hall, but loses his lodgings for ogling the dancers. Destitute, hungry, and without a decent place to live, he fortuitously encounters a crony he'd met on the ship to America, who encourages him to become a sewing machine operator in the cloak-making trade. At first life in the sweatshop is hard, but it begins to change him. "By little and little I got used to my work and even to enjoy its processes," he says. While he works, he is able to think and dream. "No one seemed to be honorable who did not earn his bread by the sweat of his brow as I did," he says. "Had I then chanced to hear a Socialist speech I might have become an ardent follower of Karl Marx and my life might have been directed along lines other than those which brought me to financial power."

Levinsky continues on his path to self-improvement. "The Ghetto rang with a clamor for knowledge," he observes, and "to save up some money and prepare for college seemed to be the most natural thing for me to do." He improves his skills at his sewing machine, and "it did not take me long to realize that the number of cloaks or jackets which one turned out in a given length of time was largely a matter of method and system." His new methods and systems eventually earn him a salary of ten dollars a week. During slow seasons, he develops a passion for the Yiddish theater. When work picks up again, he is dazzled by his ability to put one hundred dollars in the bank; his dream of attending college inches that much closer to reality. Then Levinsky expresses ambivalence about America, a feeling that will recur throughout his life.

> I knew that many of the professional men on the East Side, and, indeed, everywhere else in the United States, were people of doubtful intellectual equipment, while I was ambitious to be a cultured man "in the European way." There was an odd confusion of ideas in my mind. On the one hand, I had a notion that to "become an American" was the only tangible form of becoming a man of culture (for did not I regard the most refined and learned European as a "greenhorn"?); on the other hand, the impression was deep in me that American education was a cheap machine-made product.

Just as he is about to start a better-paying factory job comes a "calamity": the cloak makers' union goes out on strike. Levinsky reluctantly joins the union. But his shopmates reproach him for his lack of interest in union activities, and he asks them what more they want of him. They reply, "Do you think it right that millions of people should toil and live in misery so that a number of idlers might roll in luxury?"

A pragmatist with his eye on only one goal—obtaining a college degree and improving his station in life—Levinsky curtly replies, "I haven't made the world, nor can I mend it." The strike is settled, and

Levinsky is delighted that his bigger paycheck means that his dreams of attending college are that much closer to being realized. Working furiously during "the season," studying furiously for his exams during slack times, he takes only the briefest time off to attend Felix Adler's ethical culture lectures: "I valued them for their English rather than for anything else, but their spirit, reinforced by the effect of organ music and the general atmosphere of the place, would send my soul soaring."

Then a seemingly trivial incident changes the course of Levinsky's life. While working on some silk coats for a new employer, he inadvertently spills milk on them, for which his employer humiliates him. Levinsky vows revenge and decides to start his own clothes manufacturing company, partnering with his employer's talented designer. His dreams of college recede into the background, and his new venture comes to life. "I visioned myself a rich man, of course, but that was merely a detail. What really hypnotized me was the venture of the thing. It was a great, daring game of life."

After a few false starts, some bad breaks, and then a bit of luck, Levinsky's business begins to succeed. But in the process he finds himself changing into a different sort of person:

> The inadequacy of my working capital often forced me to have recourse to subterfuges that could not exactly be called honorable. One day, when we had some bills to meet two days before I could expect to obtain the cash, I made out and signed checks, but enclosed each of them in the wrong envelope—this supposed act of inadvertence gaining me the needed two days of grace. On another occasion I sent out a number of checks without my signature, which presumably I had forgotten to affix.

Time passes, and Levinsky is now a wealthy man, but then another crisis looms:

> My business was making headway when the Cloak and Suit Makers' Union sprang into life again. . . . It seemed as if this time it had come to stay. My budding little establishment was too small,

> in fact, to be in immediate danger. It was one of a scattered number of insignificant places which the union found it difficult to control. Still, cheap labor being my chief excuse for being, the organization caused me no end of worry.

Eventually Levinsky's worst fears are realized. All the cloak manufacturers form a coalition and lock out their union men. A bitter struggle ensues, with Levinsky now in the thick of it:

> I made a pretense of joining in the lockout, my men clandestinely continuing to work for me. More than that, my working force was trebled, for, besides filling my own orders, I did some of the work of a well-known firm which found it much more difficult to procure non-union labor than I did. What was a great calamity to the trade in general seemed to be a source of overwhelming prosperity to me. But the golden windfall did not last long. The agitation and the picketing activities of the union, aided by the *Arbeiter Zeitung*, a Yiddish socialist weekly, were spreading a spell of enthusiasm (or fear) to which my men gradually succumbed. My best operator, a young fellow who exercised much influence over his shop mates and who had hitherto been genuinely devoted to me, became an ardent convert to union principles and led all my operatives out of the shop. I organized a shop elsewhere, but it was soon discovered.
>
> Somebody must have reported to the editor of the *Arbeiter Zeitung* that at one time I had been a member of the union myself, for that weekly published a scurrilous paragraph, branding me as a traitor.
>
> I read the paragraph with mixed rage and pain, and yet the sight of my name in print flattered my vanity, and when the heat of my fury subsided I became conscious of a sneaking feeling of gratitude to the socialist editor for printing the attack on me. For, behold! the same organ assailed the Vanderbilts, the Goulds, the Rothschilds, and by calling me "a fleecer of labor" it placed me in their class. I felt in good company. I felt, too, that while there were people by whom "fleecers" were cursed, there were many others who held them in

high esteem and that even those who cursed them had a secret envy for them, hoping some day to be fleecers of labor like them.

Here is an amazing situation. Through Levinsky, Cahan is reasoning from the perspective of a union member who has become a capitalist, and whose ruminations are ignited by an attack on him in a newspaper for which Cahan used to write editorials attacking people much like Levinsky. And as Cahan was writing those lines, he was either doubled over in pain from an ulcer or recovering from its removal. His doctors believed the ulcer had been brought to an acute stage by the stress of a strike during which Yiddish-speaking garment workers had formed a mob outside the *Forward* Building and stoned Cahan's office. As the story unfolds, the reader can't help but feel a certain amount of sympathy for Levinsky, despite all his cynicism. At one point, as Levinsky sits in an elegant dining car speeding through the night, he imagines he is "partaking of a repast in an enchanted palace" and wonders, "Can it be that I am I?"

While Levinsky's quest for romance grows ever more frustrating, he emerges triumphant as a businessman. Toward the end of the novel, he delivers something of a paean to American capitalism. As he walks along the great Fifth Avenue shopping thoroughfare in a reverie, he refers to himself as

> a Russian Jew as head of one of the largest industries in the United States. . . . As a master of that industry he had made good, for in his hands it had increased a hundredfold, garments that had formerly reached only the few having been placed within the reach of the masses. Foreigners ourselves, and mostly unable to speak English, we had Americanized the system of providing clothes for the American woman of moderate or humble means. The ingenuity and unyielding tenacity of our managers, foremen, and operatives had introduced a thousand and one devices for making by machine garments that used to be considered only as the product of handwork. . . . We had done away with prohibitive prices and greatly

> improved the popular taste. Indeed, the Russian Jew had made the average American girl a "tailor-made" girl.
>
> When I learned the trade a cloak made of the cheapest satinette cost eighteen dollars. To-day nobody would wear it. One can now buy a whole suit made of all-wool material and silk-lined for fifteen dollars. . . . The average American woman is the best-dressed average woman in the world, and the Russian Jew has had a good deal to do with making her one.

The storyline that Cahan created for *The Rise of David Levinsky* must have been surprising even for him: a Jew transcends capitalism by using it to improve social conditions, not via philanthropy, but by running a company that uses machines to profitably make inexpensive goods available to millions of people. Suddenly we glimpse a country in which capitalism and socialism seem allied in a way that once seemed unimaginable. Certainly Cahan seemed to grasp, at least unconsciously, the paradox of America as a place where immigrants, capitalists or not, could quickly rise to power and prominence. At some point Cahan must have realized that while he was a socialist and the *Forward* a complex profit-sharing association, he had risen to great heights by bringing to light the issues of the working poor and striving immigrants. In the process, he himself had become a captain of industry.

Rival newspapers certainly noted it: one ran a cartoon of Cahan, the socialist, squeezing his writers under the caption "Free Press," which was a pun in Yiddish as well. As the cultural historian and Yiddish professor Eddy Portnoy observes, "the cartoonists of the Yiddish humor press developed a caricature of a bloated *alrightnik*, or capitalist (ironically, Cahan's own neologism), wearing the *Forward* Building as his top hat. This caricature varied in style, but remained a permanent fixture, appearing along with Cahan as representatives of the *Forverts* for nearly a quarter century in a variety of Yiddish periodicals." The fiery socialist had become, in the eyes of many of his colleagues, a sort of Eustace Tilley, the top-hatted dandy who appeared on the cover of the first issue of *The New Yorker* in 1925.

The *Forward* was hardly a sweatshop, but it made its presiding spirit a famous and powerful man. This no doubt explains the unmistakable narrative sympathy for Levinsky that appears as the novel draws to its conclusion. He falls hopelessly in love with the lively and progressive Anna Tevkin, who lives in a home full of life and culture, if not business success. Levinsky celebrates the Passover seder with her family. "She flooded my soul with ecstasy," he relates. Of her father, he observes, "Tevkin's religion was Judaism, Zionism. Mine was Anna."

After the seder meal, Levinsky takes Anna aside and says that while her brother asked the four questions, he would like to ask a fifth.

"Something about Jewish nationalism?" she asks, in one of the great lines of the book.

"About that and something else," Levinsky replies, and proceeds to propose marriage.

She rejects him, and his "crushing sense of final defeat" causes him "indescribable suffering." He blames his fiasco, in part, on the difference in their ages; had he been ten years younger, Anna's attitude might have been different. But he puts most of the blame squarely on her environment. "The atmosphere around her was against me," he muses. "I hated the socialists with a novel venom."

Levinsky never does find love. Although he has amassed an enormous fortune, at fifty-seven he is an unhappy and lonely man. For all his worldly success, he would, were he able, trade places with "the Russian Jew, a former Talmud student like myself, who is the greatest physiologist in the New World, or with the Russian Jew who holds the foremost place among American songwriters and whose soulful compositions are sung in almost every English-speaking house in the world." He engages a sculptor ("also one of our immigrants, an East Side boy who had met with sensational success in Paris and London") to create a bust of himself. "But I never left his studio without feeling cheap and wretched."

In the end, Levinsky is unable to feel comfortable in his luxurious life. He is "always more or less conscious of my good clothes, of the high quality of my office furniture, of the power I wield over the men in my pay." He confesses to a "lurking fear of restaurant waiters." And in the final paragraph, Levinsky realizes that he cannot put his past behind him. "I can never forget the days of my misery. I cannot escape from my old self. My past and my present do not comport well. David, the poor lad swinging over a Talmud volume at the Preacher's Synagogue, seems to have more in common with my inner identity than David Levinsky, the well-known cloak-manufacturer."

The Rise of David Levinsky was quickly recognized as a classic of American realism. Not all the reviews were admiring; H. W. Boynton, writing in *The Bookman*, used the phrase "spiritual obscenity" to describe the character Cahan created, and an unnamed reviewer in *The Nation* opined that Levinsky was "that type of Jew who raises the gorge of all decent human beings." But most of the notices were quite complimentary, including the glowing and insightful one that appeared on the front page of *The New York Times Book Review* on Sunday, September 16, 1917, alongside a review of a new novel by H. G. Wells:

> Among the many different kinds of immigrants who have come flocking in thousands to America, there were none to whom the change from the Old World to the New could be any greater than it was to the Russian Jew. From being one to whom practically every opportunity was denied, he became one to whom practically every opportunity was open. The rolls of the College of [the] City of New York tell us something of what certain members of the race did with one kind of opportunity, the history of the cloak and suit industry is record of their use of another. In this new novel is related, so vividly and so convincingly that it reads more like fact than fiction, the autobiography of one of these Russian Jews, his struggles and failures, his successes and his tragedy. . . . *The Rise of David Levinsky* is not a pleasant book, nor is David himself an especially likable or appealing individual. . . . But he is a very real one, a genuine human being. For the dominant quality in this novel is the effect it gives

> of being altogether real. . . . [It is] a vivid portrayal . . . of the eternal struggle between idealism and materialism, between intellectual and business interests, between selfishness and generosity, good and evil, as it was fought out in the soul of David Levinsky.

John Macy, writing in *The Dial*, described Cahan as a "seer." From the beginning, the reviewers discussed the degree to which the novel was autobiographical. They cited the obvious parallels, starting with the fact that Cahan and Levinsky were looking back on life from the same age. Both had risen from poor, Orthodox families, and both had come from small towns in czarist Russia. Both had been educated Jewishly and flirted with secular education in Russia. Both fell away from religion. Both decided as young men to go to America, where both went to night school and attempted a variety of trades before climbing to the top in one. Cahan became certified as a schoolteacher in New York before entering the newspaper business; Levinsky tried his hand at peddling before entering the garment industry. Cahan's friend William Dean Howells called *The Rise of David Levinsky* a "pretty great autobiographical novel." And Ronald Sanders remarks that one need only substitute the words "Yiddish press" for "cloak and suit trade" in the novel's first paragraph, and "David Levinsky seems to become Abraham Cahan." The young Levinsky, Sanders says, is so much like the young Cahan "that it must have been extremely difficult for Cahan to formulate the crucial point at which Levinsky's life and career diverged from his own."

The two lives do diverge, however, and as Cahan biographer Sanford Marovitz has suggested, "the differences between the author and his central character are far more important than their likenesses." Levinsky forsook political engagement and the causes to which Cahan devoted his life. Levinsky evinced little interest in Zionist issues. Levinsky was a capitalist businessman, but it was Cahan who would come to play an active role in the long struggle against Soviet Communism by supporting the anti-Communist wing of the labor movement.

It's not clear, however, if these differences were apparent, or important, to Cahan while he was writing the novel. Levinsky's struggle, his journey—and Cahan's own journey in writing it—is internal. Levinsky is extraordinarily self-absorbed. When he takes an interest in others, it is almost always in hope of gaining something in exchange. Levinsky never manages to find a wife, much less maintain a lasting relationship with one woman. His patronage of prostitutes is accompanied by loathing and self-loathing. He is obsessed with his own problems, successes, frustrations, and yearnings. He cheats, he lies, he two-times, he trades up—not only in business but also in his romantic pursuits. His association with literature and culture is superficial. His personality appears to be the very opposite of Cahan's, who maintained long and steady relationships with individuals and institutions throughout his life.

Yet Cahan appears, in *David Levinsky*, to be seeking to get past superficial similarities and differences. In the famous opening paragraph, Levinsky says that when he thinks of his past "in a superficial, casual way," the metamorphosis he has gone through strikes him as "nothing short of a miracle." He was born in the "lowest depths of poverty" and arrived in America with four cents in his pocket, and he eventually rose to become a multimillionaire and captain of industry. Then he gets to the point: "And yet when I take a look at my inner identity it impresses me as being precisely the same as it was thirty or forty years ago. My present station, power, the amount of worldly happiness at my command, and the rest of it, seem to be devoid of significance."

One clue to where the story of David Levinsky fits into Abraham Cahan's life would appear twenty years after Cahan died, in a memoir written by a staff member of the *Forward.* David Shub was a crony of both Cahan and his wife, Anna. She was, Shub writes, "a very intelligent and well-read woman. She knew not only Russian and English literature, but also French. She and her father used to correspond in French." He called her "a very skilled translator" and notes that she translated nearly all of Cahan's English stories and novels into Russian. She also translated Chekhov's stories from Russian into English. And one time she sent a story of her own to *The New York Sun.* Cahan discovered it in the paper and ran home to exclaim, "Anyuta, it is a gem." But she told Shub that she did not pursue a career as a bellettrist because she felt that Cahan didn't want her to compete with him. When Shub asked him about this, Cahan replied, "Rubbish. That's utter nonsense. She was just too lazy to write. She was always rather lazy."

Anna, in any event, declined to translate *The Rise of David Levinsky* into Russian. "Not only will I never translate his *David Levinsky*," she told Shub when pressed on the point, "I haven't even read it, and I'm not ever going to read it."

"Why not?" he asked in amazement.

"Because he chose as the hero of his great novel a Jewish immigrant, an ordinary man who worked himself up in America and became a successful manufacturer, an 'all-rightnik.' Couldn't he find a nicer, more intelligent type among all the other American Jewish immigrants to put forth for the American reader?"

Shub believed that Anna's response was an example of her "caprices, her own strong convictions, and also her own 'meshugas.'" But there was a certain truth in what she said. David Levinsky is superficially an unattractive, lonely, isolated figure, but Cahan undoubtedly portrayed him with a profound sympathy; that he chose a lonely capitalist to be the hero of his masterpiece can't be an accident. When he sat down to write the story, a great deal was going on in his life, and in the world at large, over which he had to brood. Within the next few years, all the beliefs that Cahan and his comrades on the left held so dear would be profoundly shaken. Soon the world would be engulfed in a war unparalleled in history, one that would rattle the foundations of all political ideologies save democracy. The left-of-center movement from which Cahan was emerging had, at least at the outset, sneered at the suggestion that workingmen and women had a stake in the war or its outcome. But once America entered the war, the *Forward*, like many of the skeptics at the opposite end of the political spectrum, became a supporter of the war. Then there was the matter of Soviet Communism. *The Rise of David Levinsky* was published on the eve of the Bolshevik Revolution. Cahan and the *Forward* soon grasped that Communism was a flawed, even evil enterprise.

None of it happened immediately, either at the *Forward* or at the other great American newspapers. A number of them, including *The New York Herald*, welcomed the February Revolution that, as we have seen, ended the Romanov monarchy and installed a democratic socialist government headed by Alexander Kerensky. Nor, eight months later, were they able to see immediately the catastrophe of the October Revolution, when hopes for democratic socialism died and the Bolshevik tyranny began. Cahan, whom the historian Richard Gid Powers would describe as "the most important Jewish anticommunist of the twenties," was not much quicker than others to see the Leninists for what they were. He defended the Bolsheviks, Powers says, "even when their regime was clearly indefensible according to democratic Socialist principles." When the Communists were accused of stifling civil liberties in Russia, Cahan wrote that "the fruit of the whole revolution would be . . . swept away if [the Bolsheviks] were to allow political freedom."

In Powers's telling, it was the anger of "other Jewish Socialists, who denounced him for abandoning the principles of democratic socialism out of sympathy for the Bolshevik dictatorship," that brought Cahan around. One Socialist critic of Bolshevism, Vladimir Medem, a Bund leader who had recently come to New York from Poland and carried considerable sway in the Jewish community, told Cahan that "if a reversion to the Spanish inquisition is necessary for the realization of socialism, then we can do without such a socialism." Medem's words, Powers estimates, "made Cahan take a fresh look at what the Soviets were doing to socialism." Cahan, in any event, threw the *Forward* into the fray and began to print all sorts of stories and editorials against the Bolsheviks.

One of Cahan's targets was a front organization called the Friends of Soviet Russia, whose stated purpose was to raise funds for famine relief. In the summer of 1922, the *Forward* began to expose its operations in both editorials and news articles. It accused the FSR of siphoning off funds raised for famine relief and using them instead for Communist propaganda and for subsidizing Communist newspapers through advertising; it said FSR employees were engaging in Communist Party work using money raised for relief, and that the organization was guilty of general extravagance.

The attacks were damaging enough that the FSR formed an investigating committee, chaired by American Civil Liberties Union cofounder Roger N. Baldwin; its members included a former member of the editorial staff of *The Nation* and an editor at *The New Republic*. The committee issued a report published in *Soviet Russia*, the official magazine of the FSR, which said it itemized the charges and sent the list to Cahan, who "politely declined to deal with the committee in any way, on the ground that," as the committee characterized it, "while he does not doubt its integrity, it was appointed by the organization against which the charges were brought."

Thus the FSR committee pronounced the FSR innocent. But there would never be any love lost between the *Forward* and the Communists. The *Forward*'s feud with the *Morgen Freiheit*, the Yiddish-language daily affiliated with the Communist Party USA, erupted from the *Freiheit*'s founding in 1922 and would last until the *Freiheit* folded in 1988. Cahan's anti-Communism hardened sharply after his visit in 1923 to Europe, where he gained a firsthand understanding of the irredeemable nature of the tyranny that was emerging in Russia.

When he returned, he famously proclaimed that "Russia has at present less freedom than it had in the earliest days of Romanov rule. . . . The world has never yet seen such a despotism."

The *Forward* was one of the first newspapers in America to report on the Siberian prison camps, which most people on the left steadfastly ignored. Cahan sent *Forward* reporters to Russia. Eventually, in the 1930s they filed eyewitness accounts of the mass starvation that resulted from Stalin's collectivization, during which millions of peasants died and millions more were exiled to Siberia. Cahan pushed his point so hard that some on the left began saying that the *Forward* was just as bad as William Randolph Hearst's famously right-wing publications because of its "anti-Sovietism."

Cahan's move into the hardline anti-Communist camp clearly rattled the Communists. In May 1923 he delivered the keynote speech at the eleventh national convention of the Socialist Party of America, held in New York. *The Worker*, the official publication of the Communist Party, called Cahan's remarks a "compilation of the most loathsome back stairs gossip against Soviet Russia, emanating from the journalistic house of prostitution of the entire capitalist world, combined with the vapid ravings of his own distraught mind." It called Cahan a "notorious Bolshevik baiter" and mocked those who applauded him. SPA cofounder and chairman Algernon Lee had introduced Cahan, *The Worker* reported, as "that old, loved, and trusted fighting socialist comrade." But Cahan had "immediately launched into a tirade that was so acrimonious, intemperate, and obviously false that the majority of the delegates were stunned." Only the allies of Morris Hillquit, who was in Europe and for whom Cahan was filling in, appeared pleased. The national secretary of the Socialist Party, Otto Branstetter, "smirked in the most cringing and servile manner," while Lee "grimaced like a trained baboon at each barrage of billingsgate hurled at the leaders of the World Revolution."

Cahan denounced Trotsky as a "bombastic windbag," *The World* reported, and said Trotsky's physical ailments were "undoubtedly due to his earlier complete moral collapse." *The World* continued that "the mountebank Cahan . . . screeched deliriously that the great leader of the Bolshevik revolution [Lenin] was a 'muddle head lunatic.'" Cahan apparently attacked several other Bolshevik leaders, including Karl Radek and Gregory Zinoviev, both of whom had traveled to Russia with Lenin from Switzerland through Germany and Sweden aboard the infamous "sealed train."

With this speech, Cahan took his place within the leadership of an anti-Communist movement that would not be fully vindicated until 1989, nearly forty years after Cahan's death, when the Soviet Union finally collapsed in the face of a three-pronged strategy led by President Ronald Reagan, Pope John Paul II, and Lane Kirkland of the American Federation of Labor-Congress of Industrial Organizations.

Cahan's campaign cost the *Forward*. In 1926, when the Communists tightened their grip on several unions, the *Forward* experienced a plunge in its circulation due to its unrelenting anti-Communist stance. At a meeting on this subject, Cahan declared, "I would rather see the *Forward* go under than weaken the struggle against the communists."

Cahan was facing another potential circulation problem from a different quarter: the closing off of immigration into the United States. In the early 1920s, the *Forward* was at the apex of its success. Circulation stood at nearly 250,000. The paper had a dozen bureaus across the country, in Los Angeles, Detroit, Boston, and Milwaukee, and abroad, in Warsaw, Moscow, and other European cities. A separate edition was published in Chicago.

The American public took note. In 1922 Oswald Garrison Villard, the longtime editor of *The Nation*, wrote, "Which is the most vital, the most interesting, the most democratic of New York's daily journals? . . . In my judgment it is the *Forward*, or the *Vorwaerts*, to use its Yiddish name. . . . It is printing today by far the best fiction and *belles lettres* of any newspaper in America."

The 1924 Johnson-Reed Act forever altered Cahan's readership, as it ended the era of unfettered immigration that had seen millions of Jews and other peoples from eastern Europe, Asia, and the Mediterranean come to America. "A great misfortune," Cahan called the Johnson-Reed Act, in a front-page *Forward* headline. In the early stages of the immigration debate, Meyer London had argued on the floor of the Congress that immigration was essentially self-regulating. He characterized the chauvinistic element among the anti-immigration forces as "utterly incomprehensible when found among the American people, full of the vigor of youth and absorbing unto itself all that is strong and virile in the human stock." But the trends that culminated in the Johnson-Reed Act had been evident well before it was passed, and the Socialists—even the Jewish Labor Bund—fell in with those who favored restriction.

The act had a collateral impact on the Zionist struggle, and Cahan's role in all of this was significant enough that an entire book, *Jewish Socialists in the United States: The Cahan Debate, 1925–1926*, by Yaacov N. Goldstein, has been devoted to it. The debate it refers to was about Zionism; as Goldstein explains, the closing off of Jewish immigration to the United States and the economic crisis in the newly established independent Polish commonwealth had the unintended consequence of setting the stage for the Jewish state; these factors contributed to the swelling of Jewish emigration to Palestine in the 1920s, which came to be known as the "Polish Aliyah."

In the summer of 1924 the general manager of the *Forward*, B. Charney Vladeck, made an important visit to Poland together with the director of the Hebrew Immigrant Aid Society. The report they submitted on their return was "harrowing," says Goldstein, telling of, among other signs of crisis, "six thousand Jews who were roaming around various parts of Europe with the aim of reaching the United States" but with no chance of entering the country. The *Forward*'s correspondent in Poland reported that the "Jewish surge to Palestine [was] the most important event at the moment in Poland."

Goldstein presents these developments as "a pivotal factor in the intensification of the debate in the American-Jewish workers' movement on its positions regarding Zionism and Palestine." The "general American workers' movement" supported the restrictions on immigration put into place by the American government. In 1922 the annual conference of the American Federation of Labor, held in Cincinnati, resolved to "support the policy of closing the gates despite the opposition of the Jewish unions." In this context, on July 1, 1925, the *Forward* announced that its editor would be departing for Europe in August to serve as a delegate to the second congress of the Labor and Socialist International in Marseilles and would then travel on to Palestine.

11

Cahan's trip to Palestine was more significant than that of any other American newspaper editor, a fact that no one understood more clearly than the Zionist leadership in Palestine. Max Pine, chairman of the United Hebrew Trades and also of the fund-raising campaign of the Histadrut, the labor organization in Palestine that had been founded in 1920, wanted to overcome socialist opposition to his Zionist aims. Pine encouraged Cahan to come and see "the miracle" that was being performed by the Jewish workers in "Eretz Yisrael." Two weeks before Cahan's arrival, the Histadrut newspaper *Davar* said it viewed Cahan's imminent arrival with "trepidation." Columnist David Zakai wrote that "the lion [was coming] out of his lair, the king of the *Forward* himself. . . . When he praises, millions will praise after him; and when he scorns, those millions will scorn still more than they have until now." *Davar* reported even the advance arrival of Cahan's private secretary, M. Vinograd.

This was more than just a political trip; whether they favored or opposed political Zionism, *Forward* readers were eager to hear what its editor thought about what was going on in Palestine. Such interest, Cahan knew, could only fuel the paper's sales. "The thing is of such unusual consequence and has stirred up so much discussion and curiosity all over Europe as well as in America that we cannot make it too big," he wrote Vladeck from Paris. "I am learning a good deal of the Palestine and Zionist situation. Everybody seems to be bursting with this subject. . . . You may advertise it on the largest possible scale."

So Vladeck did. The *Forward* unleashed a huge campaign to publicize Cahan's upcoming trip. It distributed ten thousand promotional matchbooks; it took out ads in nearly a dozen magazines and newspapers, including *The New York Times*, the *Chicago Tribune*, the *Los Angeles Herald*, and *The Nation*; and a big sign was put up in Times Square "proclaiming the *Forward*'s Palestine series for the whole world to see," as Vladeck wrote to Cahan, who was by then in Tel Aviv. An astonishing 25,000 posters, half in Yiddish, half in English, were placed in store windows and on the walls in New York's subway stations and the Boston El. Some 50,000 leaflets would be handed out throughout the United States, "to the kinds of Jews that the Jewish press does not usually reach," Vladeck wrote to Cahan.

On September 26, 1925, Cahan and his wife arrived in Palestine, pulling into the railway station in Lydda on an overnight train from Egypt. That day the *Forward* ran a full-page ad proclaiming, "Today *Genosse** Cahan arrived in Jerusalem. . . . Of all the assignments that *Genosse* Cahan has accepted in his many years as editor of the *Forward*, this is the greatest and most responsible one." Over the course of the next ten weeks, Cahan's dispatches from Palestine were rolled out with great fanfare, printed in both Yiddish and English ("for your children and your English-reading friends"). On Sunday, December 8, toward the end of the series, the staff printed 220,000 copies of the paper, the largest December press run in the *Forward*'s history.

Isaac Ben-Zvi, a leader of the Labor Zionists and president of the Jewish National Council of Palestine who would later serve as Israel's second president, was appointed Cahan's tour guide in Jerusalem. They were joined by Alter Kacyzne, a prominent writer and photographer based in Poland, whose images of Jewish life throughout eastern Europe and Palestine became popular with *Forward* readers.**

Monday, September 28, was Yom Kippur, and Cahan visited seven Jerusalem synagogues that one day. When he got to the Western Wall, the sixty-five-year-old atheist wept. Cahan sent one of Kacyzne's pic-

* Comrade

** In 1941 Kacyzne would flee Nazi-occupied Warsaw for Ukraine. But the German army reached Ukraine ahead of him, and on July 7 in Tarnopol, during a Nazi roundup, Ukrainian collaborators beat him to death.

tures of bearded men in caftans and prayer shawls, praying at the Wall, to New York to appear on the cover of the newspaper's rotogravure section on Sunday, November 8. Cahan was so moved by his visit that he "offered to make a substantial cash contribution to a fund for the purchase of the Wailing Wall and the area around it, so that it would belong once again to the Jewish people."

On Monday, October 5, Cahan received permission to board the Soviet ship *Lenin*, which had arrived in the Jaffa port from Odessa carrying 371 Jewish immigrants from Russia. Here is how he described the scene for *Forward* readers:

> As the ship was not anchored far offshore, I could see the crowd of relatives and the Jews who had come to welcome their dear ones. A huge iron gate separates Jaffa port from the city. . . . A few [relatives] climbed on the roofs of the low office buildings while others jostled around the gate. Almost everyone was dressed in white because it is still hot here, like New York in July, although the air is better and it is even quite cool in the shade. . . .
>
> The sea was a lovely azure color, like the sky. Tel Aviv could be seen, far off, with its low white buildings and before it a strip of yellow ground separating it from the sea. The cluster of old grey houses on the seashore is Jaffa, which is, so to speak, the forepart of Tel Aviv. A great British warship stood in the port, and eight other ships were anchored alongside each other. The harbor lighters, rowed by Arabs, plied incessantly between the ships and the shore.

At the time of Cahan's visit, there were in Palestine about 122,000 Jews, who represented 16 percent of the total population of 757,000. His arrival coincided with the peak of the immigration wave known as the Fourth Aliyah, which began in 1924 and ended in 1928. This wave brought some 80,000 Jews to Palestine, mostly from the middle class, mostly small business owners escaping eastern European anti-Semitism. They were very different from the idealistic Labor Zionist agricultural workers whom Cahan had encountered at his way station in Brody more than forty years earlier. When an economic crisis rocked the Jewish community in Palestine in 1926–27, some 23,000 Jews left. But the ones who stayed established important small businesses and light industries. They were most definitely not socialists of any kind. The battle lines were beginning to be drawn over the political character of the Jewish community in Palestine.

Five days before Cahan's arrival, *Davar* had carried an interview with him by a leader of the World Union of Poale Zion, a Marxist Zionist organization, who had buttonholed Cahan at the Labor Socialist International meeting in Marseilles, in an effort to smoke out his politics. Cahan told the leader: "I treat Zionism in an entirely non-partisan way. I do not believe in it, but there is no hatred for it in my heart." He said he "can appreciate the idealism of many Zionists, who interest me individually. But Zionism is one thing and migration to Palestine is something else; the migration is an undeniable fact."

If Cahan seemed to be weighing his words, the fact is that his trip to Palestine had stirred up quite a debate among the members of the *Forward*'s editorial board. Three opposed the journey entirely. "They feared that my journey would be interpreted as acquiescence to the Zionists," Cahan recalled. "If you are genuine socialists," he retorted, "why are you afraid of Zionism?" Three others favored the trip, two of them talking "like full-fledged Zionists," and one admitting that "for forty years he had been a Zionist at heart." Cahan considered himself part of a group of "practical men" who "expressed the view that it was ridiculous to object to the journey" because of how it might be seen. But Goldstein believes that "the dissenters seem to have been correct in seeing Cahan's journey as a public act, with all that this signified, and not the private affair of some journalist, as Cahan liked to present it."

From the moment he arrived in Palestine and began filing his stories, Cahan asserted that he was operating without preconceptions and that he would report the truth back to the readers of the *Forward*. "I came to Palestine with that single-minded resolution to describe all shades of life and each and every corner honestly," he wrote. "I wish to find out everything so as to get deep down into the problems and understand the situation correctly." He insisted that he had not been among the socialist haters of Zionism and that he "had migrated to America before the Bund was founded" and so had "played no part in its battles against Zionism." He added that "the hatred by Bund members for Zionism" was "strange" to him and "was certainly not relevant to the American reality." Cahan was certainly not being two-faced about it, but he was glossing over the *Forward*'s long-established condescension to Zionism. Nor was he shy about admitting his lack of knowledge about Palestine. He was unfamiliar with the work of Yosef Haim Brenner, for example, the Hebrew author and Zionist who had been killed by Arab rioters in Jaffa in 1921. And the names Joseph Trumpeldor* and Tel Hai meant little to him.

As he journeyed through Palestine, Cahan positively *kvelled* over the agricultural settlements and other achievements of the labor and socialist movements. On a four-day journey through "the Jewish settlements of the new kind," he took evening and morning meals with members of kibbutzim and devoted "many hours to observation, to reflection, to discussion, and to debate." His tour included five kibbutzim and also a few moshavim (collective communities in which farms or plots are privately held). One moshav was operated by Hasidim from Yablonka, in Belarus, and Cahan met with the Yablonka Rebbe. It was important, Cahan reported, "to clarify to the American reader that when one speaks of the 'communist settlements' these are not to be identified with the Bolshevik communists." A "handful" of Bolsheviks had tried to "split the Histadrut" but had "failed abysmally."

A reception was held for Cahan at Ein Harod, a six-year-old kibbutz

* Joseph Trumpeldor (1880–1920) was a Russian-born Zionist pioneer. A hero of the 1905 Russo-Japanese War, he immigrated to Palestine in 1911. In 1915 he organized the Zion Mule Corps, a division of Jews from the Middle East who fought alongside the British at Gallipoli during World War I. On March 1, 1920, responding to an alarm from the residents of the farming village of Tel Hai in the Upper Galilee that was being threatened by Arab gangs from nearby Lebanon, Trumpeldor arrived with reinforcements and died in the course of the battle.

in the Jezreel Valley. Cahan called it beautiful. "I always found it difficult to tear my gaze away from the scenery," he wrote, "the fields, the mountains, the flocks of sheep pasturing on the land, the camels moving slowly with their cautious and graceful gait."

At the Ein Harod reception, Cahan said, "I'll tell you the truth. This evening is one of the happiest evenings I have spent in all my sixty-five years. For this alone my journey would have been worthwhile. You are bringing true the best of my dreams and the dreams of my friends of forty years ago. I feel that I am surrounded by saints and pure people. I respect you. I embrace and kiss each one of you; with all my heart I am with you."

Cahan was not yet, he told his readers, in a position to finalize his views on what chance for success the Jewish National Home in Palestine had, or on what the character of this home was to be, but he had to admit "to the existence of the elevation of spirit. . . . The enthusiasm present in most people far outstrips anything I read or imagined."

Cahan sent back nearly two dozen dispatches from Palestine. He gave readers a glimpse of the range of people he was seeing ("factory owners, businessmen, and bankers . . . I was asking questions and hearing answers from one of the biggest silk industrialists in Tel Aviv"). And he displayed a keen insight into the conflicts among the various factions who were struggling to create, for the first time in almost two thousand years, a Jewish infrastructure in Palestine:

> Generally it may be said that a quiet struggle is taking place here between two trends. One represents the finest idealism and the loftiest goals of the workers and of progressive nationalism. The other is material in nature. This is a conflict between the pragmatic-economic world on the one hand and numerous workers' and Zionist factors on the other. The idealistic-ideological aspirations have taken on the character of a sort of new Jewish religion.
>
> The future of Palestine lies in industry, with attempts being made to establish it in Tel Aviv, and in the cooperative agricultural settle-

ments, which, I was told, are developing extraordinarily in the Jezreel Valley and the Haifa area. Perhaps in the future a way will be found to merge the two tendencies into a single firm trend.

Cahan also reported that he met criticism from some Jews in Palestine over the *Forward*'s support for Jewish settlement projects in the Soviet Crimean and Ukrainian republics. In the early 1920s, more than 150,000 Jews were resettled in hundreds of agricultural colonies in Crimea and Southern Ukraine, funded in part by the American Joint Distribution Committee. Cahan quoted one man who attacked the JDC "because it raised millions for the Crimea settlement instead of Palestine." Others in the conversation silenced the man, but Cahan ended his dispatch by quoting a woman who said that in Russia, "apart from the oppression and despotism, it is impossible to bear the constant fear of the Cheka.* You're afraid of your own shadow and you can go mad with this endless terror."

Cahan sent a dispatch on Jews and Arabs at the Tel Aviv Market, another on industry and the future of Palestine, and one that he called "All Kinds of People and Parties in Palestine." In the latter he wrote that "Zionist chauvinism is so strong that it has become something like a superstition" and noted that "free thinking has no meaning here, and revolutionary aims are denied everywhere." He wrote that "the fire of Zionist nationalism has melted all the class and ideological conflicts" and rhetorically asked, "In such a situation, what meaning can there be to declarations on principles, or class struggle, or social revolution?"

Cahan admitted to being slightly disappointed in the socialist comrades he encountered. "When you tell a revolutionary in Palestine that you are going to write about the greed of the property owners in Tel Aviv, for example, or about the depressed economic condition of the workers in Palestine, he finds himself in a quandary. As a socialist he has to insist that you do write about these matters, but as a Zionist he

* The first Soviet state security organization, the Cheka was a forerunner of the KGB.

is afraid that to do so may harm the endeavor in Palestine." The author of *The Rise of David Levinsky,* who had "exposed" the Jewish businessman and yet muted his exposé with Jewish sympathy and a sense of peoplehood, no doubt understood the divided impulse. "In the end," Cahan concluded, referring to the bemused revolutionary, "he is first of all a Zionist, and all the other 'isms' come only afterwards."

Cahan made a point of reporting that he found many dissenters from the official Zionist party line, people who came to him privately after official meetings. Some of them were clearly just cranks or troublemakers, but others he felt were making important points. The majority of Jews in Palestine, he insisted in several articles, were actually indifferent to Zionism and were simply seeking economic opportunity and freedom from persecution. Some of his criticisms have a contemporary ring. New arrivals were "kissing the sand dunes of Tel Aviv" only to begin, a few weeks later, to joke about their "initial enthusiasm" and to attack the Histadrut labor exchange, "claiming favoritism in giving out jobs" while they were "forced to tramp the streets searching for work until their feet were swollen." But his experiences in the Jewish homeland were obviously affecting him deeply; he saw "many dedicated youngsters who withstood this ordeal. I saw some who had gone hungry for weeks, and they suffered like martyrs. Their idealism, their loyalty to Zion, gives them strength." In one early dispatch he wrote, "I can't help it . . . I must marvel at the heroic fire that burns in them."

One individual who burned with such fire was David Ben-Gurion. The thirty-nine-year-old general secretary of the Histadrut worked hard to win over the American editor, spending hours with him, answering his questions about kibbutzim and the Histadrut and following his daily travels with great attentiveness. Ben-Gurion was well aware of the *Forward*'s influence. "The great public draws its ideas mainly from the *Forward*," Ben-Gurion had written in his diary back in 1920. After reading Cahan's first dispatch from Palestine, Ben-Gurion wrote, with evident pleasure and relief, that "even these few words will have a great impact in America." Cahan was clearly dazzled by Ben-Gurion and described him for *Forward* readers as "a genuine labor leader and not one of the dime-store variety (three for a *groschen*) . . . a man of strong character." This last phrase Ben-Gurion proudly recorded in Hebrew in his diary, underlining it for good measure.

After his return to New York in November, Cahan continued to publish articles about his visit. In "Flowering of Palestine Depends on the Welfare of the Arabs," he noted that "the Arab question is closely connected with the economic problem of the Jewish settlement in Palestine." The problem could be solved, he said, by "providing a living for the Muslim population. Wider economic opportunities and higher wages for farmers and workers, as well as more business for merchants, with the Jews playing a leading role in the improvement of conditions—this will shatter the anti-Semitic propaganda." While he was in Palestine, he had made a point of meeting with the secretary of what he called the "anti-Jewish Committee of the Effendis." He described their anti-Semitic propaganda as "obviously a constant hazard." But following the lead of the still strongly pro-British Labor Zionist leadership, he wrote that "as long as Great Britain retains the so-called Mandate I believe that there is no cause for concern. The leaders of the anti-Jewish propaganda, from their viewpoint, are very serious, more than I credited them. But on the other hand, my stay in Palestine eradicated any belief I had in the virtues of their cause from a moral perspective."

Cahan also weighed in on the ideological differences between the Labor Zionists and the Revisionist Zionists. He called the latter "extremist chauvinists." The Jews deserve a home in Palestine, he wrote, "not because this was once their home, but principally because of their splendid work and self-sacrifice, by means of which they are seeking to turn barren tracts into fertile land, and the miserable, decayed, and primitive existence that characterizes the country into a land where life is in keeping with modern civilization." The future of the Jews in Palestine, he argued, depended on their success, and rather presciently, he predicted that if they succeed in realizing the major part of their program, "then their sense of self-reliance will not be damaged even if Britain leaves Palestine to its fate."

In 1923, two years before Cahan made his trip to Palestine, Vladimir

Jabotinsky—a Russian Jewish journalist, soldier, novelist, and poet and the most controversial of the Zionist visionaries—published in Berlin, in the Russian-language journal *Rassvyet*, an essay about the Zionist enterprise, "The Iron Wall."* Both Jabotinsky and Cahan were literary men touched by history, and both were caught between political and literary careers. But the difference in their political worldviews was striking. Cahan's was the worldview of socialism, labor activism, and anti-Communism, while Jabotinsky's was Zionism and the fate of the Jews of Europe. Although the issue pulled Jabotinsky away from his literary career, he used his skills as a writer and orator to marshal a movement.

"The Iron Wall" would become his most enduring essay about the Zionist enterprise. Many considered him an enemy of the Arabs, but he denied it at the outset, saying that his emotional relationship to Arabs was, as it was to all other peoples, "polite indifference." The expulsion of the Arabs from Palestine was "utterly impossible," he wrote. "There will always be *two* nations in Palestine." He identified with the idea—endorsed at the Third All-Russian Zionist Convention, held in 1906 in Helsinki—that bringing Jews to Palestine was not the purpose of the Jewish state but the precondition for establishing it.

Jabotinsky ridiculed the idea that there could be a "voluntary agreement between ourselves and the Palestine Arabs. Not now, nor in the prospective future." History showed no example of a country being settled "with the consent of the native population." The inhabitants "have always stubbornly resisted . . . whether the colonists behaved decently or not." He rejected the assessement, made by some, that "the Arabs are either fools, whom we can deceive by masking our real aims, or that they are corrupt and can be bribed to abandon to us their claim to priority in Palestine, in return for cultural and economic advantages." On the

* Jabotinsky's essay was also published in an English translation in South Africa's *Jewish Herald* on November 26, 1937; that version of the essay is available at http://www.danielpipes.org/3510/the-iron-wall-we-and-the-arabs.

contrary, "we may tell them whatever we like about the innocence of our aims, watering them down and sweetening them with honeyed words to make them palatable, but they know what we want, as well as we know what they do not want. They feel at least the same instinctive jealous love of Palestine, as the old Aztecs felt for ancient Mexico, and the Sioux for their rolling prairies. To imagine, as our Arabophiles do, that they will voluntarily consent to the realisation of Zionism in return for the moral and material conveniences which the Jewish colonist brings with him, is a childish notion."

This "Arabophile" view reflected, he said, "a kind of contempt for the Arab people; it means they despise the Arab race, which they regard as a corrupt mob that can be bought and sold, and are willing to give up their fatherland for a good railway system." Some individual Arabs might "take bribes," he suggested, but "every native population in the world resists colonists as long as it has the slightest hope of being able to rid itself of the danger of being colonised." An Arab editor had said he believed that "Palestine has a very large potential absorptive capacity, meaning that there is room for a great many Jews in the country without displacing a single Arab." But a Jewish majority and a Jewish state would become inevitable, the editor went on to say, "and the future of the Arab minority would depend on the goodwill of the Jews. . . . Zionists want only one thing, Jewish immigration; and this Jewish immigration is what the Arabs do not want."

So, Jabotinsky concluded, there was "no likelihood of any voluntary agreement being reached" with the Arabs. Hence "those who regard such an agreement as a condition sine qua non for Zionism may as well say 'non' and withdraw from Zionism. *Zionist colonization must either stop, or else proceed regardless of the native population.*" He denied that an agreement with Arabs is impossible—only that "what is impossible is a voluntary agreement." And then he wrote the famous words: "As long as the Arabs feel that there is the least hope of getting rid of us, they will refuse to give up this hope in return for either kind words or for bread and butter, because they are not a rabble, but a living people. And when a living people yields in matters of such a vital character it is only when there is no longer any hope of getting rid of us, because they can make no breach in the iron wall. Not till then will they drop their extremist leaders whose watchword is 'Never!' And the leadership will pass to the moderate groups, who will approach us with a proposal that we should both agree to mutual concessions. Then we may expect them to discuss honestly practical questions, such as a guarantee against Arab displacement, or equal rights for Arab citizens, or Arab national integrity."

Jabotinsky ended on an optimistic note that the Jews "will be found ready to give them satisfactory guarantees, so that both peoples can live together in peace, like good neighbours. But the only way to obtain such an agreement, is the iron wall, which is to say a strong power in Palestine that is not amenable to any Arab pressure. In other words, the only way to reach an agreement in the future is to abandon all idea of seeking an agreement at present."

Jabotinsky's stark assessment of the coming struggle was far from Cahan's sense that the tension in the land was between different sectors of Jewish society: between the socialists and the capitalists, the agrarians and the urbanists, the collectivists and the individualists. After brushing aside the "chauvinists," Cahan focused on the cooperative settlements and the ins and outs of the Communist bodies in Palestine. The future depended on the success of industry, he said, but if Palestine ever became an industrialized country, "the fine things we see in it now are doomed to vanish." What Cahan called the "tragedy of the entire situation" was not relations with the Arabs but the Zionists' attempt to blend two irreconcilable opposites: the splendidly idealistic farming collectives in the Jezreel Valley and the highly industrialized urban economy that would be needed to make possible significant immigration.

If, in his reporting from Palestine, Cahan seemed to veer from wide-eyed exhilaration and reportorial earnestness to armchair philosophizing and socialist condescension, he certainly ignited a debate among his colleagues at the *Forward* and, presumably, among its quarter-million daily readers. But he had succeeded in creating a newspaper flexible enough to accommodate a no-holds-barred debate on what he now, belatedly, comprehended was a defining issue of Jewish identity in the twentieth century. And he opened this debate at a time when mainstream American Jewish organizations evinced little interest in it.

A long, mocking piece by Ben-Zion Hoffman, writing in the *Forward* under the name Zivion, began: "Comrade Abe Cahan declared that despite the fact that the work being accomplished in Palestine aroused considerable emotions in him, he has not become a Zionist. If this is indeed so, I have nothing to argue about. . . . I will not try to persuade Comrade Cahan that he is a Zionist when he himself admits that he is not." Hundreds of words later, many of them excoriating Cahan for his new passion, Zivion concludes that in the same way that messianic Judaism exists because of the Messiah's nonappearance, "Zionism likewise will continue to exist, for the reason that it cannot be realized."

Then Max Pine weighed in with a long attack on Zivion. Pine conceded that "we are not Zionists" in Zivion's sense of a movement that wanted to restore the throne of King David and bring all Jews to Israel, he said. But "we are Jews!" and therefore "have something to discuss on the subject of Palestine." Cahan's reporting "had only deepened our sympathy," and one day "a great change will take place in the minds and hearts of our workers regarding their attitude toward our brothers, the workers of Palestine."

Against charges that Cahan had abandoned the principles of international socialism, B. Charney Vladeck defended him, proclaiming that a close reading of "all the telegrams and articles sent by Comrade Cahan from Palestine" enabled one to conclude that "the affair between Madam Zion and Comrade Cahan is up in the air." Cahan, he said, "did not go beyond making a few compliments. For a couple of charming remarks you don't get the electric chair." As long as Cahan's position remained "Palestine *also*" and not "Palestine *alone*," Vladeck had no problem with his boss's Zionist enthusiasm. Then he spent a few thousand words reiterating Cahan's arguments, concluding that the socialist position should be not "Palestine alone" but "Palestine also."

Some prominent secular American Jews, such as future Supreme Court justice Louis Brandeis, had come to Zionism earlier than Cahan; Brandeis became formally involved with the movement in 1913. If Cahan was lagging behind him and other Zionists, he was running ahead of important sectors of the American Jewish community. Not until the rise of Nazism in Germany in the 1930s would the Reform movement depart from its long hostility to the idea of a Jewish nationality and officially come out in favor of Zionism. Before World War II even the Orthodox Agudath Israel of America declined to support political Zionism on religious principles; it played an increasingly involved role in the Israeli government after statehood was declared in 1948. The American Council for Judaism, which opposed the idea of Jewish nationhood, didn't even get incorporated until 1942.

Within the pages of the *Forward*, the debate raged well into the spring of 1926. Scores of other publications followed its progress, reprinting and commenting on the impassioned articles that were running in the paper. It is hard to think of another editor in the history of American journalism who permitted such brutal articles to be published about himself in his own newspaper. Cahan finally did call a halt to the feud by running a series of "summing up" articles, which appeared in the paper beginning May 6. "I am not a Zionist," he wrote, "but I have never defined myself as an opponent of the Palestinian movement. Furthermore, I have always shown sympathy toward the idealists in Palestine, even though I did not believe at all in their ideology or in their program. My visit to Palestine increased my sympathy significantly. I returned from my visit and I am still not a Zionist, just as before. On the other hand, my feelings have changed, positively, toward the socialist segment of the Zionist movement. Had I known about and understood the communes and the Histadrut, with all its ramifications and enterprises, I would have treated it previously with far more friendly warmth."

It was a rare admission of error.

No sooner had Cahan closed the *Forward*'s debate on Zionism than he began planning a trip to the Soviet Union, which took place in 1927 and might be described as the reverse of his tour of Palestine. He had visited Palestine as the head of a movement that was skeptical about Zionism, only to be surprised, even floored, at the positive things that were happening there. That visit set in motion a long, slow turn that would cause the *Forward* to joyously greet the partition of Palestine in 1947 as one of the most significant events in the long history of the Jews. In the case of his trip to the Soviet Union, Cahan went as a representative of a movement that had been overjoyed at the downfall of the Romanovs and the rise of democratic socialism in Russia, only to become increasingly disillusioned by the Bolshevism that replaced it. What he saw and personally experienced there solidified his contempt for Communism, and his determination to fight it in the pages of his newspaper obtained for the rest of his life.

David Shub, Cahan's sometime deputy, was put in charge at the paper while the editor was away. Before Cahan left, he later recalled, rumors had it that the *Forward* was "going to be pro-Soviet." Cahan, trying to keep to his standards of unbiased reporting, told Shub that while he was in the Soviet Union, Shub "should be discreet" in his editorial writing and "avoid any themes that are critical of Soviet Russia."

For more than a month, Cahan visited Moscow, Leningrad, Kiev, Odessa, Minsk, and other cities as well. As with the Palestine trip, the *Forward* widely publicized his journey. "No American journalist is better qualified to understand and interpret Soviet Russia than Abraham Cahan," the paper proclaimed in an advance advertisement. "He combines a thorough knowledge of the Russian language and literature with a profound sympathy for the Russian masses." Cahan claimed that "I went everywhere as a Russian like all other Russians. For the most part no one knew that I was a guest," but that is doubtful. He neither dressed nor talked like an ordinary Russian, and ordinary Russians didn't arrive at agricultural settlements in automobiles, as Cahan did, accompanied by officials from the Joint Distribution Committee.

Shub recalled that Cahan "decided from the very beginning not to have any interviews with any of the Soviet bigwigs, members of the

Soviet government, or leaders of the Communist Party." He was given leave to travel wherever he wanted, but almost every day a former labor editor of the *Forward*, using the name Max Goldberg, would call on Cahan at his hotel. Goldberg had returned to Russia after the 1917 revolution and had been, as a Bundist, mayor of the city of Berdichev. "In the summer of 1918, however, he betrayed the Bund and became a secret member of the Communist Party," according to Shub. Another frequent visitor to Cahan's hotel was a man named George Vishniak. Vishniak had been a member of Daniel De Leon's Socialist Labor Party and a leader of the Cloak Makers Union in New York, before switching allegiances and becoming an employee of the Soviet government. "Cahan told me later," recalled Shub, "that he had wondered how come that no matter what city he was in, at whatever hotel, he would encounter Vishniak the next day, who happened to be on 'Soviet business' in the exact same place." Cahan became convinced that Vishniak's "business" was to keep tabs on him and find out whom he was seeing.

The *Forward*'s Moscow correspondent, Z. Vendrov, also visited Cahan frequently; Vendrov was considered a Soviet sympathizer, if not a party member. After Cahan returned from Russia, Shub noted, "Vendrov was still the *Forward* correspondent, and when I sometimes changed the lead of an article of his, he would write to Cahan that under no circumstances should his articles be edited, because that could lead to serious reprisal."

When Cahan made an expedition to the Jewish colonies of Crimea, he was accompanied by Dr. Joseph Rosen, the director of the American Jewish Joint Agricultural Corporation, a program under the umbrella of the American Jewish Joint Distribution Committee. Rosen was personally opposed to Bolshevism but managed to avoid criticizing the Soviets; the mood of fear and self-suppression was everywhere evident.

The highlight of Cahan's trip was a visit to the revolutionary Vera Figner, whom he had long admired and whose memoir he had published in the *Forward*. Born in 1852 into a well-to-do family, Figner had trained as a doctor in Switzerland (Russia didn't allow women to attend medical school at that time) and returned to Russia to work as a paramedic and an antigovernment agent. As a member of the radical terrorist group Narodnaya Volya, she had helped plan two of the assassination attempts on Alexander II in 1881. When the group was betrayed by one of its members,* Figner was arrested, tried along with other members of Narodnaya Volya, and sentenced to death. Her sentence was eventually commuted to life in prison. She served for twenty years, plus two additional years of internal exile, before being allowed to leave Russia in 1906. In Europe she traveled widely and advocated for political prisoners in Russia. Her autobiography, *Memoirs of a Revolutionist*, published after she returned to Russia in 1915, made her an international celebrity. It is still in print.

In the years after her return, Figner had grown disillusioned with the revolution, criticizing the Soviet dictatorship until it drove her into silence. Introducing Cahan to a group of surviving members of Narodnaya Volya, she referred to him, sotto voce, as "one of us." As Cahan listened intently, this aging band of revolutionaries expressed their opposition to the Soviet regime. To protect them, Cahan did not write about this meeting in the *Forward*, but he confided to Shub that it was "one of the most moving moments" in his life. It only increased his contempt for the Soviet regime.

The America to which Cahan returned in 1927 was hardly concerned about repression in the Soviet Union. The country was busy toasting its newest hero, the aviator Charles Lindbergh, who had just completed the first solo nonstop transatlantic flight, from New York to Paris. The economy was booming, and unemployment, which had peaked at 21 percent in 1921, had fallen to a little more than 3 percent. The anarchists Ferdinando Nicola Sacco and Bartolomeo Vanzetti were executed in August of that year, after a highly politicized murder trial and in the face of widespread opposition to the verdict among the Jewish labor unions. It

* Sergey Degayev, a police informer who later changed his name to Alexander Pell, eventually moved to America and founded the school of engineering at the University of South Dakota.

was to the growing tensions in Palestine that Cahan would next turn his attention.

As European Jews continued to immigrate to Palestine in record numbers, the Arabs of Palestine responded with increasing fury. In the late summer of 1929, tensions were running high as false rumors that Jews were massacring Arabs in Jerusalem and seizing control of Muslim holy places swept through Arab communities. On August 17 a Jewish boy was stabbed to death in Jerusalem, a crime that a week later led to a catastrophe: a massacre in Hebron, home to the Tomb of the Patriarchs, where Abraham and Sarah, Isaac and Rebecca, and Jacob and Leah are buried. Jews had lived harmoniously with Arabs in Hebron for centuries. After fleeting warnings of trouble, the killing started on Saturday, August 24. During the "affray"—the word that *The New York Sun* used in its editorial to refer to the massacre—sixty-seven of Hebron's Jews perished.

The *Forward* published an editorial on August 29, referring to the massacre as "The Third Destruction," intentionally linking it in significance to the destruction, in 586 B.C.E. and 70 C.E., of the First and Second Temples in Jerusalem. The attacks on Jews had been made by "savage Arab masses, incited by their own leaders and permeated with dark chauvinism—the root of all wars, of all misfortunes." Clearly understanding the scale and significance of the story, Cahan returned to Palestine to report on it himself. The confidence that he had expressed back in 1925 in the ability of the British Mandatory authorities to keep peace between the Jews and the Arabs had proved to be overly sanguine.

Cahan's editorial, the *Forward* would observe nearly seventy years later, was noteworthy "not only because it marked a milestone in the *Forward*'s swing behind the idea of a Jewish state but also because of the long view it took, drawing distinctions between what was happening in Palestine and what happened at the massacres at Kishinev and Proskurov." In the Russian pogroms, the 1929 editorial declared, Jews had been "literally slaughtered like oxen in a butcher shop." But in Eretz Yisrael "Jews put up resistance wherever they could. Even in the Slobodka yeshiva in Hebron, the boys fought back and built fortifications with tables and chairs." The details of the struggle, the editorial confidently predicted, would include examples "of great heroism and self-sacrifice" that would "fill everyone with pride at the combative spirit and courage of Jewish youth." The editorial was startling not only for its support of the religious Jews, but also for its break with the left, which sided with the Arabs at Hebron. The Communist newspaper *Freiheit* initially supported the Jews of Hebron but then promptly fell in with the Soviet line, calling the pogrom a revolt against British and Zionist imperialism. The *Freiheit* even organized a pro-Arab, anti-Jewish demonstration at Union Square.

The *Freiheit*'s posturing infuriated Cahan, but it proved a boon to the *Forward*, as readers decamped from the *Freiheit* and switched their allegiance to the *Forward*; so did three of the *Freiheit*'s important writers, H. Leivick, Menachem Boraisho, and Avrom Reisin. Cahan filled the *Forward*'s pages with letters from angry *Freiheit* readers, some of them accusing the *Freiheit* of treason. The debate over Zionism that Cahan launched in the pages of the *Forward* had, however awkwardly, put the *Forward* on a trajectory toward growing support for the Jewish state. The Abraham Cahan who was about to lead the *Forward* into its fourth decade was a different person from the impassioned revolutionary who arrived in New York in 1882. There was only one other major issue on which Cahan needed to find his way home.

12

Cahan returned from Palestine in October 1929, just as the stock market was crashing and America was plunging into an economic depression that would last for just about a decade and leave millions unemployed. In its most severe months, more than 25 percent of American job seekers were out of work. That same year Jay Lovestone was ousted as the head of the Communist Party USA on orders from Joseph Stalin. In the wake of his feud with Stalin, Lovestone vowed to bring down the entire Soviet Union. As a place to weave his plots, Lovestone was given a cubicle at the office of the International Ladies' Garment Workers' Union, which was the *Forward*'s arm in the labor movement. From that cubicle he would forge an alliance with David Dubinsky, president of the ILGWU and, later, with James Jesus Angleton, the chief of counterintelligence at the CIA.

By taking in Lovestone, the *Forward* was providing seed money for one of the greatest, if least-known, efforts in the struggle against Communism: the drive, after World War II, to organize throughout liberated Europe free trade unions that were answerable not to a government, a corporation, or a political party but to a vote of their members. These unions operated under the umbrella of the International Confederation of Free Trade Unions, based in Brussels; they battled the Communist-influenced unions that were under the influence of the World Federation of Trade Unions, based in Prague. At the end of World War II, Lovestone sent to Europe a young organizer named Irving Brown, who helped break the Communists' control of the Western European docks, enabling aid from the Marshall Plan to arrive. A generation later he brought in labor union members to help break the effort of Communist-backed students to topple France's Fifth Republic. It was with Brown's International

Confederation of Free Trade Unions that there eventually affiliated a little-known free trade union in Gdansk, Poland, named Solidarity, which would later rise up and crack Soviet rule in the East Bloc.

All this, however, lay in the future. In the 1930s Cahan had come to recognize that the Yiddish-speaking labor unionists who read the *Forward* needed to start moving away from the Socialist Party, and to give them a way out the *Forward* helped establish the American Labor Party. By 1934 a rift had developed within the Socialist Party: a radical and pacifist faction had developed, led by Norman Thomas, that unlike the *Forward* was prepared to work with various affiliates and fronts for the Communist Party. The American Labor Party endorsed Franklin Roosevelt in the 1936 election, enabling the *Forward*'s socialist readers to vote to reelect the president without also voting for the corrupt, Tammany Hall–backed Democratic Party machine. Eventually, however, the American Labor Party was also infiltrated by Communists, and by the 1950s its membership had migrated over to the newly established Liberal Party of New York. It ceased functioning in 1956.

Such a short summary skims over a story that is worth a book of its own,* one chapter of which would no doubt cover the growing distance between Cahan and Vladeck. In addition to being the general manager of the *Forward* for twenty years, Vladeck was also a public figure in his own right and a particularly compelling orator. Far more engaged politically than Cahan, Vladeck was a member of the New York City Council and played a leading role in building low-cost housing for workers in the city. He was well to Cahan's left.

Vladeck doubtless aspired to succeed Cahan as editor of the paper, and it was widely assumed that he would. But Vladeck was, at bottom,

* One contemporary writer, Simeon Strunsky, once summarized the complexities of labor politics at the time with the following report: "It seemed that in Philetus' district the Republican candidate for Congress was a Communist who had carried the Republican primary and the Socialist primary but who had been defeated in the Communist primary. Against him ran a Socialist who had carried the Democratic primary and Communist primary, but had lost the Socialist."

a politician; Cahan was, at bottom, a newspaper editor. Their private correspondence offers glimpses of the disdain with which Cahan dealt with Vladeck, assigning him chores while he was off on one grand trip or another. According to David Shub, Cahan thought Vladeck "absent minded and too busy with other things, and not really capable of managing the *Forward*."

In October 1938, Vladeck died of a heart attack at the age of fifty-two. By then things had grown so distant between the two men that Cahan fled New York to avoid attending his colleague's funeral. "The minute Cahan learned of Vladeck's death," Shub wrote, "he ran off to Lakewood because he didn't know how else he could not be at Vladeck's funeral and not speak, and he did not want to do that." The funeral, held in front of the *Forward* Building, attracted a half-million mourners, including New York governor Herbert Lehman.

This story illuminates not only an aloofness but a certain caginess, even cowardice, in Cahan that conflicts with his popular reputation. We get another glimpse of this side of the man in Shub's account of another story, from sometime in late 1937 or early 1938. Shub was writing a column in the *Forward* called "The Most Interesting and Important Events in the Socialist World" and regularly read the European socialist press as well as *Pravda*, the official newspaper of the Soviet Communist Party. He began to notice intimations that Stalin was, as Shub put it, "getting ready to join Hitler against the West." Shub found the possibility unthinkable, so shocking as barely to be uttered.

One day, however, while they were sitting in the Garden Cafeteria, an eatery on the corner of Rutgers and East Broadway that was the regular haunt of the *Forward* crowd and other Yiddish journalists of the Lower East Side, Shub mentioned the story to Cahan.

"Are you going to write about that?" Cahan snapped.

Shub said he had just finished writing the column.

"But then you must write just the opposite," Cahan responded, "that the Moscow leaders were never so hostile to Nazi Germany as now." He added that "Duranty is in Moscow, and he knows what's going on in the

Kremlin circles." Walter Duranty was the *New York Times* leg in Moscow and notoriously sympathetic to Stalin. The *Forward* had long since abandoned hope that Stalin might emerge as a more democratic figure than Lenin.

"Duranty writes what Stalin wants him to write," Shub replied.

Cahan referred to one of Duranty's recent dispatches to show Shub that he was wrong. He "used to sit against the wall with his face toward the door, and I would sit opposite him," Shub wrote, and so Shub failed to notice that at a table nearby were a few colleagues from *Der Tag*, a Yiddish daily less to the left and higher-brow than the *Forward*.

This may, or may not, explain why Cahan was so cagey. Was he trying to protect a scoop? Shub, in any event, was unable to hold back, and replied, "You're reading only what Duranty says in the *Times*, but I read the European Socialist press and the Soviet papers and magazines."

Cahan did not answer. But several days later Shub discovered that Cahan had come into the office early and "with his own hands" had removed key text and "destroyed the type and torn up the proofs." Knowing that Shub might try to publish the piece in another paper, the Bundist *Der Veker*, he had also taken the manuscript.

Whether Cahan did this because he was angry at Shub for setting into type such an explosive story without first consulting with him, or because he just did not want to believe that the Soviet government, however much he hated it, was about to join forces with the Nazis, we may never know. We can only speculate about Cahan's motives. My own conclusion is that the first possibility is correct; he was, at bottom, a careful and controlling editor who wanted to play the scoop on his own terms. It was not one of Cahan's finer moments, but he would no doubt keep it in mind as the *Forward* covered World War II using the methods that had made his paper great: gathering the news, however dark, at its sources in Russia and throughout Europe and interpreting it in light of Jewish history.

The roots of Cahan's next great battle extended back a few decades. On May 17, 1911, Cahan had published in the *Forward* a piece attacking

Jewish *apikorsim*, or learned Jewish apostates. He likened *apikorsim* to the character in Turgenev's novel *Rudin* who hates all women because his wife betrayed him. "So it is with the 'apikores'—when it comes to his former religion," Cahan wrote. "His ability to think no longer functions. He can only deny and mock in anger. . . . Various peoples celebrate their holidays with dance, song, and special folk theater. Would the Jewish heretic consider it an insult if a Jew went to hear these songs, see these dances? It would not even enter his mind to question that. Yet when it comes to Jewish holiday scenes like the Passover Seder, the 'apikores' becomes enraged. The free-thinking Jew, naturally, won't wear a kittel, read a Hagaddah, observe all the religious ceremonies; yet on that night, he might long for the scenes of his childhood, the scenes of the nest in which he was born."

The pogroms that swept through Russia during the late nineteenth century and the early twentieth were at least partially responsible for Cahan's change of heart about the value of Jewish traditions. "The place of the 'free-thinker' has become occupied by the 'freer' thinker, and the pogroms have awakened a feeling of self-respect in the enlightened Russian Jew," he wrote.

> When the pogroms began, enlightenment began to spread among Russian Jews. The number of enlightened, progressive Jews grew quickly. The learned person took the place of the type who nourished himself with a few Hebrew pamphlets; circumstances led well-read, developed thinkers and the thinking modern Jew to the conviction and feeling that a Jew was also a person, and that for a Jew to be ashamed of Jews was not only inappropriate, but also unproductive. In the first years of the revolutionary struggle in Russia, the Jewish revolutionaries put their lives in danger working for the spiritual development of the Russian peasantry. They "went to the people," as they say in Russian. That Jews were also a people never occurred to anyone.

Eventually, Cahan noted, "people got around to realizing this," but the *apikorsim* "continue to advocate the older brand of heresy" and "usually also stick to the old position about the association of the Jewish socialist with the Jewish people. . . .

> It often turns out that this same type believes that German socialism can concern itself with the German people and Russian socialists with Russian peasants and workers, but a Jewish socialist who interests himself in Jewish problems is, according to them, a traitor to his ideals. Too often this question about the feelings of Jews toward Jews becomes mixed up with the question of religion. That is, as soon as a Jewish melody interests someone, they are abandoning themselves to superstition. You can sing a Russian tune, but a Jewish song has no "right of residence" in your aesthetic heart.

Cahan acknowledged that there was a time, "in the first days of Russian nihilism," when it might have been reasonable for a thinking person to conclude that "it was senseless to display any feelings—no matter what feelings. . . . Then, a Jew didn't dare reveal a special affinity for Jews, but that was not a contradiction. Then, a person's own mother was no better than a stranger." But those "infantile times" had passed, Cahan declared.

> It has long been acknowledged that even the greatest revolutionaries' souls are not made of iron, and that his mother is dearer to him than your mother. Today, if you demand of a Jewish socialist that a pogrom in Kishinev should not interest him more than a pogrom against the Armenians, it would sound like one of those exclusionary laws from which Jews are used to suffering. Yes, we can confess that our mother is closer to us than a stranger. We can (or we ought to be able to, at least) confess that Jews are, naturally, closer to us than other people.

The essay must rank as one of the most remarkable of Cahan's career, though it would not be considered so were he himself not such an avowed freethinker, the phrase Cahan long favored for describing his religious views—or rather his lack of them. He had started describing himself in this way long before he left Russia, probably at the same time as he stopped laying tefillin, the phylacteries (leather boxes containing scriptural passages) that are strapped on the head and left arm during weekday morning prayer. Yet the tug of Sinai that he felt so strongly as a youngster clearly began to reassert itself as the years passed. Late in Cahan's career it triggered his bitter and dramatic showdown with the *Forward*'s most famous writer over the laws of Sinai and the issue of apostasy.

Sholem Asch was not just any apostate. Born in 1880 at Kutno, Poland, into a Hasidic family and traditionally educated, he became attracted by secularism at a young age and left home to make his way as a writer in Warsaw. In 1900 he began publishing short stories, plays, and novels about Jewish life in Europe, Palestine, and America; they brought him international acclaim and an honored place in the pantheon of noted Yiddish writers. Settling in New York in 1914, he became a regular contributor to the *Forward* and by 1920 had become so famous that a twelve-volume edition of his collected works was published on the occasion of his fortieth birthday. In 1932 he was elected honorary president of the Yiddish PEN, an international writers' organization, and in 1933 he appeared on the short list for the Nobel Prize in literature. In 1936 the critic Ludwig Lewisohn named him one of the ten greatest living Jews—the only writer on a list that included Albert Einstein, Sigmund Freud, Martin Buber, and Louis Brandeis.

In the spring of 1938, as conditions for Europe's Jews deteriorated and war loomed, Asch, then in France, began sending to the *Forward* chapters from his novel-in-progress, which he had entitled *Der Man Fun Natseres* (*The Nazarene*). The novel was a retelling of the story of Jesus, depicting him as an observant Jew. Asch, who was best known for what the journalist Ellen Umansky calls "sepia-tinged portrayals of shtetl life" as well as for sweeping family sagas, had been toying with the idea of a novel about Jesus since 1908, when he made his first trip to Palestine. "Since that time I have never thought of Judaism or Christianity separately," Asch told a reporter for the *New York Herald Tribune*. "For me it is one culture and one civilization, on which all our peace, our security, and our freedom are dependent."

Umansky speculates that there were "other, perhaps less conscious factors at play." After his *Three Cities* (1929–31), a sprawling, multigenerational novel that earned him his greatest acclaim ("One of the most richly creative works of fiction that have appeared in our day," trumpeted *The New York Times*), Asch "yearned for another success, one that would broaden his readership beyond its traditional base." His biographer Ben Siegel maintains that Asch had long coveted literary accolades and calculated that the subject of Jesus might be attractive to the Nobel committee.

The Nazarene is a complex work in which figures in twentieth-century Warsaw turn out to have lived previous lives in the time of Jesus. One of the characters is an anti-Semitic history professor, Pan Viadomsky, who had a past life as the right-hand man to Pontius Pilate, the prefect who presided at Jesus's trial. Viadomsky's Jewish assistant turns out also to have had a past life, as a rabbi who witnessed Jesus's last days. Bizarre though the plot is, it is a testament to Asch's storytelling powers that he could write a compelling narrative that re-creates the sounds, smells, and other sensory features of Jerusalem in the time of the Second Temple. His goal, as Umansky characterizes it, was "to reclaim Jesus" with an "earth-bound Rabbi Yeshua ben Joseph" who is "unquestionably grounded in his Jewish faith." Umansky puts it this way:

> Asch introduces us to a "lean and hungry-looking" Jesus preaching to the poor fishermen by the harbor, with his dark beard and traditional sidelocks, clad in a tallis with the "ritualistic fringes hanging down almost to the ground." This is a rabbi who followed Hillel's teachings, who was well-liked and respected by his fellow clergymen, who declared while speaking from a tiny synagogue pulpit (with his mother, Miriam, proudly watching with the other women in the balcony) that he had come "not to destroy the Law and prophets, but to fulfill them."

None of this is necessarily a sign of apostasy, and it can even be seen as something to the contrary, as a Judaization of Jesus, of a kind that has, in recent times, become part of mainstream Jesus scholarship. What Cahan divined in the general tenor of the book, however, was that as Asch made Christianity feel Jewish, he was simultaneously negating Jewish particularity. The idea that there exists a "Judeo-Christian" religious tradition emerged in America only after World War II, as a response to the Holocaust and to prewar Christian anti-Semitism; it was an attempt to fight the religious marginalization of the Jews but at the same time maintain the validity of two distinct religious theologies. Asch, however, explicitly stated that he did not see the two religions as separate. That was what enraged Cahan. Not only did he refuse to publish the novel, he demanded that Asch destroy his manuscript, which Asch of course refused to do. Instead, he arranged for its translation and publication in English. Critical reception for *The Nazarene*, which was translated by Maurice Samuel and published in 1939 by G. P. Putnam, was largely positive. It was praised by Alfred Kazin in *The New Republic*, by Clifton Fadiman in *The New Yorker*, and by Philip Rahv in *The Nation*.

It was a remarkable situation, distinguished Jewish critics failing to comprehend Asch's defection. That role fell to the editor of the *Forward*, who launched an all-out literary war against Asch and his novel. Other Yiddish literary figures joined him. The *Forward* also published Asch's "My Response," in which Asch confronted the criticism that rained down on him from within the Jewish community. He also defended his views in a 1940 article for *The Atlantic Monthly*. The controversy stretched into the early years of World War II, a war against the Jewish people in which Cahan and the *Forward* were engaged in the defense of both America and the Jews.

Asch's next book, *What I Believe*, published in 1941, was his attempt to explain to his critics that he did in fact value Judaism. It not only failed to appease Cahan but also inspired him to publish a book-length response, which he called *Sholem Asch's New Direction*. He began by insisting he had "never had any unfriendly feelings of a personal nature toward Sholem Asch." They had known each other "for more than thirty years and during this entire time nothing serious enough ever occurred to destroy our friendship." Cahan noted that he had even recently praised Asch's novel *The Song of the Valley*. The current controversy, he said, was "of an entirely spiritual and Jewish-social nature," and he confessed that Asch's new direction "has caused me heartache"—a heartache in which, he insisted, he was not alone.

Cahan took pains to point out that he himself was "absolutely not religious." On the contrary, he described himself as "a free-thinker in the fullest sense of the word, as are most radical people." At the same time, he wrote respectfully and even defensively of Jewish practice, noting that there are "a substantial number of religious Jews in America" and that "kashruth [Jewish dietary law] is observed by a large percentage of Jews." He noted that "almost all Jews observe circumcision" but acknowledged that "in most cases this is considered to be more of a national custom than a religious one." He asserted that Jews "have a well-rooted respect for our faith because it is that of our parents and forefathers. We honor the Jewish faith as a tradition of our people." He called the feeling a "deep and intimate one."

As regards Christianity, Cahan maintained:

> We respect similar feelings among Christians because to them their religion is also one of the traditions of their forefathers. However, their religion has no relevance to us as Jews. In such liberal countries as America and England, Christians do not expect us to accept their religion. . . .
>
> The Christian religion is foreign to us as Jews and will remain so. It can be no other way. However, this has nothing to do with our attitude toward Christians as citizens and human beings and with their attitude toward us. A Jew remains a Jew even when he is an atheist. However, he ceases to be a Jew when he accepts another religion. One cannot believe in two religions simultaneously.

Cahan said that he tried to deal with Asch respectfully and complained that Asch, in his eight-column response to his critics, "barely touched on the real question," devoting barely a third of a column "to anything which had any connection at all to the main topic." The rest, Cahan said, "was devoted to complaints about his critics." What Cahan called the "actual subject" was:

> The fact that Jews do not recognize Jesus as a holy and godly man and Sholem Asch does recognize him as such; that Jews do not recognize the Holy Book of the Christian Religion (the New Testament) and Sholem Asch does. Not only does he recognize he who is considered to be the founder of the Christian religion but he exhibits great enthusiasm for him and places him above Moses and the Jewish Prophets. . . .
>
> During the almost two thousand years of the existence of the Christian religion millions of Jews sacrificed their lives because they refused to accept it. He, Sholem Asch, propagandizes in favor of this belief in *The Nazarene*, in American newspapers and in a French weekly publication, as well as in his book, *What I Believe*. In many places in his two books and articles, he sharply exhibits his Christianity more clearly than even a bishop could express.

To read these words in the cold light of history is to sense a kind of primal scream. Then Cahan turned on the critics in the secular press who gave the book positive reviews; they were, he said, obviously unfamiliar with the centuries of Christian persecution of Jews who refused to accept Christ as the Messiah. The critics in the Jewish newspapers, he said, "unanimously tore this book apart," and "more than one article" appeared in "every Jewish newspaper in New York . . . each of them with negative comment."

"Most American Christians" he said dismissively, "considered this book to be a belletristic work, nothing more" or as that of "a literary dreamer, free from any other direction, bent on ambition." It may also have rankled Cahan that many of those who gave the book a literary imprimatur in the secular press were members of the Jewish literary elite who did not see fit to review his own novels with the same enthusiasm. The remainder of the book is Cahan's evisceration, sentence by sentence, of Asch's work. Cahan accused him of relying solely on the New Testament and of being disingenuous about his belief that Jesus is the Messiah.

Cahan ridicules Asch's and Putnam's use, in publicity materials for *The Nazarene*, of a blurb in support of the book from Albert Einstein. Cahan concluded that Einstein had never read the book but was merely praising Asch's writing in general, and in any event, he mocked the suggestion that Einstein's opinion amounted to much because "Professor Albert Einstein is an absolutely outspoken atheist. He believes in neither any god nor godliness as the words are commonly understood. . . . That a heretic should endorse a book that is full of enthusiasm for a godly man and the miracles he performed makes about as much sense as saying two times two is thirteen." Cahan was particularly galled by Asch's suggestion that, as Cahan characterizes it, "every religious Jew . . . is awaiting Jesus' arrival as the Messiah." Wrote Cahan, "One's blood boils when reading these words!"

Asch was hurt by Cahan's campaign against him, not only personally but professionally. Thereafter the pages at all the Yiddish papers were closed to him—except for the mouthpiece of Stalinist Communism, the *Freiheit*. One *Forward* writer, Melech Epstein, recalled encountering Asch at the Garden Cafeteria while all of this was going on. "Asch," Epstein would later write, "spoke like a deeply wounded man, and could not conceal his apprehension that Cahan was succeeding in isolating him. 'Cahan will not drive me away from Jewish life and literature,' he kept repeating."

Over the next half dozen years, Asch continued to publish both fiction and nonfiction that supported his ideas about the commonality of Christianity and Judaism, books that continued to enrage his critics but received acclaim in certain literary quarters. Then he apparently had a change of heart and returned to writing about traditionally Jewish subjects. Asch eventually moved to Israel, and after his death in 1957, his home in a suburb of Tel Aviv was turned into a museum.

One gets the sense that Asch failed to appreciate what he was up against with Cahan. By the time the showdown with Asch took place, Cahan was approaching eighty. When David Levinsky, Cahan's greatest literary creation, looks back on his life, he speaks of feeling that, despite all his worldly achievements, his inner being is the same as it was when he was a young student in the yeshiva swaying over his religious text. This was the sentiment on which Cahan would make his last stand, even while he denied it. At the conclusion of his attack on Asch, Cahan insisted, one last time, "I am not religious. I am a total free-thinker. However, I respect the traditions of our people, and the attitude of our free-thinkers towards such a new direction is the same as the attitude of religious Jews towards it." And that is where he left it; after eighty years, the great freethinker had driven out the apostate, only to find himself back where he started, in league with the religious Jews who had given birth to him, half a world and nearly a century away.

13

The *Forward* was one of the few American newspapers that maintained a clear-eyed view of Hitler during the 1930s. Even such a distinguished newspaper as *The Wall Street Journal*, which would emerge as a stalwart supporter of America's hard line during the Cold War, greeted Neville Chamberlain's appeasement of Hitler at Munich in September 1938 with an editorial advising its readers to place their hopes in the 1928 Kellogg-Briand Pact, which renounced aggressive war and was signed by America, France, Germany, Italy, Japan, and Britain, among other countries.

In sharp contradistinction, the *Forward* reacted to the Munich Agreement on October 1, 1938, the day after it was signed, with a mixture of fury and ridicule, calling it a "shameful document" and referring to Hitler as the "Fascist devil" who had "made a fool of his terrified opponents, of the democratic countries, and of the whole civilized world." The *Forward* imagined Hitler rolling around in his bunker, laughing. "I, Hitler, now appear as the defender of the Holy principle of the self-determination of peoples," it imagined him telling his camarilla. "The truth," the *Forward* said, "is that what has been achieved by the agreement is not really peace, and that we have simply postponed the danger of war for a later date, but not avoided it."

The *Forward*'s prediction came true when Hitler invaded Poland on September 1, 1939, one week after the signing of the nonaggression pact between Germany and the Soviet Union. Cahan wrote in the newspaper:

> Hitler has allies in his enterprise of setting the world on fire, and one of them—and probably the most important one—is Stalin. Look at what happened the night the world got incinerated. Hitler's parlia-

ment was gathered in Berlin and Stalin's parliament was gathered in Moscow. In Stalin's parliament the democratic republics of England and France were made fun of. [The Jewish diplomat Maxim] Litvinov was attacked for having been preoccupied with the insane notion that fascism had to be conquered. Stalin's friendship with Hitler was praised. Immediately thereafter, Hitler made a speech in his parliament, saying he's signing with both hands everything that was said in Stalin's parliament. And immediately, the next minute, Hitler took matches in hand and went off into the bitter night to set the world aflame. Was this all a coincidence? Can such dramatic occurrences happen by accident? Or do they harmonize because they are logically tied to one another, as if one conductor had designed the whole thing—one bloody conductor? Stalin is Hitler's partner in his setting the world in flames. Let us remember that. Let us pass it down to our children's children.

In March 1940, Cahan's longtime nemesis, the Revisionist Zionist leader Vladimir Jabotinsky, arrived in New York to raise an alarum over the gathering catastrophe and recruit a Jewish army to fight alongside the allied countries at war with Hitler. Cahan and Jabotinsky had corresponded as early as 1926. The writer Louis Gordon has recently speculated that having written a novel about the Kishinev pogroms, Cahan was "most certainly was aware of Jabotinsky's role as the leader of the Jewish defense in the aftermath of that anti-Semitic violence, as well as the numerous parallels between Jabotinsky's novel *The Five*, a tale of assimilation in interwar Russia, and Cahan's own masterpiece, *The Rise of David Levinsky*."

On March 19, 1940, Jabotinsky addressed an audience of 5,000 people at the Manhattan Opera House on West 34th Street, calling for "an exodus from Europe and the settlement of six million Jews on both sides of the Jordan," in Gordon's words. Cahan was not present at the event, but his friends were, and Cahan published his response in the *Forward*.

He had first encountered Jabotinsky's writings, he recalled, at the office of a friend in Paris. He realized that Jabotinsky possessed a "superb" writing style, but "a certain opposite opinion" was forming within him with respect to the substance of Jabotinsky's work. He arrived at the view that Jabotinsky's "abilities are a lot greater than his practical sense and seriousness." He worried "when Jabotinsky began to imitate the outward forms of Hitler and Mussolini's forces by instituting in his organization the brown-shirt uniform, with certain Nazi-like ceremonies included." He noted ruefully that "on inexperienced young people, such comedy sometimes works like a charm."

"Gigantic" is the word Cahan used to describe the meeting at the Manhattan Opera House, though he also wrote of Jabotinsky's "laughability as a leader." Then Cahan began temporizing. "How to take care of five million or six million homeless Jews and provide them with homes is a question that is loaded with incredible difficulties and problems," he proclaimed. "He, Vladimir Jabotinsky, however, doesn't know of difficulties. . . . One would have to be a prophet to be able to foretell the character of tomorrow's problems." He then mocked Jabotinsky's call for the establishment of a Jewish army that would enter the war on all fronts. He denigrated Jabotinsky's earlier warnings about anti-Semitism in Germany. And he disagreed with Jabotinsky's assertion that were the Jews of Europe to be evacuated to the Middle East, a substantial nation would be created. "Six million is a pretty small state," Cahan caviled.

For all his verve as an editor over a great span of time and through a magnificent fight against international Communism, Cahan, in his final decade, was floundering badly. Perhaps he knew it. Certainly Jabotinsky did. After reading Cahan's full-page attack on him in the *Forward*, the Revisionist Zionist wrote to Cahan saying that he had read it with great interest. "The question of whether AK or VJ does or does not believe in the possibility of a mass exodus is one that it would be useless to argue," he wrote. Then he pleaded: "Speaking as one old Jewish journalist to another, I still expect you to warn American Jews of this situation, for it will be theirs to deal with its unprecedented burdens, and it is you who are the doyen of the Jewish press."

Cahan's reply, dated April 17, 1940, dripped with condescension.

> To be sure, you and I look at things from two different points of view, but as I tried to make clear in my article about you, I sincerely admire your talent. So much so that the part you play in the Zionist movement is of secondary importance from my point of view. . . . Frankly speaking, I regret that you have not devoted your great gifts to journalism and literature.

In May, Germany invaded France. In August, Jabotinsky traveled to Hunter, New York, a town in the Catskill Mountains, to visit a training camp of Betar, the Revisionist Zionist youth movement he had founded in 1923. Its name alluded to the last Jewish fort in Palestine to fall during the Bar Kochba revolt against the Romans in 136 C.E., and it honored as well the Zionist hero Joseph Trumpeldor. On August 4, while at the camp, Jabotinsky lay down for a nap and died in his sleep from a heart attack. He was fifty-nine years old.

Years later Harry Lopatin, who had been a young staffer at the *Forward* in the summer of 1940, recalled that Cahan had tried to get one of his regular reporters or editors to cover Jabotinsky's funeral. But they all refused, so Cahan sent Lopatin. Then Cahan sat down to write what was undoubtedly one of the most remarkable editorials in the history of the *Forward.*

"The death of Vladimir Jabotinsky at this grim time for the Jewish people is, in the true sense of the word, a national catastrophe," he began, then proceeded to laud Jabotinsky as a person, a writer, and an orator. When Jabotinsky spoke, "even the deaf could hear." But what struck with particular force was Cahan's prediction that Jabotinsky would be missed "not only now, in the middle of the storm, but also later, when the storm is over and the time comes to heal the wounds and rebuild Jewish life on new foundations in a new time."

The editorial has been dismissed by some as a typical obituary in which nothing ill about the deceased is mentioned. But it was so at odds with everything Cahan had been writing, not only as recently as a few weeks before but also throughout his long career, that it is hard to avoid the conclusion that it came from a deeper recognition than any he had previously articulated: that for all the greatness of the movement Cahan led and the struggles into which he had thrown himself, the crisis that was about to befall the Jews, and the free world, was bigger than any one ideology.

So it proved to be. During the war, the *Forward* reported on the annihilation of Europe's Jews in greater detail than other newspapers. The paper also reported on the fate of a number of Russian Bundists, particularly Henryk Ehrlich and Victor Alter, who had moved east with the outbreak of the war, only to be murdered in the 1940s on orders of Stalin. According to David Shub, Cahan was "heavily embroiled in the fight against the Nazis" and said he wanted to live to see Hitler's downfall.

"I don't care what happens to me after that," Cahan said from time to time, as Shub recalled. "Today I am hale and healthy and tomorrow I could suddenly die."

It was Anna who faltered first. While alighting from a Fifth Avenue bus one day, she broke her foot and, after it healed, was left with a limp. She suffered a heart attack in 1946, and Cahan himself was felled by a stroke a few weeks later. He lay in a coma for more than a week, while his wife was in another hospital and did not know of his fate.

Cahan recovered and, after several months in the hospital, was able to return to the paper, greeting Shub and others with a rousing "Hello, Socialists!" He complained that the paper was "going in all directions," grumbling that one of the editors, Herman Lieberman, whom he liked a great deal, was writing "Orthodox religious articles," as Shub recalled.

"Lieberman has a window into the women's section of the shul and he's saying the *Tseneh Reneh*," Cahan remarked, referring to the popular Yiddish commentary on the Bible that was intended for women.

Shub pestered Cahan for permission to visit the convalescing Anna, but Cahan put him off and, in Shub's telling, Anna eventually called Shub herself and invited him to visit her in their apartment in the Algonquin

Hotel. "But God forbid, under no circumstances, don't tell Cahan," she said. It turns out that Anna was worried about Cahan's growing stinginess and his complaints about expenses. "If he can't work anymore, will the Forward Association still continue to pay his salary?" she asked, noting that her husband had a lot of enemies at the paper. Shub reassured her that they would both be properly taken care of. As her health worsened, Cahan himself encouraged Shub to visit, and he was saddened to find her failing so quickly; she died on May 1, 1947, a week after Shub last saw her. Cahan was with her when she passed away but for a week could not accept it, mumbling over and over, "How can it be, that Anyuta is dead? Anyuta is no longer here?"

No doubt Cahan's misery was compounded by the fact that his clout at the paper was dwindling. After the war, none other than Kurt Schumacher, chairman of the newly formed Social Democratic Party in West Germany and a staunch anti-Nazi and anti-Communist, came to New York and made a point of calling on Cahan at the paper. Schumacher had been imprisoned by the Nazis and sent to a series of concentration camps; he had a well-deserved reputation for great integrity and devotion to the principles of democratic socialism, the latter of which brought him into conflict with the chancellor, Konrad Adenauer. Cahan understood that a strong Social Democratic Party was vital to defeating Stalin's machinations in West Germany, and he invited a number of his colleagues into his office to meet Schumacher and to be photographed with him. Afterward he wrote an account of Schumacher's visit, but the *Forward* editors refused to print it. He was stung. Then board member Nathan Chanin threatened to take the matter to the full membership of the Forward Association. The article was printed, and the *Forward*, Shub noted, "did not lose even one single reader."

In 1947 the *Forward* celebrated its fiftieth anniversary, and on May 25 more than 20,000 people crowded into Madison Square Garden to pay tribute to the paper that had paved their way to life in America. A full orchestra performed on the bunting-festooned stage, a larger-than-life flag proclaimed the jubilee in Yiddish, and congratulatory messages were read from President Harry Truman, former Governor Herbert Lehman, *New York Times* publisher Arthur Hays Sulzberger, and other luminaries. While the *Forward* had much to celebrate, all in attendance must have understood that the best days of Yiddish newspaperdom were behind them.

European Jewry, the wellspring of Yiddish language and culture from which the *Forward* had drawn its immigrant readership, was virtually destroyed by the Holocaust. The survivors who had managed to make their way to New York for the most part made their homes on Manhattan's Upper West Side and in Brooklyn's Borough Park and Williamsburg neighborhoods. Yiddish socialism was not of interest to them. Some of the Lower East Side newspapers remained, but the old urgencies were gone, except as memories. The *Forward*'s erstwhile competitor, the *Tageblatt*, had closed its doors in the 1920s. The *Morning Journal* would be taken over in the early 1950s by the *Day*, which had risen out of the ashes of the *Warheit*, which had stopped publishing in 1918. The Communist *Freiheit* managed to persist through the Hitler-Stalin Pact, the revolution in Hungary in 1956, and the Prague Spring in 1968, but it finally expired in 1988, a year before the Soviet Union itself became part of history.

In September 1950, a banquet was held at the Hotel Commodore to mark Cahan's ninetieth birthday (which was actually on July 7). Cahan had been hospitalized beforehand and was unable to read, but he was determined to go to the last great event in his honor. Seated on the platform alongside him were William Green, the president of the American Federation of Labor; David Dubinsky, president of the ILGWU; Jacob Potofsky, president of the Amalgamated Clothing Workers of America; and other labor leaders. Cahan beamed, even though near total deafness prevented him from hearing their speeches and the messages from President Truman, Governor Thomas E. Dewey, Senator Herbert Lehman, and Prime Minister David Ben-Gurion. When the toastmaster invited him to say a few words, Cahan proclaimed, "This is the happiest day of my life."

His health continued to decline. He was hospitalized for the last time in August 1951, and Shub rushed over to see him on Friday afternoon, August 24. He found Cahan lying in bed, very pale, with his mouth open and his eyes closed. Shub thought he had died. But when the nurse awakened him, Cahan recognized his aide, declared him to be "my everlasting friend," and burst into tears. He died a week later, on August 31, 1951.

Cahan's funeral was held on September 5, 1951, at the *Forward* Building on East Broadway. When the crowd in the auditorium reached five hundred, the Fire Department refused to allow anyone else inside. *The New York Times* estimated that 10,000 people had gathered outside the building, in Strauss Square and in Seward Park; others were seen leaning out of tenement windows and standing on fire escapes so they could hear the service, which was broadcast on loudspeakers. Music by Chopin and Grieg was played. The *Forward*'s business manager, Alexander Kahn, who led the gathering, specifically mentioned Cahan's fight against Communism. "He was one of the first to fight Communists. He was one of the first to relegate party tradition and support Roosevelt. His idealism was always guided by a sense of the real, and when the interests of the people and his country came into conflict with any tradition or dogma, he resolved it in favor of the interests of the people."

Representing President Truman, Secretary of Labor Maurice Tobin spoke of the importance of the free trade union movement and declared, "We should as Americans say 'Thank God' for the day Abe Cahan arrived in the United States." It was one of the few mentions of God in the entire ceremony. David Dubinsky spoke of Cahan's courage in fighting the Communists for control of the United Garment Workers Union. Absent Cahan, he asked, "How many unions would have been captured and how many workers would have been enslaved?"

Representing the Jewish state, Abba Eban, Israel's ambassador to the United States, brought what the *Times* called a "tribute from the Government and the people of Israel," though he seems to have been a bit careful, given Cahan's mixed record on Zionism and his continued advocacy of Yiddish, which at the time was anathema to the Hebrew-speaking Israelis. The diplomat who became world famous for his impassioned and soaring rhetoric focused his remarks on Cahan's contributions to what the *Times* called "furthering social progress and Yiddish journalism." Eban lauded Cahan for preserving Jewish consciousness and culture against a tide of assimilation. A message in Hebrew from President Chaim Weizmann and one in Yiddish from Prime Minister David Ben-Gurion were read as well.

Remarks were also made by New York City mayor Vincent Impellitteri, by representatives of the Workmen's Circle and the United Hebrew Trades, by *Forward* editor Harry Rogoff, and by Adolph Held, president of the Forward Association. At the conclusion of the event, five cars banked with flowers led a motorcade of fifty vehicles to Mount Carmel Cemetery in Queens, where Cahan was laid to rest.

For all their mournful and noble grandeur, the eulogies missed the essence of Cahan. Those who were closest to him had long since come to understand that the union work and the political struggles were not the heart of Cahan's story. David Shub summed up Cahan's lasting achievement as being "a great scholar of literature." He had, in his long life, read widely in American, English, French, German, and Scandinavian literature. But his real love was Russian literature, which he believed surpassed all others. His favorites were Chekhov and Tolstoy, and he had read *Anna Karenina*—the novel Anna had urged on him early in their romance—four or five times.

What Abraham Cahan really longed for was to create literature that immortalized his own culture in the way that his literary heroes had immortalized theirs. *David Levinsky* was so unquestionably a step in that direction that one is left to wonder why he stopped writing fiction after its publication. Cahan's many friends and admirers wondered about it as well, most notably H. L. Mencken, who expressed his admiration for Cahan in his memoir, *My Life as Author and Editor*. They had enjoyed a lively correspondence about the Yiddish language and a long, if intermittent, acquaintanceship. Back in 1930 the publication of Mencken's

Treatise on the Gods had provoked public controversy because of its anti-Semitic comments about the Jews,* but according to Mencken, at least, he and Cahan had later agreed over lunch at the Algonquin Hotel, that the offensive remarks were "only a small part of a discussion that was generally favorable to them."

Whatever else one can say about Mencken, he knew a great novel when he read one, and twenty-five years after the publication of *The Rise of David Levinsky*, on the occasion of Cahan's eightieth birthday, the editors of the *Forward* invited him to write about Cahan the novelist. His essay appeared, in Yiddish and in English, in a special edition of the paper published on June 7, 1942. *The Rise of David Levinsky*, Mencken wrote, "sticks in my mind to this day as one of the best American novels ever written." There had been, Mencken noted, "high hopes" that the novel's "distinguished success would draw Mr. Cahan away from the razzle-dazzle of daily journalism, and set him up as what might be called a career novelist." But Mencken said he understood Cahan's choice, even if he regretted it. "The merits of *The Rise of David Levinsky* do not dim as the years pass," he wrote. He called it

* Wrote Mencken: "The Bible is unquestionably the most beautiful book in the world. Nearly all of it comes from the Jews, and their making of it constitutes one of the most astounding phenomena in human history. Save for a small minority of superior individuals, nearly unanimously agnostic, there is not much in their character, as the modern world knows them, to suggest a genius for exalted thinking. As commonly encountered, they strike other peoples as predominantly unpleasant, and everywhere on earth they seem to be disliked. This dislike, despite their own belief to the contrary, has nothing to do with their religion: it is founded, rather, on their bad manners, their curious lack of tact. . . . Yet these same rude, unpopular and often unintelligent folk, from time almost immemorial, have been the chief dreamers of the Western world, and beyond all comparison its greatest poets." Terry Teachout's biography cites an earlier version of this passage, in which Mencken describes the Jews as "the most unpleasant race ever heard of" and adds: "As commonly encountered, they lack many of the qualities that mark the civilized man: courage, dignity, incorruptibility, ease, confidence. They have vanity without pride, voluptuousness without taste, and learning without wisdom. Their fortitude, such as it is, is wasted upon puerile objects and their charity is mainly only a form of display. Yet these same Jews, from time immemorial, have been the chief dreamers of the human race, and beyond all comparison its greatest poets."

> the mature and painstaking work of an artist with long experience behind him, and an extraordinary talent. . . . No better novel about the immigrant has ever been written, or is likely to be written. The proletarian authors of our own day have devoted themselves heavily to the subject, and brought out a great many indignant and shocking books, but none of them has ever come within miles of the philosophical insight of Mr. Cahan. His David Levinsky is not a mere bugaboo in a political pamphlet; he is an authentic human being, shrewdly observed and very adroitly carved and painted.

Levinsky, he added, "takes on, in the end, a kind of representative character, and becomes the archetype of a civilization now greatly changed, and in most ways not for the better." He doubted whether "any more vivid presentation of the immigrant's hopes and disappointments, thoughts and feelings, virtues and vices has ever been got upon paper," adding, "All other novels upon the same theme fall short, in one way or another, of this one."

David Shub gave us, in his memoir, the most insightful summing-up of Cahan's life and legacy.

> Abe Cahan was never a sworn Jewish nationalist. He was nevertheless a warm Jew. His socialism never interfered with his Yiddishkeit—he was a nonbeliever but never made fun of the Jewish traditions, as some of the radicals of his generation would do. Even eighty years earlier Cahan had preached tolerance for religious Jews. In his later years he was an ardent enthusiast and supporter of Israel. Cahan until his last breath remained a convinced Social Democrat. But in the last few decades he would put the accent on the last word—democrat. He put political and spiritual freedom of the person in first place. Just like in his youth, Cahan thought that poverty, exploitation, and injustice should be outlawed. All men should be equal, all should be brothers and all should be free. But after the terrible events of the Communist Revolution in Russia he, like all the other thinking and righteous socialists, came to the conclusion

> that this can be achieved in the free countries not through a revolution, but through the step by step, gradual further development of democracy in all aspects of life in society.

After Cahan died, his legacy and his beliefs carried the *Forward* through another half century. The *Forward* opposed Senator Joseph McCarthy in the early 1950s, but in later years its editor collaborated with the FBI in the effort to expose and defeat Communists. The *Forward* continued expressing its virulent hostility to Communism during the rise of Solidarity and the fall of the Berlin Wall and the Soviet Union. Cahan was still alive in 1950 when the Communists attacked the Korean peninsula; the newspaper mocked the sham of the peace movement that fronted for the Kremlin and said that if Moscow failed to retreat, there would be a world war.

Regarding Vietnam, Cahan's successors gave full-throated support to America's entry into the fighting, and when Saigon fell to the North Vietnamese in 1975, the *Forward* warned that only then would the killing begin in earnest. The *Forward* never forgot that during the Holocaust, the grand mufti of Jerusalem, Haj Amin al-Husseini, had collaborated with Hitler while the Jews of Palestine fought with the Allies. After the war, the *Forward* would often remind its readers that Egypt, Syria, and other Arab countries were harboring Nazis. With the liberation of East Jerusalem from Arab occupation in 1967, the *Forward* vowed that the city would never be divided again.

How Cahan would have come out on all of this, had he lived another fifty years, is a matter of conjecture. One doesn't have to accept the suggestion that crops up from time to time that Cahan was the first neoconservative.* But strikingly, in the closing decades of the twentieth century, the issues Cahan championed in his later years at the *Forward* were picked up not by partisans of the left but by factions that had moved to the right, by those who had departed from a Democratic Party

* Or, as one wag put it, neo-Cahan.

that had no place for George Meany, the labor leader who presided over the merger of the AFL-CIO and was shut out of the New York delegation to the Democratic National Convention in 1972. When America's highest civilian honor, the Medal of Freedom, was bestowed on Irving Brown, the labor organizer whom Jay Lovestone sent to Europe, it was done by President Reagan.

It would be a mistake to carry all that too far—Cahan was no Republican. But it would also be a mistake not to understand it. Cahan certainly deserves a place in the pantheon of America's greatest newspaper editors—William Lloyd Garrison, Charles Dana, Henry Luce, and Robert L. Bartley, to name but a few. But above all, the words Cahan wrote in the closing paragraphs of *The Rise of David Levinsky* keep coming back to any student of his life:

> I cannot escape from my old self. My past and my present do not comport well. David, the poor lad swinging over a Talmud volume at the Preacher's Synagogue, seems to have more in common with my inner identity than David Levinsky, the well-known cloak-manufacturer.

Or newspaper editor.

ACKNOWLEDGMENTS

This book grew out of my years at the *Forward*. It is neither an authorized nor an official biography of Abraham Cahan and does not reflect the newspaper's institutional view. But I benefited from many friends and colleagues who were connected to the *Forward* and who shared with me their personal knowledge of the newspaper Cahan created and, in some cases, of Cahan himself. These include Dr. Barnett Zumoff, who has several times been president of the Forward Association and is a translator of the Yiddish poets, and Elie Wiesel, who, among other things, covered the liberation of Jerusalem for the *Forward*. I was helped by others who are now, sadly, gone, including I. B. Singer; Judith Vladeck, the Forward Association's counsel; Harold Ostroff, its general manager; William Stern, its president for several of the years that I was there; Motl Zelmanovicz, a member of the Association of the Jewish Labor Bund; and Gus Tyler, who joined the paper in 1934 as assistant labor editor and continued writing for it into the twenty-first century. I found great inspiration in Mordechai Strigler, a towering figure who edited the Yiddish *Forward* during the years that I edited the English one and whose own literary output was so great that it is measured in cycles.

On the *Forward*, I learned from many brilliant colleagues and particularly from two intellectual partners who played outsize roles at the paper. Jonathan Rosen was cultural editor of the *Forward* during the years that I edited it, and he built its widely admired cultural section. He went on to become editorial director of Nextbook and general editor of the Jewish Encounters series of which this volume is a part. David Twersky was associate editor of the *Forward* during those years and built its Washington bureau. Once, at the age of ten or so, Twersky was sent by his father to the newsstand to fetch a copy of the *Forward* only to bring home, by accident, a copy of the Communist *Freiheit*. The lad was thrown out a window, the *Freiheit* fluttering after him. That story may—or may not—be apocryphal, but until the day in 2010 when Twersky died, he never stopped searching for the right newspaper.

Help in navigating the paper's Yiddish-language morgue—and much else in twentieth-century Jewish history—was provided, in the years before her death, by Lucy Dawidowicz, in whose apartment the newspaper installed a microfilm reader. Jeremy Dauber of Columbia University also provided translations. Ruth Wisse, a professor at Harvard University, provided many insights into the history and ideological struggles of the *Forward* and into Yiddish literature, of which she has an unparalleled knowledge. Gennady Estraikh, a professor at New York University and Oxford University, shared his time and knowledge. I am grateful to Samuel Norich, publisher and chief executive of the *Forward* newspapers, not only for his insights into the Yiddish world but also for permission to include photographs from the *Forward*'s archive, whose Chana Pollack was of great assistance. Gene and Gloria Sosin were exceptionally helpful in sharing, in addition to their own sage advice, excerpts from Gloria's translation from the Yiddish of extensive parts of a two-volume memoir by David Shub, who had been one of Cahan's deputies and who produced the most intimate account of Cahan's modus operandi as an editor and of his views on politics, literature, and various personalities. I am grateful as well to Neal Kozodoy, who on the double jubilee of the *Forward* in 1997 commissioned me to write for *Commentary* the article that began my thinking of a biography of Cahan; some of its language is echoed herein.

This book is the work of a journalist but is at least partly derivative of academic studies and specialized biographies of Cahan. Authors of those works include Moses Rischin, Sanford Marovitz, and Yaacov Goldstein, as well as four who are now deceased: Irving Howe, Theodore Marvin Pollock, Ronald Sanders, and Melech Epstein. They are, in contradistinction to myself, scholars; collectively they have produced a far more detailed history of the period than I have assembled here. I recommend each of their books warmly to those who wish to know more about Abraham Cahan.

I am grateful to the staff at the YIVO Institute for Jewish Research, the American Jewish Historical Society, the Tamiment Library and Robert F. Wagner Labor Archives at New York University, the Dorot Jewish Division at the New York Public Library, and Adrienne Fischier, James Harney, and their colleagues at the Harvard Club Library in New York. Ellen Umansky, formerly of the *Forward* and *The New York Sun*, led the research and fact-checking. Gary Shapiro, formerly of the *Forward* and *The New York Sun*, and Gabrielle Birkner, formerly of the *Sun* and now of the *Forward*, provided research help, as did John Bennett, who also read the manuscript for proof and style. All errors herein are my own.

Financial support for the research for this book was provided by the Alice and Thomas Tisch Foundation via the American Jewish Historical Society and by the Robert and Ardis James Foundation via the Hudson Institute, and is gratefully acknowledged. I am grateful, as well, to Michael Steinhardt, Joseph Steinberg, and Robert Rubin, who were my partners in Lipsky-Steinhardt LLC, which owned an interest in the *Forward*.

I owe a particular debt of gratitude to Simon Weber, who in the decades before he died was the editor of the Yiddish *Forward*. He was the person I first approached about the future of the paper when, in 1983, it announced its retreat to weekly publication. Not only did he welcome me into its world, but it was with Weber and his wife, Sylvia, that I went to dinner on the first date with the woman who would become my wife, Amity Shlaes. She has, in the years since, given me, among many other gifts, our four children—Eli, Theo, Flora, and Helen—and shared with all five of us her own profound understanding of Russia, the Pale of Settlement, and the Europe from which so much of this story springs.

NOTES

Preface

6 "had come to despise": William and Sarah Schack, "From the American Scene: The Schooling of Abraham Cahan," *Commentary*, November 1954.

Chapter 1

9 "Sometimes, when I think of my past": Abraham Cahan, *The Rise of David Levinsky* (New York: Modern Library, 2001).

10 "Had I been a painter": Abraham Cahan, *The Education of Abraham Cahan*, trans. Leon Stein, Abraham P. Conan, and Lynn Davison (Philadelphia: Jewish Publication Society of America, 1969), p. 3.

10 "an old sofa, torn and with its stuffing coming out.": Ibid.

10 "I remember . . . a boot falling": Ibid., p. 4.

11 "Somewhere, in one of the other houses": Ibid.

11 Russia's conscription laws: *Encyclopaedia Judaica*, 2nd ed., s.v. "Russia."

11 "kindliest prince who has ever ruled Russia": Irving Howe, *World of Our Fathers* (New York: Harcourt Brace Jovanovich, 1976), p. 7.

12 "The most intense of my first memories": Ernest Poole, "Abraham Cahan: Socialist-Journalist-Friend of the Ghetto," *Outlook*, October 28, 1911, cited in Theodore Marvin Pollock, "The Solitary Clarinetist: A Critical Biography of Abraham Cahan, 1860–1917," Ph.D. diss., Columbia University, 1959, p. 9.

12 "entered the service of God.": Pollock, "Clarinetist," p. 10.

12 "The Jerusalem of Lithuania": Ibid., p. 3.

12 "The stench in the courtyards": Cahan, *Education*, pp. 12ff.

13 "a lower order of human being": Ibid., p. 13.

13 a culture war was brewing: William and Sarah Schack, "From the American Scene: The Schooling of Abraham Cahan," *Commentary*, November 1954.

13 "two Jews stop in the street": Cahan, *Education*, p. 30.

14 "Vilna, the city of the Gaon": Ibid.

14 situated in a lively part of town: Ibid., p. 12ff.

14 "Russian Hebraist, poet, and grammarian": *Jewish Encyclopedia*, s.v. "Lebensohn, Abraham."

14 "treasured the singing": Cahan, *Education*, p. 15.
15 "irresistibly drawn to secular books": Ibid., p. 33.
15 "the time of my greatest religious fervor.": Ibid., pp. 62ff.
16 uncle's business spiraled downward: Ibid., p. 66.
16 "If I had studied at a gymnasium: Ibid., pp. 72ff.
16 "I was no longer pious." The quotes in this paragraph, Ibid., p. 76.

Chapter 2

17 "I felt as if I had suddenly grown": Pollock, "Clarinetist," p. 36.
17 "The Vilna Public Library": Cahan, *Education*, pp. 95ff.
18 "Clearly, there were no mysteries!": Ibid., p. 89.
18 "on rare occasions, however": Ibid., p. 100.
18 "A Jewish man told me": Ibid., p. 101.
19 less a university than what today we might call: Pollock, "Clarinetist," p. 45.
19 "to insure that future Jewish teachers of Jews": Cahan, *Education*, p. 107.
19 "Each new terrorist deed": Ibid., p. 140.
19 relaxation of the laws regarding military service: Howe, *World*, p. 7.
20 "hunchbacked son of a cantor": Ibid., pp. 140–41.
20 "Even though they dressed and chatted": Ibid., p. 141.
20 "I walked in a daze as one newly in love.": Cahan, *Education*, pp. 146ff.
20 "You will bring misfortune on your own head": Ibid., p. 151.
21 On Sunday morning, March 1, 1881: On Alexander II's assassination, see Ronald Sanders, *The Downtown Jews: Portraits of an Immigrant Generation* (New York: Harper & Row, 1969), pp. 11–13.
21 "Our czar is dead": Cahan, *Education*, p. 152.
21 "Every day the press blazoned a new sensation,": Ibid., p. 154.
22 "Even though the pogrom": Ibid., p. 158.
22 thrilled to be in the big city: On Cahan's St. Petersburg trip, see ibid, pp. 160–62.
23 "We kissed and embraced": Ibid., p. 163.

Chapter 3

24 the tension between Cahan's universalist, radical self: Ronald Sanders makes this point in *The Downtown Jews*, p. 38.
24 "the principle of the revolutionaries": Cahan, *Education*, p. 165.
24 "I began to burn with blushing": Ibid, p. 166.
24 a Russian translation of volume one of Marx's *Das Kapital*: Ibid., p. 168.
25 "Your darkly charming friend": Ibid., p. 171.
25 "If I loved my mother": Ibid., p. 146.

25 "an uneasy sleep.": Ibid., p. 171.

25 "When the interrogation was ended": Ibid., p. 174.

26 When complications arose: The details about Cahan's escape are drawn from ibid., pp. 176ff.

26 "We are your brothers. We are Jews": Ibid., p. 182.

26 "the beginning of the nationalist movement": Ibid.

26 "stopped talking in Russian": Ibid., p. 182ff.

27 "were an instinctive outpouring": Ibid., p. 183.

27 "the Ukrainian pogrom makers": Ibid.

27 "Two groups emerged": Ibid., p. 185.

28 "a pioneer of this pro-Palestine movement.": Ibid. On Belkind's life, see *Encyclopaedia Judaica*, 2nd ed., s.v. "Belkind, Israel."

28 "first of all a socialist": Ibid.

28 "And what would he be giving his life for?": Ibid.

28 "imagined a wonderful communist life": Ibid., p. 186.

29 "I paced my room in a fever.": Ibid.

29 "On that Saturday night there began": Ibid., p. 196.

29 "We made a strange group": Ibid., p. 199.

30 thousands of Jewish refugees: The estimates of arrivals are from Howe, *World*, pp. 29–30.

30 "with their feminine black feathered hats": Cahan, *Education*, p. 202.

30 "The sad tones touched the sorrowing ears": Ibid., p. 203.

30 "I was not just running away": Ibid., p. 205.

30 "a long coat that was a cross": Dr. Charles Rayevsky, "My First Meeting with Ab. Cahan," in *Jubilee Writings on the Occasion of Ab. Cahan's 50th Birthday*, quoted in Cahan, *Education*, p. 206.

30 "bitterly disappointed": Cahan, *Education*, p. 204.

31 "Who needs you?": Ibid., p. 207.

31 "Long live freedom in the American republic!": Ibid., p. 209.

31 "for the first time I could see": Ibid., p. 210.

31 "bicycles, bootblacks, and hansom cabs": Ibid., p. 212.

31 "that all Americans were tall and slender": Ibid., p. 216.

31 "the water and the sky were blue": Ibid., pp. 215–16.

32 "literally overcome with the beauty": Abraham Cahan, *The Rise of David Levinsky* (New York: Modern Library, 2001), p. 86.

Chapter 4

34 no Statue of Liberty stood guard: The description of New York in 1882 is drawn from Sanders, *Downtown*, pp. 40–41.

34 a "heartless bourgeois.": Cahan, *Education*, p. 218.

34 "the first Russian-Jewish intellectuals": Ibid., p. 225.
34 "considered us to be atheists": Ibid.
34 "was not really my dream": Ibid., p. 226.
34 at the beginning of an enormous transformation: Howe, *World*, pp. 69–70.
35 "two dozen Christian churches, a dozen synagogues": Ibid.
35 "I learned more English from him": Cahan, *Education*, p. 233.
35 "Every hour of work seemed like a year,": Ibid., p. 230.
36 "contained a large class of proletarian intellectuals: Sanders, *Downtown*, p. 53.
36 "The worker was being reduced": Cahan, *Education*, p. 231.
36 among the longshoremen: For the longshoremen's strike, see Sanders, *Downtown*, pp. 56–59.
36 "we were scabs who": I. Kopeloff, *Amol in Amerika* (Warsaw, 1928), cited in Howe, *World*, pp. 102–3.
36 Eisler's Golden Rule Hall: Howe, *World*, p. 103.
37 "thumping heart.": Cahan, *Education*, p. 236.
37 "started for the door"; "hero of the day": Ibid.
37 "If it is for Jewish immigrants": Ibid., p. 237.
38 a hall in the back of a German saloon: Sanders, *Downtown*, p. 64.
38 "the first socialist speech in Yiddish": Cahan, *Education*, p. 237
38 "kindled a wave of excitement": Bernard Weinstein quoted in Howe, *World*, p. 103.
38 "with elaborate Vilna curses": Cahan, *Education*, p. 238.
38 "typical of the moment": Howe, *World*, p. 104.
38 "It is a joke,": Cahan quoted in Melech Epstein, *Profiles of Eleven* (Detroit: Wayne State University Press, 1965), p. 63.
38 "The anarchists and even the socialists": Cahan, *Education*, p. 282.
39 "careful but tortured English": Ibid., pp. 239ff.
39 "religion of humanity": Howe, *World*, p. 104.
39 "for me the sermons": Cahan, *Education*, p. 249.
40 "filled with a crushing longing.": Ibid., p. 241ff.
40 "determined"; "only a few years earlier": Ibid., p. 273.
40 "I call them socialist meetings,": Ibid., p. 297.
41 "How would it look for a socialist": Ibid., p. 283.
41 "For Russian socialists": Sanders, *Downtown*, p. 84.
41 "almost my entire first presidential": Cahan, *Education*, p. 289.
42 "first lesson in American politics": Ibid., p. 292.
42 "rum, Romanism, and rebellion": Ibid.
42 "criticized the two capitalist parties": Ibid., p. 289.
42 "read and reread": Ibid., p. 292.
42 "What is a ghetto?": Ibid., p. 355.
43 "a woman with a mournfully pious face": The facts about this meeting come from ibid., pp. 298–99.

Chapter 5

44 February 1885: Sanders, *Downtown*, p. 75.
44 "much admired for her discriminating intelligence": Cahan, *Education*, p. 306.
45 "proofreader, manager, bookkeeper": Ibid., p. 308.
45 Chicago's Haymarket Square: This account of the Haymarket affair is drawn from Sanders, *Downtown*, pp. 80ff, and from Howe, *World*, p. 51.
45 "bloody fruit," "Anarchy's Red Hand": *New York Times*, May 6, 1886.
45 "For us, the thirteenth of March": Sanders, *Downtown*, p. 84.
46 skeptical of anarchism as a viable movement: Ibid., pp. 84–86.
46 "When I got my membership card": Ibid., p. 86.
46 "both more necessary and more possible": Ibid.
46 "There had been, we knew, unions": Ibid., pp. 91ff.
47 "Me, I'm from the town of Proletarishok": Ibid., p. 110. On the founding of the *Arbeiter Zeitung*, see ibid., pp. 97–110.
48 "Today our biblical portion": Cahan quoted in ibid., p. 97.
49 "caused a revolution in my brain": Pollock, "Clarinetist," p. 194.
49 "Reform is chloroform,": Gus Tyler, *A Vital Voice: 100 Years of the* Jewish Forward (New York: Forward Association, 1997), p. 9.
49 "that the place of the socialists": Ibid.
50 "how to put an end to the endless persecution": Ibid., p. 19.
51 "widely recognized as the most articulate": Sanders, *Downtown*, p. 148.
51 "He's a clown, a comedian": Quoted in Pollock, "Clarinetist," p. 146.
51 "We Jews have a special obligation": Sanders, *Downtown*, p. 152.
51 "emancipation of society from Judaism": Karl Marx, "On the Jewish Question," in *The Marx-Engels Reader*, ed. Robert C. Tucker (New York: W. W. Norton & Company, 1978), p. 52; also see Bernard Lewis, *Semites and Anti-Semites: An Inquiry into Conflict and Prejudice* (New York: W. W. Norton, 1999), p. 112.
52 "He was always telling jokes": Sanders, *Downtown*, p. 153.
52 "a lively and happy girl": Ibid.
52 "I had never had such a strong feeling of life": Ibid., p. 154.
53 "Eloquently you spoke of the freedom": George Leonard quoted in Pollock, "Clarinetist," p. 144.
53 "What shall be the stand of the organized workers": Sanders, *Downtown*, p. 149; The account of the showdown in Brussels has been widely written about and has been drawn here from, among others, Tyler, *Vital Voice*, and Sanders, *Downtown*.
54 "were in no way prepared to assume": Sanders, *Downtown*, 151.
54 "did not permit a heroic and pure-hearted": Ibid., pp. 151–52.
55 "That was my father's chair: Abraham Cahan, "Ab. Cahan Meets Friedrich Engels," an excerpt from *Bleter fun mayn lebn*, trans. Yankl Stillman, *Jewish Currents* (November 2008), at http://jewishcurrents.org/2008_nov_cahan.htm.

55 "the Jews are not drinkers": Pollock, "Clarinetist," p. 165.

55 "I wanted to have the pleasure": Cahan, *Bleter fun mayn lebn*, quoted in Pollock, "Clarinetist," p. 197.

56 "I will close with a name": Howells quoted in Sanders, *Downtown*, p. 191.

56 "I feel so not only as the socialist editor": Pollock, "Clarinetist," p. 197.

57 "I have read your story": On Cahan's meeting with Howells, see Pollock, "Clarinetist," pp. 198ff, citing Cahan, *Bleter fun mayn lebn*.

57 "Imagine then what an effect": Pollock, "Clarinetist," p. 199.

58 "He found work for her and for himself": Excerpt from "A Sweat-Shop Romance," in Abraham Cahan, *Yekl and the Imported Bridegroom and Other Stories of the New York Ghetto*. (New York: Dover Publications, 1970), pp. 201–2.

59 "I rang the bell and heard sounds inside": This account of Cahan's meeting his parents is drawn from Yankl Stillman's translation of Cahan, *Bleter fun mayn lebn*, published in the November 2008 issue of *Jewish Currents*.

61 "an entrapped swindler": J. C. Rich, *Sixty Years of the* Jewish Daily Forward (New York: Forward Association, 1957), p. 13.

61 "a Bolshevik before there were Bolsheviks": Ibid.

61 "labor fakers": Ibid.

61 "dual unionism": Howe, *World*, p. 523. The account of the fight was drawn from several sources, principally Sanders, *Downtown*, and Tyler, *Vital Voice*.

61 "Though led by men who regarded themselves": Howe, *World*, p. 523.

62 "was startled to hear the lecturer": Sanders, *Downtown*, p. 167.

62 "nervous and extremely temperamental.": Ibid., p. 177.

62 "House of Lords": "House of Commons" Ibid.

63 "my hat became so heavy": The facts in this paragraph are from Pollock, "Clarinetist," p. 186, citing Cahan, *Bleter fun mayn lebn*.

63 "hold high the flag of international class conflict": Ibid.

Chapter 6

64 "At Basel, I founded the Jewish State": *The Complete Diaries of Theodore Herzl*, ed. Raphael Patai, vol. 2 (New York: Herzl Press and Thomas Yoseloff, 1960), p. 581. Diary entry of September 3, 1897, written in Vienna.

64 "Zionists with seasickness.": Georgi Plekhavov quoted in Howe, *World*, p. 293.

65 Some fifty-eight dailies in New York alone: Joseph W. Campbell, *1897: The Year That Defined American Journalism* (New York: Routledge, 2006), p. 74.

66 the *Forward* jumped into this mix: The first edition's headlines are noted in Tyler, *A Vital Voice*, inside front cover.

66 the smell of fresh wood filled: Rich, *Sixty Years*, p. 18. Also see Pollock, "Clarinetist," p. 187.

66 The *Forward*'s first Sunday edition: Pollock, "Clarinetist," p. 187.
66 "the only good novelist in England": Ibid., p. 188.
66 Cahan opposed using the *Forward*: Sanford E. Marovitz, *Abraham Cahan* (New York: Twayne, 1996), pp. 39ff.
67 "People love a fight,": Pollock, "Clarinetist," p. 189.
67 succeeded in ousting hundreds of them: Tyler, *Vital Voice*, p. 13.
67 "the more voracious and penetrating reader": Pollock, "Clarinetist," p. 194.
68 "painfully reluctant to part with his": Abraham Cahan, *Yekl and the Imported Bridegroom and Other Stories of the New York Ghetto.* (New York: Dover Publications, 1970), p. 89.
68 "grew shy and could not say a word": Pollock, "Clarinetist," p. 205.
68 "Not *Yekl the Yankee . . . Yekl.*": Ibid.
68 "Our editors have their own": Ibid.
68 from the Russian master Ivan Turgenev: Sanders, *Downtown*, pp. 201ff. This lively account of Cahan's encounter with Howells draws on Cahan, *Bleter fun mayn lebn.*
69 Jewish life on the Lower East Side: Sanders, *Downtown*, pp. 201–2.
69 "You know, dear Mr. Howells,": Ibid., p. 202.
69 "You describe only Jews": Ibid.
69 The *Arbeiter Zeitung*'s readers loved it: Pollock, "Clarinetist," pp. 206ff.
69 Couldn't the novelist have painted: Sanders, *Downtown*, p. 203.
70 "You can betch you' bootsh!": Cahan, *Yekl*, pp. 2, 19.
70 "the most hideous jargon": Pollock, "Clarinetist," p. 220, citing review of August 1, 1896 in the *Commercial Advertiser*. On the critical reaction to *Yekl*, see Pollock, "Clarinetist," pp. 220–25.
70 "from beginning to end throughout": Pollock, "Clarinetist," p. 221, citing review from October 1896 issue of *Bookman*.
70 Yekl "and his fellow-personages": Pollock, "Clarinetist," p. 221, citing review in *New York Times*, July 12, 1896.
70 "new star of realism": Sanders, *Downtown*, p. 204.
70 "Novels dealing with the Irish": Moses Rischin, "Abraham Cahan and the *New York Commercial Advertiser:* A Study in Acculturation," *Publications of the American Jewish Historical Society* 43, no. 1 (September 1953), pp. 10–11. Rischin quotes from Cahan's memoir.
71 freelance journalism work: Ibid., pp. 11–12.
72 "for its influence, the resultant prestige": Ibid., p. 12.
73 "Belles lettres is one thing": Quoted in Sanders, *Downtown*, p. 211.
73 "'We' had use for anyone": Lincoln Steffens, *The Autobiography of Lincoln Steffens*, vol. 1 (New York: Harcourt, Brace and Company, 1931), pp. 314–15.
73 "We are doing some things": Steffens quoted in *Grandma Never Lived in America: The New Journalism of Abraham Cahan*, ed. Moses Rischin (Bloomington: Indiana University Press, 1985), p. xxi.
73 "I love you . . . clever good fellows": Ibid., p. xxii.

73 "Give me assignments that will bring": Cahan quoted in Pollock, "Clarinetist," p. 235.

74 "The duties of a police reporter": Abraham Cahan, "Police Headquarters with Jacob Riis," trans. Leizer Burko, *Jewish Daily Forward*, May 19, 2010, www.forward.com/articles/128149/.

74 "Riis was not a tall man": Ibid.

74 "At the words 'call it in' ": Abraham Cahan, "I Need to Make a Call But Can't," trans. Leizer Burko, *Jewish Daily Forward*, May 19, 2010, http://forward.com/articles/128147/i-need-to-make-a-call-but-can-t/.

75 "I had become as infatuated": Steffens, *Autobiography*, vol. 1, p. 244.

75 "a socially prominent Jewish lady": Ibid., p. 243.

76 "As he chanted his poems": Hutchins Hapgood, *The Spirit of the Ghetto*, ed. Moses Rischin (Cambridge, MA: Harvard University Press, 1967), p. 94.

77 "Cahan took us, as he could get us": Steffens, *Autobiography*, vol. 1, pp. 317–18.

78 "was a dark-eyed young woman": Abraham Cahan, "East Side Talks Maine," Feb. 22, 1898, in Rischin, *Grandma*, pp. 4–5.

79 "the same penetrating intensity he had come": Pollock, "Clarinetist," p. 253.

79 "who disbelieves in or who is opposed to all": Immigration Act of 1903, text of law via: http://library.buffalo.edu/exhibits/panam/law/images/alienact1903.html.

79 "The deeper you probe into corruption,": Pollock, "Clarinetist," p. 254.

80 "Oh, let's rather talk about socialism": Ibid., p. 255.

Chapter 7

81 Cahan found himself gravitating: For this period in Cahan's life, I have relied on Sanders, *Downtown*, p. 246ff, drawing on Cahan, *Bleter fun mayn lebn*.

81 "Socialism occupies the place of religion,": Sanders, *Downtown*, p. 248.

82 "When I was a fool, a socialist,": Ibid., p. 249.

82 two advertising agents for the *Forward:* The details of this meeting and Cahan's accession are from Sanders, *Downtown*, pp. 250ff, citing Cahan, *Bleter fun mayn lebn*

84 "There will be much more to read": Ibid., p. 256, citing Cahan, *Bleter fun mayn lebn*.

84 "a kind of highbrow Yiddish": Pollock, "Clarinetist," p. 299.

84 "In Love with *Yiddishe Kinder*": On Cahan's first *Forward* issue, see Sanders, *Downtown*, pp. 257–262.

85 "the three stages in the life": Ibid., p. 258.

85 "*Mazel* is somebody else's *schlimazel*": Ibid. [Sanders spells the words "Mazzel" and "shlim-mazzel"], p. 263.

86 By midsummer, 19,000 copies: Ibid., p. 268.

86 "I wanted to know what sort of impression": Abraham Cahan, "I Go Among the Public to Study How to Write for It," trans. Leizer Burko, *Jewish Daily Forward*, May 19, 2010, www.forward.com/articles/128154/.

86 "Sometimes somebody did recognize": Ibid.

86 "If you want to pick a child up": Cahan quoted in Pollock, "Clarinetist," pp. 302-3.

87 "more socialistic": Ibid., p. 307.

87 the locals called him the "bird-man.": Sanders, *Downtown*, pp. 273ff, and Pollock, "Clarinetist," p. 307, both citing Cahan, *Bleter fun mayn lebn*.

87 "In the bird manual you would read": Sanders, *Downtown*, p. 274.

88 the Kishinev massacre: Ibid.

88 "In the march on the first of May": Editorial, *Jewish Daily Forward*, April 30, 1903.

89 "the stupendous growth of the revolutionary": Abraham Cahan, "Jewish Massacres and the Revolutionary Movement in Russia," *North American Review*, July 1903, p. 58.

89 "Russia seems to be on the eve": Ibid., p. 62.

90 New York was home to one million Jews: Sanders, *Downtown*, p. 350.

90 "Judaism [had] not much of a chance": Abraham Cahan, *The Rise of David Levinsky* (New York: Modern Library, 2001), p. 95.

90 "stood mutely by his side": Pollock, "Clarinetist," p. 308.

91 the *Bintel Brief* ("bundle of letters"): For the case that the *Bintel Brief* arose from competition with other Yiddish papers, see Sanders, *Downtown*, pp. 350–71.

92 "Send us interesting true novels": Sanders, *Downtown*, p. 356.

92 "Not an invented one but a *real* tragedy": Ibid., pp. 357–58.

92 "which didn't seem suited": Abraham Cahan, "A Bintel Brief Is Born," *Jewish Daily Forward*, reprinted May 19, 2010, http://forward.com/articles/128152/a-bintel-brief-is-born/. Cahan's account of the birth of the *Bintel Brief* column appears in Sanders, *Downtown*, pp. 361–63.

92 "It's a Godsend": Pollock, "Clarinetist," pp. 323–24, citing George M. D. Wolfe, "The *Bintel Brief* of the *Jewish Daily Forward* as an Immigrant Institution and a Research Source," M.A. thesis, Graduate School for Jewish Social Work, 1933, p. 88.

92 "poor working woman": Sanders, *Downtown*, p. 362.

92 "because he had a beard": Ibid,. p. 363.

93 "Among the letters the *Forward* receives": Ibid., p. 361.

93 "What a picture of workers' misery": Ibid., p. 362.

93–94 "Permit me to convey"; "Well, we can give no better": Ibid., p. 365.

94 "I must write to you about my situation": Ibid., p. 366.

94 "Many of these encounters took place": Cahan, "Bintel Brief" *Forward*, reprinted May 19, 2010.

95 "comparing their litany": Sanders, *Downtown*, p. 369.

Chapter 8

96 "draw a graphic picture of conditions.": "A Revolutionary Novel of Russia," *New York Times*, April 22, 1905.

96 "were moving about musingly,": Abraham Cahan, *The White Terror and the Red: A Novel of Revolutionary Russia* (New York: A. S. Barnes, 1905), p. 388.

97 "Does the Zionist idea have any reality to it?": Editorial, *Jewish Daily Forward*, July 9, 1904.

97 "About socialists . . . there is nothing to say": Ibid.

97 60,000 people jammed into Seward Park: Pollock, "Clarinetist," p. 328.

98 "Modern Jewish life has been characterized": Howe, *World*, p. 289.

98 "The Jew's conception of a labor organization": John Commons quoted in ibid., p. 290.

98 "The interests of the workingmen": Morris Hillquit, quoted in ibid., p. 314.

99 "They don't begin to ask": Pollock, "Clarinetist," p. 329.

99 "Thank God! . . . A stone has been rolled off": Ibid.

99 "your mind's eye travels to the West": Ibid., p. 331.

99 "300 People Burned in a Theater": Ibid., p. 334.

100 His wildly popular novel *The Brothers Ashkenazi*: Rebecca Goldstein, "Love, Tough and Not Tough," *New Republic*, July 27, 2010.

100 the overall tone of the *Forward*: Howe, *World*, pp. 529–30.

100 We used to write that one side: Adolph Held, YIVO interview, May 23, 1964, quoted in Howe, *World*, p. 531.

101 Cahan could be ruthless: Epstein, *Profiles of Eleven*, pp. 94–95; For Cahan's dispute with Gordin, see pp. 151–57.

101 his attacks on Gordin were not soon forgotten: Sanders, *Downtown*, p. 390.

101 "Jewish in WORD—American in THOUGHT": *Printers' Ink*, February 26, 1920.

101 "Our One-Quarter-of-a-Million Readers": Circulation figures are from Pollock, "Clarinetist," pp. 335–36.

102 a Yiddish-language history of the United States: Sanders, *Downtown*, pp. 386–87.

102 "How did you become a socialist?": Pollock, "Clarinetist," p. 335.

102 "holy duty": Ibid., p. 337.

103 "I'm tired of listening to speakers": Sanders, *Downtown*, p. 400.

103 "You are on strike against God and nature": Ibid., p. 401.

103 "Medieval America always": George Bernard Shaw quoted in both Sanders, *Downtown*, p. 401, and Howe, *World*, p. 299.

103 "The girls, headed by teenage": Howe, *World*, p. 299, citing Coleman McAlister, "All of Which I Saw," *Progressive*, May 1950.

104 "Stay firmly together, sisters and brothers!": *Forward*, February, 9, 1910, in Pollock, "Clarinetist," p. 338.

104 The paper itself donated $2,000: Ibid., p. 340.

104 The Protocols of Peace: Sanders, *Downtown*, p. 403; Howe, *World*, pp. 301–2; and Tyler, *A Vital Voice*, p. 32.

105 "At his birth Nature said to Cahan": "Karnegie Hall gepakt mit toyznter Ab. Kahan tsu bagrisn oil zany yubileum," *Forward*, November 12, 1910, quoted in Pollock, "Clarinetist," p. 342.

105 "A fifty-year-old smiling public man": Sanders, *Downtown*, p. 391.

106 "Above all, he kept pounding": Leon Wexelstein, "Abraham Cahan," *American Mercury*, September 1926, p. 92.

106 "One girl after another fell": Rosenfeld quoted in Sanders, *Downtown*, pp. 394–95. The excerpt from his poem can be found in Tyler, *Vital Voice*, p. 33.

107 "The entire neighborhood is sitting shiva": Abraham Cahan, "The Blood of the Victims Calls to Us" (March 27, 1911), trans. Chana Pollack, *Jewish Daily Forward*, March 15, 2011, www.forward.com/articles/136161/.

107 "Come and pay your last respects": Sanders, *Downtown*, p. 396.

Chapter 9

108 "to bestride the Lower East Side like a colossus": Sanders, *Downtown*, p. 405.

108 "only the electric sign of the *Jewish Daily Forward*": Alfred Kazin, *A Walker in the City* (New York: Harcourt, Brace and Company, 1951), p. 107.

109 "restless and unsettled,": Abraham Cahan, "The Dreyfus Trial," trans. Chana Pollack, *Forward*, May 19, 2010, www.forward.com/articles/128150.

110 " 'You probably want to be with your Jewish friends' ": Ibid.

110 "inexplicably nervous": Pollock, "Clarinetist," p. 351.

110 "pleasant, almost childish smile": Ibid., p. 351.

110 Dreyfus "viewed himself as merely a symbol,": Ibid., pp. 351–52.

111 Lenin was living incognito: Ibid., p. 353.

112 "When I had immigrated to America": Ibid, p. 355.

112 "our politics is that Jews must": Ibid p. 356.

112 "when whole days are spent on such": Ibid., p. 357.

113 "as healthy as a brick building": Ibid, p. 358.

113 "Tailors on Brink of a Complete Victory,": Sanders, *Downtown* p. 405.

114 "The Great Tailors' Strike Settled": Ibid., p. 407.

114 "To the *Warheit*!"; "The *Warheit*, the Center of the Revolution": Ibid., pp. 408–9.

115 "The hungry expressed satisfaction"; "unruly children": Ibid., p. 410.

115 "felt years younger and took juvenile pleasure": Pollock, "Clarinetist," p. 362.

115 a circulation of nearly 140,000: Ibid., p. 362.

116 "a condition which provided grist": Leonard Dinnerstein, *The Leo Frank Case* (Athens: University of Georgia Press, 2008), p. 1.

116 "We believe the reasons there are the same": Pollock, "Clarinetist," p. 366.
116 "trying harder to understand his position": Ibid., p. 367.
116 "irrational race hatred; fanatic, ingrained": Ibid., pp. 368–69.
117 "many kindnesses,": Ibid., p. 369.
117 most likely contributed to Frank's lynching: Steve Oney, *And the Dead Shall Rise* (New York: Pantheon, 2003), pp. 590–92.
117 The heady optimism among European socialists: Sanders, *Downtown*, pp. 428–29.
118 "Stories of Tammany violence and fraud": Epstein, *Profiles of Eleven*, p. 173.
118 "I do not expect to work wonders in Congress,": London quoted in Howe, *World*, p. 315.
118 "the special representative of the alleged": Ibid., p. 314.
119 "fountainhead of socialist thought and doctrine": Pollock, "Clarinetist," p. 371.
119 "The Great War came closer": Henry Roth, *Mercy of a Rude Stream: A Star Shines Over Mt. Morris Park*, vol. 1 (New York: St. Martin's Press, 1994–98), pp. 74–75.
119 "The blood curdles, the brain splits": Pollock, "Clarinetist," p. 371, citing *Forward* editorial of Sept. 3, 1914.
120 "I am convinced that in the interests": This quotation and those in following paragraphs are drawn from Pollock, "Clarinetist," pp. 371ff.
120 Germany certainly did its best: See Howard M. Sacher, *A History of the Jews in America* (New York: Vintage Books, 1993), pp. 239–40.
121 "Nearly all the public expressions": Zosa Szajkowski, *Jews, Wars and Communism: The Attitude of American Jews to World War I, the Russian Revolutions of 1917, and Communism (1914–1945)*, vol. 1 (New York: KTAV Publishing House), p. 8.
121 Philipp Scheidemann: Gennady Estraikh, "The Berlin Bureau of the New York Forverts," in *Yiddish in Weimar Berlin: At the Crossroads of Diaspora Politics and Culture*, eds. Gennady Estraikh and Mikhail Krutikov (Oxford: Legenda, 2010), p. 144.
121 "Mecca of socialism,": Ibid., p. 141.
122 "adopt Germany's proposal that he forbid": Pollock, "Clarinetist," p. 377.
122 "not renounce its convictions,": Howe, *World*, pp. 539–40.
122 "It is a fact, and we may as well": Pollock, "Clarinetist," pp. 376–77. It is unclear whether the interview was ever published.
123 "at no time could Cahan's motives be suspect": Ibid., p. 377.
123 "The Twilight of the Kings,": Quoted in Lloyd Wendt, Chicago Tribune: *The Rise of a Great American Newspaper* (New York: Rand McNally, 1979), pp. 407–8.
124 "That which has long been awaited": Ronald Sanders, *Shores of Refuge: A Hundred Years of Jewish Emigration* (New York: Schocken, 1988), p. 296.
124 "As if by magic,": B. Razman, *Forward*, March 30, 1917; quoted in Pollock, "Clarinetist," pp. 378–79.
124 "His Majesty's Government view with favor": Text from Balfour Declaration in Simon Sebag-Montefiore, *Jerusalem* (London: Weidenfeld & Nicolson, 2011), p. 415.
125 "Declaration should really be named for Lloyd George": Ibid., p. 415.

125 "we should be able to carry on extremely useful propaganda": Sebag-Montefiore, *Jerusalem*, p. 414.

125 "the friendship of the Jews of the World": Ibid.

125 "mighty change that socialist enlightenment has brought": Abraham Cahan, "The 'Victory' of Zionism and the Socialist Enlightenment of the Masses," *Forward* editorial, December 1, 1917.

126 "This changes none of our problems": Ibid.

126 "Economic interests will ensure that": Ibid.

127 "personally . . . sympathetic to the movement": Quoted in Moses Rischin, "The Promised Land in 1925: America, Palestine, and Abraham Cahan," *YIVO Annual* 22 (1995), p. 85.

127 "Let us stop pretending about the Jewish past": Quoted in Roberta Strauss Feuerlicht, *The Fate of the Jews: A People Torn Between Israeli Power and Jewish Ethics* (New York: Times Books, 1983), pp. 113–14.

Chapter 10

129 "to eat a mint cake": This phenomenon is described in John Geiger, *The Third Man Factor* (New York: Viking, 2009), reviewed in *Wall Street Journal*, August 24, 2009.

130 David Levinsky was born: This and all subsequent passages from the novel in this chapter are from Abraham Cahan, *The Rise of David Levinsky* (New York: Modern Library, 2001).

136 "the cartoonists of the Yiddish humor press": Eddy Portnoy, "Ab. Cahan Hates Cartoons," reprinted in *Jewish Daily Forward*, May 19, 2010, http://forward.com/articles/128146/ab-cahan-hates-cartoons/.

138 "spiritual obscenity": Marovitz, *Abraham Cahan*, p. 163.

138 "that type of Jew who raises the gorge": Ibid., p. 164.

138 "Among the many different kinds of immigrants": "Vital Problems in Current Novels," *New York Times*, September 16, 1917.

139 John Macy, writing in *The Dial*, . . . seer": Marovitz, *Abraham Cahan*, p. 163.

139 "pretty great autobiographical novel.": Ibid., p. 153.

139 "David Levinsky seems to become": Sanders, *Downtown*, p. 419.

139 "the differences between the author and his central character": Marovitz citing Jules Zanger, *Abraham Cahan*, p. 154.

140 "a very intelligent and well-read woman": David Shub, *On the Revolving Stage of History: Recollections of People and Events in Russia and the West* (New York: Cyco, 1970), chap. 80. The quotations are translated from the Yiddish by Gloria Sosin.

140 "Anyuta, it is a gem.": Ibid.

141 "Not only will I never translate": Ibid.

142 "the most important Jewish anticommunist": Richard Gid Powers, *Not Without Honor: The History of American Anticommunism* (New Haven: Yale University Press, 1998), p. 49.

142 "if a reversion to the Spanish inquisition": Ibid., p. 50.

143 "politely declined to deal with the committee": "Report of the Investigating Committee of Five," *Soviet Russia* [published by of Friends of Soviet Russia], Nov. 1, 1922, p. 238.

143 "Russia has at present": Powers, *Not Without Honor*, p. 50; also Howe, *World*, p. 542.

143 one of the first newspapers in America: Howe, *World*, p. 542 and J. C. Rich, *Sixty Years of the* Jewish Daily Forward (New York: Forward Association, 1957), p. 30. Howe writes of the comparison of the *Forward* to Hearst's publications because of "anti-Sovietism."

144 "compilation of the most loathsome back stairs gossip": "Socialist Party National Convention Delegates Remain Silent in Face of Attack on Soviet Russia: Cahan Rages in Attack on Soviet Rule." *The Worker*, June 2, 1923, online at http://www.marxists.org/history/usa/parties/cpusa/1923/06/0602-wicks-spconvention.pdf.

144 "notorious Bolshevik baiter": Ibid.

144 "bombastic windbag": Ibid.

144 "I would rather see the *Forward* go under": Epstein, *Profiles of Eleven*, p. 103.

145 "Which is the most vital,": Oswald Garrison Villard quoted in Tyler, *A Vital Voice*, p. 41.

145 "A great misfortune,": 1924 *Forward* headline quoted in Moses Rischin, "The Promised Land in 1925: America, Palestine, and Abraham Cahan," *YIVO Annual* 22 (1995), p. 86.

145 "utterly incomprehensible when found among": Gordon J. Goldberg, *Meyer London: A Biography of the Socialist New York Congressman, 1871-1926* (Jefferson, NC: McFarland & Company, Inc.), p. 129.

146 "Polish Aliyah": Yaacov N. Goldstein, *Jewish Socialists in the United States: The Cahan Debate, 1925–1926* (Brighton, U.K.: Sussex Academic Press, 1998), p. 13.

146 "harrowing": Ibid., p. 14.

146 "a pivotal factor in the intensification": Ibid., p. 13.

146 "support the policy": Ibid.

Chapter 11

147 "the miracle": Goldstein, *Jewish Socialists*, p. 20.

147 "the lion [was coming] out of his lair": Ibid., pp. 20-21.

147 "The thing is of such unusual consequence": Forward Association minutes, August 7, 1925, quoted in Moses Rischin, "The Promised Land in 1925: America, Palestine, and Abraham Cahan," *YIVO Annual* 22 (1995), pp. 88–89.

148 "proclaiming the *Forward's* Palestine series": Vladeck to Cahan, September 21, 1925, quoted in Rischin, "Promised Land," pp. 89–90.
148 "Today *Genosse* Cahan arrived in Jerusalem": Ibid., p. 90
148 Cahan's dispatches from Palestine: Rischin, "Promised Land," pp. 88–96
149 "offered to make a substantial cash": Ibid., p. 96.
149 "As the ship was not anchored far offshore": Abraham Cahan quoted in Goldstein, *Jewish Socialists*, p. 73.
150 "I treat Zionism in an entirely non-partisan way": Ibid., p. 21.
150 "They feared that my journey": Ibid., p. 23.
150 "the dissenters seem to have been correct": Ibid., p. 23.
150 "I came to Palestine with that single-minded resolution": Ibid., pp. 71–72.
151 "had migrated to America before the Bund": Ibid, p. 24.
151 "the Jewish settlements of the new kind": Ibid., p. 80.
151 "to clarify to the American reader": Ibid.
152 "I always found it difficult to tear my gaze": Cahan quoted in Goldstein, *Jewish Socialists*, p. 97.
152 "I'll tell you the truth": Ibid., p. 26.
152 "factory owners, businessmen, and bankers": Ibid., p. 70.
152 "Generally it may be said that a quiet struggle": Ibid., p. 71.
153 more than 150,000 Jews were resettled: Jonathan Dekel-Chen, *Farming the Red Land* (New Haven: Yale University Press, 2005), p. 4.
153 "because it raised millions for the Crimea settlement": Goldstein, *Jewish Socialists*, p. 76.
153 "apart from the oppression and despotism": Ibid.
153 "Zionist chauvinism is so strong that it has become": Ibid., p. 89.
153 "When you tell a revolutionary in Palestine that you": Ibid.
154 "kissing the sand dunes of Tel Aviv": Ibid., p. 92.
154 "I can't help it": Cahan quoted in Sanders, *Downtown*, p. 441.
154 "The great public draws": Quote from Ben-Gurion diary in Rischin, "Promised Land," p. 98.
154 "a genuine labor leader and not one of the dime-store": Ibid.
155 "the Arab question is closely connected": Goldstein, *Jewish Socialists*, p. 94.
155 "extremist chauvinists"; "not because this was once their home": Ibid., pp. 94–95.
156 "The Iron Wall": from "utterly impossible" . . . to "abandon all idea of seeking an agreement at present": Originally printed in *Razsviet*, April 11, 1923. English translation via Jabotinsky Institute, online at http://www.jabotinsky.org/multimedia/upl_doc/doc_191207_49117.pdf [minor typographical errors corrected].
158 "the fine things we see in it now are doomed to vanish": Goldstein, *Jewish Socialists*, p. 112.
159 "Comrade Abe Cahan declared that despite": Ibid., p. 136.
159 "we are not Zionists" in Zivion's sense . . . But "we are Jews!": Ibid., p. 48.

159 "all the telegrams and articles sent by Comrade Cahan": Ibid., p. 161.

160 "I am not a Zionist . . . but I have never defined myself": Ibid., p. 230.

161 his trip to the Soviet Union: see chapter 80 of Shub, *On the Revolving Stage of History.*

161 "going to be pro-Soviet.": Ibid., chapter 80.

161 "No American journalist is better qualified": Daniel Soyer, "Abraham Cahan's Travels in Jewish Homelands: Palestine in 1925 and the Soviet Union in 1927," in *Yiddish and the Left: Papers of the Third Mendel Friedman International Conference*, eds. Gennady Estraikh and Mikhail Krutikov (Oxford: Legenda, 2001), p. 70.

161 "I went everywhere as a Russian like all other": Ibid.

161 "decided from the very beginning not to have any": Shub, *On the Revolving Stage*, chapter 80.

162 "In the summer of 1918, however, he betrayed the Bund": Ibid.

162 "Cahan told me later . . . that he had wondered how": Ibid.

162 "Vendrov was still the *Forward* correspondent": Ibid.

163 "one of us" . . . "one of the most moving moments": Ibid.

164 tensions were running high: For an account of the Hebron massacre, see Jerold Auerbach, *Hebron Jews* (New York: Rowman & Littlefield, 2009), chapter 4.

164 "savage Arab masses, incited by their own leaders": "The Next Destruction?" editorial, *Jewish Daily Forward*, August 29, 1929.

164 "not only because it marked a milestone": Ibid.

164 "literally slaughtered like oxen in a butcher shop": Ibid.

165 examples "of great heroism and self-sacrifice": Ibid.

165 initially supported the Jews of Hebron: "Remembering the Hebron Riots, 1929," *Jewish Daily Forward*, August 20, 2004.

Chapter 12

167 "It seemed that in Philetus' district the Republican candidate" Stephen Beisman Sarasohn, "The Struggle for Control of the American Labor Party, 1936–1948," M.A. Thesis, Columbia University, 1948, p. 1.

167 aspired to succeed Cahan as editor: Baruch Charney Vladeck Papers, Tamiment Institute Library, Bobst Library, New York University.

168 "absent minded and too busy with other things": Shub, *On the Revolving Stage of History*, chapter 97.

168 "The minute Cahan learned of Vladeck's death": Ibid.

168 "getting ready to join Hitler against the West": Ibid.

168 "Are you going to write about that?" . . . : Ibid.

170 "So it is with the 'apikores'—when it comes": Abraham Cahan, "Away Ye

'Apikores,' Hello to the Jewish Revolutionary Heart" (May 17, 1911), reprinted *Jewish Daily Forward*, May 16, 1997.

170 "The place of the 'free-thinker' " . . . : Ibid.

172 "sepia-tinged portrayals of shtetl life": Ellen Umansky, "Asch's Passion," *Tablet*, April 24, 2007.

172 "Since that time I have never thought": Ibid.

173 "other, perhaps less conscious factors at play": Ibid.

173 "One of the most richly creative works of fiction": Ibid.

173 Asch had long coveted literary accolades: Ben Siegel, *The Controversial Sholem Asch* (Bowling Green, OH: Bowling Green University Popular Press, 1976), p. 144.

173 "to reclaim Jesus" . . . "earth-bound Rabbi" . . . "lean and hungry-looking": Ellen Umansky, "Asch's Passion."

174 "never had any unfriendly feelings" and subsequent: Abraham Cahan, *Sholem Asch's New Direction*. The text quoted here was translated by Mindle Gross, commissioned by the author.

177 closed to him: Siegel, *Controversial*, pp. 150, 197–98.

177 "spoke like a deeply wounded man": Epstein, *Profiles of Eleven*, p. 105.

178 "I am not religious. I am a total free-thinker": Abraham Cahan, *Sholem Asch's New Direction.*

Chapter 13

179 a "shameful document" . . . "Fascist devil": Editorial, *Jewish Daily Forward*, October 1, 1938.

179 "Hitler has allies in his enterprise of setting the world on fire": "The World is Burning," editorial, *Jewish Daily Forward*, reprinted May 28, 2010. Translated by Chana Pollack and Myra Mniewski.

180 Cahan and Jabotinsky had corresponded: Louis Gordon, " 'An Old Jewish Journalist to Another': The Private Correspondence of Ze'ev Jabotinsky and Ab. Cahan—'I Still Expect You to Warn America's Jews,' " *Jewish Daily Forward*, May 26, 2000, referencing Abraham Cahan archives, the YIVO Institute for Jewish Research, New York.

180 "most certainly was aware of Jabotinsky's role": Louis Gordon, " 'An Old Jewish Journalist to Another.' "

180 "an exodus from Europe and the settlement of six million": Ibid.

181 "a certain opposite opinion": The text quoted here is from the English-language translation reprinted in Louis Gordon, " 'An Old Jewish Journalist to Another': The Private Correspondence of Ze-ev Jabotinsky and Ab. Cahan—'5 Million or 6 Million is a Pretty Small State,' " *Jewish Daily Forward*, May 26, 2000.

181 "How to take care of five million or six million": Ibid.

181 "The question of whether AK or VJ does or does not believe": Louis Gordon, "'An Old Jewish Journalist to Another': The Private Correspondence of Ze-ev Jabotinsky and Ab. Cahan—'I Still Expect You to Warn America's Jews,'" *Jewish Daily Forward*, May 26, 2000.

182 "To be sure, you and I look at things": Ibid.

182 "The death of Vladimir Jabotinsky at this grim time": "The New Foundation," editorial, *Jewish Daily Forward*, May 26, 2000, citing editorial of August 6, 1940.

183 "heavily embroiled in the fight against the Nazis": David Shub, *On the Revolving Stage of History*, chapter 107.

183 "I don't care what happens to me after that": Ibid.

183 "Hello, Socialists!": Ibid.

184 "But God forbid, under no circumstances": Ibid., chapter 111.

184 "How can it be, that Anyuta is dead?": Ibid.

184 "did not lose even one single reader": Ibid.

185 The *Forward*'s erstwhile competitor, the *Tageblatt*: Sanders, *Downtown*, pp. 448–49.

185 "This is the happiest day of my life": Shub, *On the Revolving Stage of History*, chapter 111.

186 "my everlasting friend": Ibid.

186 "He was one of the first to fight Communists": "10,500 Pay Tribute to Abraham Cahan," *New York Times*, September 6, 1951.

186 "We should as Americans say 'Thank God' for the day": Ibid.

186 "How many unions would have been captured": Ibid.

186 "tribute from the Government and the people": Ibid.

187 "furthering social progress and Yiddish": Ibid.

187 "a great scholar of literature": David Shub, *On the Revolving Stage of History*, chapter 111.

188 "The Bible is unquestionably the most beautiful book in the world.": H. L. Mencken, *Treatise on the Gods* (Baltimore, MD: Johns Hopkins University Press, 2006, with text of 1946 revised edition), p. 286.

188 "the most unpleasant race ever heard of": Citing 1930 edition of *Treatise on the Gods* in Terry Teachout, *The Skeptic: A Life of H. L. Mencken* (New York: HarperCollins Perennial, 2003), pp. 247–48.

188 "only a small part of a discussion that was generally": H. L. Mencken, *My Life as Author and Editor* (New York: Alfred A. Knopf, 1993), p. 247.

188 "sticks in my mind to this day": H. L. Mencken, "Abraham Cahan," in *A Second Mencken Chrestomathy* (New York: Alfred A. Knopf, 1995), p. 282; first published in the *Forward*, April 21, 1940.

189 "the mature and painstaking work of an artist": Ibid., pp. 283–4

189 "Abe Cahan was never a sworn Jewish nationalist": David Shub, *On the Revolving Stage of History*, chapter 111.

191 "I cannot escape from my old self": Abraham Cahan, *The Rise of David Levinsky* (New York: Modern Library, 2001), p. 518.

INDEX

NOTE: Initials AC refer to Abraham Cahan in this index.

Index

Index

Index